THE SECOND FLOOR

Todor Zhivkov in his study during the visit of a delegation.

Kostadin Tchakarov

THE SECOND FLOOR

An exposé of backstage politics in Bulgaria

Macdonald

A *Macdonald* Book

First published in the United Kingdom in 1991 by
Macdonald & Co (Publishers) Ltd
London & Sydney

Typeset by Selectmove Ltd, London

Printed and bound in Great Britain by
BPCC Hazell Books
Aylesbury, Bucks, England
Member of BPCC Ltd.

A CIP catalogue record for this book
is available from the British Library

ISBN 0-356-20621-1

Macdonald & Co (Publishers) Ltd
165 Great Dover Street
London SE1 4YA

A member of Maxwell Macmillan Publishing Corporation

CONTENTS

Introduction

I have written this book to expose some events and facts of backstage politics of the upper echelon of power in Bulgaria over the last two years. I have also focused on some other political events in my country in so much as they are connected with the political processes of that period.

I make no claim to have exhausted my subject. I describe things as I have witnessed them. To some of my colleagues, some of the events or facts in question may seem quite different. This depends largely on the tasks which were assigned to each of us. Everything which I have been forced to do as a participant in the day-to-day running of the country was a mandatory part of my job. To me this was the main and most important aspect in the discharge of my official duties.

I want my readers to know that I feel a moral apprehension. Because I am writing about my work from my own point of view, I may easily lapse into self-assertion or overstate my personal role in the events. I would like to emphasize that I was only one participant in these processes; I have no right to speak for my colleagues.

I cannot underrate the role played by scores of political figures. But now Todor Zhivkov's comrades-in-arms are silent; so are scores of his associates and 'statesmen' with whom he had worked for several decades. This is why I put pen to paper to express my civil protest against this silence and lying-low.

I would emphasize that I do not seek to whitewash my involvement in these political processes about which rightly or wrongly everybody is now directing abuse. I am not trying to say in justification of myself that if it had not been me, it would have been someone else, even worse than me. And besides, I do not want to be taken as a penitent or, God forbid, as a victim of Todor Zhivkov's repressions. To put the record straight, I underline that my participation in the key stratum of our political system was the historical chance of a lifetime which only few Bulgarians have had. Irrespective of all evaluations and feelings which now run high around Todor Zhivkov, I should recall that he ruled the

110-year-old Bulgarian state for nearly 35 years, which is longer than the reign of Tsar Ferdinand. This cannot and should not be underestimated.

What I fear more is something else.

I have never tried to appraise my time or the events in which I have taken part in artistic, historical or journalistic terms. I hesitate because years will have to pass before our time can be judged fairly. Historians call this 'the distance of time', which is a 'must' for a mature and detached reassessment of the past. I would call it 'the patina of time' – a necessary condition without which any recollection of the past would trap us in personal bias.

At this stage Bulgarian society is strongly divided, literally split over the events surrounding the ousting of Todor Zhivkov. Feelings have been running high; new political forces and names have appeared on the scene; figures and groups, formerly at the top, are struggling to hold ground which until recently seemed immovable; public malice, political jealousy and the lust for revenge have all reached incredible proportions.

Much to my chagrin, I can see top people in the party who would resort to political cannibalism to save their positions and interests.

I bow to the wisdom of the common people who are the power-base of this party. To those who earned their living by the sweat of their brow and who maintained their dignity. Despite everything, this party demonstrated a phenomenon. While governments in other East European countries were removed after a relatively short period of time, this party displayed enviable endurance. Most of the twentieth century in Bulgaria has passed under this party, whether underground or ruling. It has had its ups and downs but, in the long run, the political and social ideals of the people have been closely linked with its struggles. What Bulgaria takes into the twenty-first century, for better or for worse, belongs to it.

Many people now simply want to humiliate or to degrade others. Their excuse – trivial and seeking psychological justification – is: 'We have been neglected, wronged and insulted. Now we have to recover our self-confidence by offending those who used to live better than us.'

Every day I hear and learn about the statements and declarations of political figures. They distort facts and truths and 'arrange them' in tones and undertones to tune up and harmonize a shattered orchestra. Alas! One conductor – Todor Zhivkov – has been calling the tune of this orchestra and has been composing its score for 35 years.

I would not venture to predict what will happen in the coming months and years. Some events in the former German Democratic Republic and in Czechoslovakia could have been explained by past phenomena, as a drive towards German unity or a revenge for the defeat after the Prague Spring of 1968.

Here in Bulgaria everything is rather different and unpredictable. The West has already found with professional and political accuracy that the Bulgarian opposition is the weakest in ideological, organizational and personal respects compared with its counterparts in Eastern Europe. Some consider that an intellectually mediocre totalitarian regime can only bring forth a mediocre opposition. Such maxims, however, are cold comfort for Bulgarian society which found itself plunged into a total crisis and which is looking for new footholds to get out of it.

One should not forget that Bulgarians want to stand firmly on the ground. They do not like to take risks preferring instead power, security and support. They gave an enthusiastic welcome both to the Teutonic 'eagles' in 1942 and the Russian boys in 1944. They mourned the death of both Tsar Boris II and Georgi Dimitrov. They shouted 'hosanna' and after that 'crucify him' to almost every socialist leader in contemporary history including Stalin, Khrushchev, Brezhnev and Traicho Kestov. Now they enact the same melodrama with their recently ousted leader, Todor Zhivkov.

I do not know whether this is due to a historical memory ingrained in our genes by ages of struggle for survival or whether it is due to the 'human material' which is currently available in Bulgaria, but throughout our public and private life we Bulgarians have always vacillated between two lines of conduct and development of human civilization – the Eastern and the Western. We still do. Which will take the upper hand: 'European egocentricity' or 'Asian collectivism'? Time will soon tell.

I do not intend to give the world a simple and easy insight to Bulgarian social consciousness nor do I seek a clue in the understanding of world and Bulgarian history. These notes by no means claim to rationalize scientifically the stages, processes and objective laws of history. This can only be achieved after the full information on our political economic and social life is 'leaked'.

I do not seek hard and fast judgments of good or evil or to label people as good or bad. Certainly, I cannot and do not want to hide my personal attitudes, my sympathies or antipathies to a given event or person. But then, I do not claim to be their judge. On these matters history alone has its say.

I could define *The Second Floor* as an account of people, facts, documents and events which I have witnessed. At some points the assessments and conclusions may fall short of an analysis. Mere facts, however, are also helpful; most of them are to be obtained only from a sole witness. I have simply had the unique opportunity in Bulgaria to work as a political aide to Lyudmila Zhivkova – a well-known figure in recent Bulgarian history, for around two years until her death – as well as for two years as a close political aide to Todor Zhivkov until his overthrow on 10 November 1989. During the rest of the time I have served in different departments and councils in the State Council and the Central Committee of the party. In other words, for almost 15 years I have been involved with the system which helped run the party and the state and which was controlled by the general secretary, Todor Zhivkov. In this capacity I have had numerous contacts and ample opportunities to observe, reflect and conclude.

I have entitled these notes *The Second Floor* because for 15 years my office was on the second floor of the State Council and of the Central Committee of the party where the head of state and the general secretary invariably had their offices. Here the state did not just have its brain trusts; these corridors also served as its large intestine. It was there that plots, traps and ambushes were conceived and human fates were sealed. That floor is a witness, a participant and memory of Bulgaria's contemporary history.

List of Names

Alexandrov, Choudomir	Member of the Politburo
Atanassov, Georgi	Prime minister of the People's Republic of Bulgaria
Balev, Milko	Member of the Politburo
Bogdanov, Peter	Member of the Bulgarian Communist Party's Military Operations Organizations
Bogdanov, Stefan	Chief of State Security Counterintelligence immediately after 9 September 1944
Chankov, Georgi	Politburo member of the Communist Party until 1958
Chervenkov, Vulko	General secretary of the Bulgarian Communist Party's Central Committee 1949–54
Damyanov, Georgi	Politburo member of the ruling party
Damyanov, Raiko	Former member of the Communist Party
Delius, Dr (Otto Wegner)	Resident of the Abver in Bulgaria
Dimitrov, Lyuben	Police inspector
Djourov, Dobri	Minister of defence
Doynov, Ognian	Former member of the Politburo, left one year before Todor Zhivkov's resignation
Evren, Kenan	Former president of Turkey
Filipov, Grisha	Former prime minister (1981–86)
Fol, Alexander	Minister of education
Fol, Nikolai	Famous Bulgarian publicist, playwright and author
Ganev, Dimitar	Politburo member of the ruling party
Genchev	Counsellor to the Tsar
Geshev, Nikola	Chief of State Security Department A
Hristov, Emil	Secretary of the ruling Communist party
Hristozov, Roussi	Former State Security chief
Ivanov, Anton	Secretary of the Bulgarian Communist Party's Central Committee
Kostov, Traicho	Former member of the Politburo, executed during the Stalin trials in Bulgaria
Koubadinski, Pencho	Member of the Politburo

Lilov, Alexander	Leader of the Bulgarian Socialist Party
Loukanov, Andrei	Party and state leader
Loulchev	Counsellor to the Tsar
Minchev, Georgi	Member of the Bulgarian Communist Party's Military Operations Organizations
Mladenov, Peter	Former minister of foreign affairs
Ozal, Turgut	Former prime minister of Turkey, now president
Palin, Velko	Head of the Military Academy
Pavlov, Pavel	Chief of State Security
Petkov, Nikola	Leader of the Agrarian party, sentenced to death and hanged in 1947
Popov, Anton	Member of the Bulgarian Communist Party's Military Operations Organizations
Popov, Zhivko	First deputy minister of foreign affairs
Pramatarov, Andrei	Chief of State Security Department B
Radev, Yaroslav	Deputy State Council president
Rainov, Bogomil	Writer, member of the Central Committee of the Bulgarian Communist Party
Romanov, Atanas	Member of the Bulgarian Communist Party's Military Operations Organizations
Russev, Svetlin	Well-known Bulgarian artist
Sankov,	Chief inspector at National Police Headquarters
Sevov, Architect Yordan	Counsellor to the Tsar
Shopov, Grigor	Deputy minister of the interior
Spassov, Mircho	Former first deputy minister of internal affairs
Staykov, Encho	Member of the Politburo
Stoyanov, Dimitar	Former minister of the interior
Tanev, Georgi	Former minister of the interior
Todorov, Stanko	Former prime minister and National Assembly president
Tsanev, Angel	Former minister of the interior
Yugov, Anton	Politburo member and chairman of the Council of Ministers
Vanga	World-famous Bulgarian clairvoyant
Vaptzarov, Nikola	Member of the Bulgarian Communist Party's Military Operations Organizations
Yakovlev, Alexander	Politburo member of the Soviet Union Communist Party Central Committee

LIST OF NAMES

Yordanov, Georgi	Minister of culture
Yotov, Yordan	Member of the Politburo
Zhivkov, Todor	General secretary of the Central Committee of the Bulgarian Communist Party and State Council President
Zhivkov, Vladimir	Todor Zhivkov's son
Zhivkova, Lyudmila	Todor Zhivkov's daughter and Politburo member

1. The Ram

Many years ago an expert on Bulgarian history told me, 'If you want to understand what drives certain events and people and what is going on in this country, you should know Geshev.'

I often recalled that phrase when, in the course of my political work, I ran into people who, each in his own way, tried to explain many events and reactions by this mysterious chief of Department A – the royal state security unit operating against the Communist party.

I am far from convinced that the course of human history can be predetermined and explained by intelligence operations and spying stunts. Somehow, unnoticeably however, I developed an interest in this top political spy, an obscure and remote figure for our generation, who had left an indelible imprint on the life of the Bulgarian Communist Party, one of the oldest and most conspiratorial parties in Europe.

A former political prisoner, who happened to be interrogated by Nikola Geshev, told me that during a moment of candour Geshev had said to him, 'If you only knew what hopes I pinned on the Bolshevik revolution and how I was disappointed. You communists cannot realize that Hitler and Stalin are one and the same thing.'

On another occasion Geshev continued, 'You communists will seize power. This is quite obvious [it happened in early 1944]. But I'll take away all your smart people, and I'll leave you only the cobblers. It serves you right to have your state run by cobblers.'

Another communist also arrested and interrogated by Geshev told me, 'He sent for me in the dead of night and offered me a drink. I refused. Tired, he sighed and said: "I hate you communists. You're all falling over yourselves to betray each other. I bought Anton Ivanov for two bottles of brandy and he betrayed you all – the contact points, the safe houses, the people and the network."'

Many years later I found out that Geshev had been right. According to evidence preserved in the party archives, Anton Ivanov was indeed responsible for the arrest of a great number of people, and he was really addicted to alcohol.

In the official political literature and party history, however, the secretary of the Central Committee of the Bulgarian Communist Party, Anton Ivanov, is presented as a legendary and selfless hero of the great trial in the summer of 1942.

He took 28 hours to reel off everything he knew about the communist movement in Bulgaria: contact points, rendezvous, words, decisions taken at meetings of the Central Committee, names and connections abroad.

The secretary of the Central Committee, Traicho Kostov, was arrested on the strength of Anton Ivanov's testimony. Three hours after his arrest, Geshev confronted the two. Anton Ivanov identified Traicho Kostov and testified that he had given him US$2,000 for the communist movement in the country and told everything he knew about his activities. Nikola Vaptsarov, Atanas Romanov, Peter Bogdanov, Anton Popov and Georgi Minchev were sentenced to death in that trial and faced the firing squad.

The confessions did not save Anton Ivanov and he shared the tragic fate of the five. Traicho Kostov was sentenced to life imprisonment. Nikola Geshev registered yet another brilliant move on the chessboard of the Bulgarian political police. His ingenuity and perfect knowledge of how the human mind worked enabled him to crush an old and experienced Bulgarian Communist who had been sent back to the country from the Soviet Union on an important political mission after suffering a stroke.

The abundant memoirs published by a number of party functionaries whetted my interest in Geshev. They recounted episodes from the life of that gifted policeman whose accomplishments and methods of work were rated as top class even by the fastidious KGB.

In his memoirs the famous banker and politician Atanas Bourov writes, 'Why did you communists shoot Loukov, Pantev and others while no one contrived to gun down that smart alec?' Even that Bulgarian, famous for his intellect, cunning and foresight, was surprised that during the period of anti-fascist resistance in Bulgaria (1941–44), the communist combat cells managed to eliminate outright fascists such as General Loukov and Colonel Pantev, who had made their mark by propaganda rather than in action, but no one even tried to attack the policeman at whose hands the revolutionary movement suffered one blow after another.

In this way I gradually began to picture a remote and at the same time palpable presence of someone whose deeds still seemed very much alive. I could almost feel this presence physically. My suspicions proved to be well-founded. Later on, events, facts and documents fitted into a jigsaw puzzle revealing Geshev's shadow behind a number of party functionaries who had rushed up the ladder after the uprising of 9 September 1944. Some of Todor Zhivkov's most intimate friends and comrades from that period also found a place in that shadow. A number of documents and the comparison of various circumstances led me to believe later on that hand, the intellect and the willpower of that gifted policeman had directed many steps in the underground communist activity of a number of top party leaders before 9 September 1944.

Let me add yet another peculiar event which is little known in Bulgarian history.

Several years ago I went to General X's office on some business. He was talking on the phone and mentioned that Colonel Nedev from the Intelligence Division had died. When he hung up, I asked him whether he was talking about Colonel Nedev, the chief of the Royal Military Intelligence Division, known as RO-2. He answered curtly, 'Yes, it's the same person.' I exclaimed, 'How did he survive under this government without being tried and executed?'

That is how I became familiar with a paradoxical fact. Colonel Nedev, a general staff officer, was sent on the eve of World War II on a diplomatic mission as a military attaché to Bucharest. He was recruited by the Soviet Intelligence Service. The German station in Bucharest found out that he had contacts with Soviet embassy officials which went beyond his duties. The German embassy in Sofia was notified. For its part, the embassy raised the question with the Bulgarian Ministry of War. Colonel Nedev was recalled and later sent to the headquarters of the Occupation Corps in Skopje. According to some evidence, he was closely related to General Nikola Mihov, the then Minister of War. That proved decisive for his career which was almost unaffected by the German *démarche*.

Later on he was called back to Bulgaria and appointed head of RO-2, the division which struck terror into underground communist activists in the army. While he served there, Colonel Nedev was in contact with the Soviet intelligence station in

Bulgaria whose chief was Savchenko, himself one of the highest ranking diplomats in the Soviet mission at that time.

Colonel Nedev later recalled that in those years he had a friendly working relationship with Geshev. This is quite understandable: one of them was fighting the communist movement in civilian life, the other one countered communist actions in the army. The two may well have been rivals in the profession.

Even today civilian and military intelligence compete, Colonel Nedev, however, was helpless when it came to the actual workings of his colleague's intelligence gathering. He knew that Geshev's plants had infiltrated all levels of the party. He knew that Geshev had photos of the headquarters of the 12 insurgent operative zones and of the commanders of the partisan detachments. 'Once I needed one of Geshev's agents for a joint operation,' Colonel Nedev recalled, 'But he flatly turned me down: "If you want information, I can give you information on the latest meeting of the Communist Politburo, but I won't give you a single man."'

This and other facts confirm that Geshev was a real professional: he retrieved information from spies and plants not listed in the official police files and personally recruited by himself. This personal spy network was probably the most important reason for his success in the fight against the communist movement.

Colonel Nedev's fate turned out to be a series of absurd and dramatic ups and downs. Around 9 September 1944 he went into hiding at a weekend house in the village of Dragalevtsi, near Sofia, provided by the headquarters of the Ukrainian Third Front to save him from the retribution of numerous communists, repressed by Intelligence Division RO-2.

His wife, however, was at large, and former police and royal army officers put complete confidence in her. She personally helped detect a number of channels, connections and the conspiratorial organization of many underground opposition groups set up at that time.

Colonel Nedev's wife was instrumental in the crackdown on the underground organizations 'Tsar Kroum', 'Neutral Officer' and 'Military League' which between 1945 and 1947 were important centres of underground activity against the Communist party and the Fatherland Front government. Notably she worked directly with representatives of the Soviet intelligence services in Bulgaria and the newly established services of the young socialist state were unaware of her activity.

In the 1950s Colonel Nedev tried to have his former activities legalized and acknowledged. He formally applied for it and requested a confirmation from the Soviet Union. Such confirmation, however, arrived neither in the 1950s nor in the 1960s. It was only in the 1970s that his activity was acknowledged in a document signed by Yuri Andropov, then head of the KGB. The secretariat of the Central Committee of the Bulgarian Communist Party adopted a special resolution to grant him a pension of around 160 leva. Colonel Nedev was supported by relatives who sold their real estate to give him some sort of allowance. Until his death he lived modestly and kept a low profile. Many people probably had no idea of the absurdities in the life of the old man who got trapped in the whirl of events.

The case of Colonel Nedev once again brings us to the mysterious figure of Nikola Geshev. Even to senior officers he remained inaccessible and secretive. He had the same way with his colleague, Colonel Andrei Pramatarov, chief of the State Security Division B, the counterintelligence service. He survived 9 September 1944 and served his sentence in the prison of Pazardjik. Apart from the most general impressions of Geshev's work, Pramatarov knew nothing specific. No person is in a position to unravel the work and the life of the man who for years ran a powerful police system.

What about the plain facts?

His application for a police job contains only scraps of information:

> Nikola Hristov Geshev – born 13 April 1896 in Sofia.
> Address – 193 Hristo Botev Blvd.
> Father – Hristo Geshev; a notary, deceased.
> Mother – Raina Manolova.
> Religion and nationality – Eastern Orthodox; Bulgarian.
> Education – secondary; certificate no. 825 dated 7 April 1917.
> Military service – Second Lieutenant discharged in 1919 from the Artillery Regiment Headquarters, Sliven.
> Police school graduate, single.

This is the typical career of a Bulgarian police officer who comes from a middle-class family, gets an officer's commission in the army and takes a job in the security services. Nothing particular or remarkable, which could motivate or at least suggest that this was a born policeman.

There is one more detail concerning Geshev's education: he studied law in Sofia and Rome, although he never graduated. He spoke French and Italian.

We now know Geshev to be a police officer with some legal schooling, definite proficiency in foreign languages and an exposure to European culture. He saw action in the first Balkan war as a volunteer paramedic and later in World War I as a mountain artilleryman. At one point in his life therefore, he was a front-line soldier who daily confronted death.

Let us briefly retrace his police career on the basis of details known to date.

Geshev had a middle class background. After finishing his secondary education at Boys' High School No.2 in Sofia, he enrolled at Sofia University to study law and completed one term. Later he left for Rome, where he pursued his law studies and finished two more terms. However, he did not manage to graduate. He enlisted as a paramedic volunteer at Regimental Hospital 4/1 during the first Balkan war. He also took part in World War I from 17 November 1917 to 18 October 1918 as a member of the 6th Artillery Detachment. He was a member of the Democratic Alliance. He graduated from a reserve officer school and was discharged from service into the reserve as a Second Lieutenant (recruitment 1940).

By order no. 288, dated 1 August 1925, his application to the police was granted and he was appointed Agent Class I. Before getting a full-time job as an agent, he worked as a police surveillance operative. At that time Kovachev was director of the police and General Roussev was minister of the interior.

By order no. 34, dated 13 February 1930, Police Director Preslavski appointed Geshev as team chief in the internal political police in place of Peter Dimitrov. That same order reads: 'For his diligent work and very good performance in the police force course examination, I hereby promote State Security Division Agent Class II Nikola Geshev to team chief . . .'

By order no. 544, dated 30 August 1937, Geshev was appointed deputy chief of Department A.

The order was signed by Police Deputy Director B. Mihailov.

Geshev was promoted to the position of Chief of Department A, State Security Division of the Police Force as of 1 December 1941.

At that time P. Gabrovski was minister and General Konov was chief inspector of State Security.

A police force certificate issued to Geshev for his job grading, details that in 1930 he had completed a course in the following subjects: criminal justice, police, criminal law (special section), identification, police techniques, political police, prevention and control of banditry, desertion and political emigration. He achieved an aggregate rate of 34 in the examination – order no. 40, dated 14 February 1930.

In 1942 Geshev drew a large monthly salary of 7,010 leva.

In October 1942 the former minister of the interior, Peter Gabrovski, sent him a personal thank you letter:

> Dear Geshev,
>
> Leaving the post of minister of the interior and public health, I feel bound to thank you with all my heart for your invaluable and loyal cooperation, especially in combating seditious elements and law, order and security violators.
>
> You should know that not only I as your superior, but every Bulgarian who had shown interest in the work of state security pinned great hopes on you. And just as everybody else, I too, not only wasn't deceived in these hopes but saw them lived up to in great proportion. Great success has been achieved, dear Geshev, particularly during the last two years, in this dogged struggle which the Bulgarian police has been leading and probably will follow for a long time to come.
>
> Undoubtedly, you and your experience and loyalty to the service have contributed enormously to these achievements. I appreciate all that, and you can rest assured that the entire Bulgarian society appreciates and will judge on their merits your great services. . . .

This is nearly everything which can be found in Geshev's personal file. We perused it not out of sheer curiosity but seeking to document as fully as possible a successful police career. To the cited facts we will only add that Geshev and all high-ranking officers in the Bulgarian State Security at that time drew their knowledge, methods of work, professional skills and habits on the ample experience of the German and the Austrian police schools.

The radical political change in September 1944 put an end to his career. The roles were reversed; this time he was the hunted and wanted political criminal.

Bulletin no. 553, 20 May 1946, placed Geshev on the wanted list. The bulletin gave the following description:

'Build: heavy, broad shouldered; height:medium, almost tall; Head: big, long; complexion: dark; hair: black, bald patch on the top; eyes: brown, alert; eye brows: slightly set apart, thick; forehead: high; nose: straight; mouth: medium large; beard and moustache: none; peculiarities: stooping; character: reserved and very artful.'

But even now, when the new authorities looked through his official record, a peculiar episode of his life still remained undisclosed. According to circles close to the Tsar, Geshev had begun his career as an ardent young communist activist. He went to study in Moscow at the youth section of the Comintern. There he was recruited by the Soviet Intelligence Service and was trained as a spy. Maybe because of this, some years later, he told an arrested communist he was interrogating: 'What great hopes I pinned on the Bolshevik revolution.'

He returned to Bulgaria and, for some unknown reasons, nobody asked for him until 1925. There is evidence that then he requested an appointment with the Tsar whom he told about his life and asked for a job in the police.

If that is the case, Geshev was a typical political renegade, as were a number of prominent historical figures in the interwar period. Take, for example, the socialist youth of Benito Mussolini. The encounter with the harsh reality of Soviet Russia was probably instrumental in Geshev's swing from one political pole to the other. Like every political renegade, he turned into the fiercest opponent of the idea of which he was an ardent and selfless champion when he was on the other side of the barricade.

Not surprisingly then, in 1925 Geshev was a member of the Democratic Alliance. This right wing political formation was set up in August 1923 by the Popular Alliance, the United People's Progressive party and part of the democrats and radicals. Some of its representatives gravitated toward fascist ideas. Geshev's membership in their organization, however, was motivated by an element of pragmatism. The Democratic Alliance was a ruling political coalition and that was important for a policeman at the start of his career.

Geshev's real police activity remained unknown even to his closest aides. This policeman undoubtedly knew the real value of silence, cunning and reserve; he passionately and fanatically built a dense personal spy network in the communist party. The crackdown on several groups in its Central Committee, the capture of the underground groups – submarined and parachuted into Bulgaria from the Soviet Union in the summer of 1941 – and scores of other great anti-communist coups were his work. Interestingly enough, the department which fought the sweeping partisan movement of 1941–44 and the communist combat actions had a relatively small personnel. Geshev had only 60 men in the State Security Division. At the beginning of World War II the 'Royal State Security' employed 800 people and at the end of the war, 1100 people. This figure suggests that his work could not have been successful if he had not relied on a dense network of informers and confidential people and if he had not been so good at running his agents.

Here is what one of his former operatives said during an interrogation. He is Dimitar G. Chobanov, born on 28 February 1912. Before 9 September 1944 he served as a State Security Department A agent. Here is the verbatim record of his interrogation:

Question: What was the task of the State Security Department A?

Answer: State Security Department A combated the Bulgarian Communist Party and its branches. It was also spying on the Soviet Union and its embassy in Bulgaria.

Question: How did Department A combat the Bulgarian Communist Party and its branches?

Answer: Department A combated the Bulgarian Communist Party by watching people involved in communist activity, by detecting communist conspiracies and the Bulgarian Communist Party's printing houses and by holding investigations into these disclosures. Department A also fought the strike movements.

Question: How did Department A detect communist conspiracies?

Answer: The detection and the frustration of communist conspiracies was greatly helped by surveillance teams outside police headquarters. The Department A plants, belonging to the circles of the Bulgarian Communist Party, played the most important role in the detection and frustration of communist conspiracies.

Question: Who recruited these undercover agents of Department A?

Answer: The undercover agents of Department A were supposed to be recruited, as I was taught at police school, by the chief of the department but they were also recruited by Geshev, although he was an inspector.
Question: How did Geshev recruit his agents?
Answer: Geshev picked out important figures in the Bulgarian Communist Party who were in touch with the Central Committee.
Question: Do you know how many undercover agents he had?
Answer: I do not know their number but I have heard from his trusted spy Boncho Bourovski that Geshev had many agents, but I do not know how many. Boncho used to say that Geshev had an underground printing press in each of his pockets. Boncho also used to say that Geshev's undercover agents all had aliases and that nobody knew their real names.
Question: Who arranged the rendezvous with Geshev's spies?
Answer: I was under the impression that Geshev himself arranged all rendezvous with the informers.
Question: Who else arranged such rendezvous?
Answer: I suppose that such rendezvous were also arranged by Boncho Bourovski and Boncho Mehandov. The surveillance team chief, Strelkovski, also arranged such rendezvous. He might have sent others, but I do not know about them.
Question: Where did Geshev rendezvous with his agents?
Answer: I cannot say because I don't know.
Question: Where did Geshev keep the reports of his informers?
Answer: Geshev had an iron safe in his office where he kept the informers' reports.
Question: Which of Geshev's closest aides can identify his informers?
Answer: I suppose that some of the informers might be identified by Bourovski, Boncho Mehandov and Dimitar Donchev (the 'Sea Wolf'). His inspector, Lyuben Dimitrov, may also know some of his undercover spies. But I suppose that State Security Chief Pavlov knew most of them, as he himself had handed him over some of his own informers.
Question: Do you know any of Geshev's informers, how many and who they were?
Answer: I know only three of them.
Question: How did you come to know them?
Answer: In early 1942 I worked in Department G. One day, on my way to the tram stop, one Department A agent, I think

it was Georgi Koukov, told me that a participant in the Spanish revolution had been detained in the headquarters. He had been writing a deposition and seemed to have an incredible memory. He had listed 380 persons, including 250 with their full names and whereabouts and their functions in the Spanish revolution. He was held in very decent conditions and received a special ration.
One day, Department G agent Ivan Gorchanov and I decided to see him out of curiosity. The 'Spaniard' was writing his testimony in the corridor of the first floor, next to Geshev's office. Boncho Mehandov was with him. We got in through the back entrance and saw him writing. Boncho asked us why we were there. We told him we wanted to see the Spaniard. We exchanged a few words and left. The Spaniard was dressed in a new ash-grey suit, of medium height and with light-brown hair. He was in a very good mood and seemed to be cracking jokes.

About a year and a half later, in the summer of 1943, at the intersection of Graf Ignatiev Street and Lyuben Karavelov Street, I was accosted by a stranger who asked me: 'Do you know me?' I answered that I didn't. He told me that he was 'the Spaniard' and I recalled that this was the same person who provided information at the beginning of 1942. He told me he had just been detained at the police station, but had phoned Geshev and the latter had ordered his release. I do not remember what suit he wore then but I noticed that he was smartly dressed.

I suppose that person wasn't released by chance on Geshev's orders. He might have been one of his undercover agents.

So, we have here aliases, shady characters and shadows which vanish once you try to touch them.

And yet the nervous answers of the ex-spy and subordinate to the great cop throw some light on some aspects of Geshev's day-to-day work. They tie some tiny 'knots', the undoing of which produces leads to betrayal and sting operations which can be followed to the present on unmasking people of whom society has a very different idea. These 'knots' are Geshev's work.

In our unadulterated notions of the past, amidst the doubts of our somewhat confused present, and in the face of an insecure future, we will increasingly often browse the secret pages of history. I venture to assume that many of these pages in the history of the Bulgarian communist and workers' movement will be signed by Geshev.

Let us trace some aspects in the career of a person who held many knots of the visible and invisible power in Bulgaria.

For many years after 9 September 1944 – in fact until 1983 – Mircho Spassov, deputy and, later on, first deputy minister of internal affairs (1957–83), was a key figure in the security services. He enjoyed the complete confidence, personal friendship and favour of Todor Zhivkov.

Like the former general secretary of the Central Committee of the Bulgarian Communist Party and State Council president, Todor Zhivkov, Mircho Spassov was also born in a village near Sofia. Born in 1911, this coincidence of birth dates was not the only reason for their close friendship, which lasted several decades.

In a memorandum recently circulated in Parliament as well as in some other circles, Mircho Spassov rejected the accusations of crimes and corruption in which he was allegedly involved while he had unlimited control of the security services.

Judging by that memorandum, Mircho Spassov was a Komsomol activist and a communist functionary as long ago as 1927. He served time in prison and in concentration camps, and in March 1944 he joined the partisans. After 9 September 1944 he was first provincial and then district chief of the Ministry of the Interior headquarters in the cities of Rousse, Sofia and Pleven, then deputy minister and first deputy minister of internal affairs, head of 'The Party Organizations, Cadres and Business Trips Abroad' department of the Central Committee of the Bulgarian Communist Party, member of the Central Committee and member of Parliament. He retired in 1982 and as he modestly ends his memoirs, 'now I am a retired colonel-general, holder of the title "Hero of Socialist Labour", four on the orders of Georgi Dimitrov and many other decorations.'

This, however, was only the tip of the iceberg. In March 1990, the Bulgarian public was shocked by the disclosures about the camps near the town of Lovetch and the village of Skravena where 'security risks' were confined in the late 1950s and the early 1960s. The camp inmates were held in conditions similar to the Nazi concentration camps. It turned out that in his capacity as deputy minister of internal affairs, Mircho Spassov was directly in charge of those camps and quite often he was personally involved in the tortures.

The terrible disclosures offset that memorandum. An investigation was ordered against Mircho Spassov. What proved hidden under the varnish of his denials was most of the underwater part of the iceberg. On the strength of information available to us, we can characterize this person as one of the most sinister figures in Bulgarian history after 9 September 1944. He is associated with most of the extrajudicial killings and repressions in this period.

In this respect Mircho Spassov was in his element. He repressed scores of people. In his capacity as chief of the provincial headquarters of the Ministry of Internal Affairs, he killed off some of the ancestors of Tonka Obretenova, a renowned patriot and champion of Bulgarian national liberation. As in most other similar cases the pretext was an absurd technicality: Tonka's son, Nikola Obretenov, who was also an active revolutionary during the National Revival Period, had been provincial governor in the city of Russe.

General Kostadin Hristov reminisces, 'Mircho Spassov and I arrested a police officer nicknamed "Chicken", We were escorting him to the police station to hand him over. I fell behind ten metres or so to relieve myself and heard several shots. I rushed and saw "Chicken" had dropped dead. I asked Mircho why he had killed him and he said, "It served him right, that bloody bastard of a cop."'

In a recently published account of Roussi Hristozov, formerly chief of State Security and minister of the interior, Mircho Spassov was a most active member of a squad formed at the National Police Headquarters immediately after 9 September 1944 to shoot down the detainees. I have personally heard Todor Zhivkov say with some fear that he knew of no person who had killed as many people in those years as Mircho Spassov.

It was hardly accidental that Mircho Spassov was in the front rank of the raiders of the police headquarters on 9 September 1944. He was one of the first who gained access to the police archives.

In a declaration, Mircho Spassov denies that he wanted to obtain those archives in order to cover up the evidence of his own activity as an *agent provocateur*. His arguments, however, are flimsy; they are not founded on documented facts.

Interestingly enough, in his younger years Mircho Spassov had a penchant for crime. He was nicknamed Mircho the Menace. Some people from the area of the town of Belovo recall that he often ambushed people on their way back from the market in the town of Pazardjik and, threatening them with a knife, robbed them of the money they had earned on vegetable sales.

Mircho Spassov had also caught Geshev's eye. Spassov wrote in his own hand: 'There is further information on one Mircho Hristov Spassov with the inspector of Department A, 1940, Geshev.' The high-ranking policeman however, refused to share that information with a colleague of his. The affair looks suspicious. Didn't Geshev shield his trusted men in this way? And how could Mircho Spassov move freely from place to place in areas blockaded by the police? The implications of parts of his memorandum are also suspicious, for example: 'In November 1943, after I was released from the concentration camp, I went underground. In this capacity I was secretary of the Third Sofia District of the Bulgarian Communist Party. In February 1944, by a decision of the Central Committee of the party I joined the partisans and in June 1944, by a decision of the party's Central Committee, I was transferred to the Second Sofia District of the Bulgarian Communist Party.' How was he moved from one area to another and how did he infiltrate various structures of the underground party committees and partisan units? And what invisible agency propelled such a fiend to the top job at the Ministry of the Interior?

It was in this ministry that his character manifested itself fully demonstrating his propensity for cruelty, violence and gross physical brutality. Runaway inmates of the Lovetch camp, captured at the Yugoslav border, recall: 'We ran away because we could no longer endure the sadistic treatment of Mircho Spassov. He used to visit the camp at least once a month, closeted himself in a room, drank with his aides and sent for inmates whom he personally battered to death. They stuffed the dead bodies in sacks and stacked them by the wall until he had had enough and was tired.'

On other occasions, however, Mircho Spassov showed 'striking magnanimity'. The recollections of T. Zahariev, former district chief of the Ministry of the Interior headquarters in the town of Pazardjik illustrate this well: 'I learned that Gavril Dimitrov, former agent of Geshev's Department A, was given a job in Belovo. I decided to recruit him. I went in person to the office where he worked as an accountant. I introduced myself and he immediately reacted as a professional and put two and two together. I asked him how he managed to survive. He replied that Mircho Spassov himself knew about him and had secured that job for him. I suggested that we meet and talk. He realized that he was to be recruited and suggested we meet in Pazardjik. We fixed a day and a time for the rendezvous. He did not turn up on the appointed day. I looked for him and found that he had left for Sofia. There he had had a heart attack and, as a result, had died.'

Obviously, Mircho Spassov hastened to break any lead which could expose his association with Geshev. Yet the intercession for the ex-police agent and his unexpected death aroused Zahariev's suspicion and led him to believe that there was some kind of a connection between Mircho Spassov and Gavril Dimitrov. Spassov's high rank, however, dampened his enthusiasm for taking a closer look at the matter.

The operation through which he invested in the purchase of western companies is another mystery. The records at the lawyers' and notary offices in Vadz, Liechtenstein, can shed light on the matter.

According to the recollections of one of the State Security chief investigators in the 1973 proceedings against Kyuchukov, deputy minister of transport and chief of civil aviation, the names of Mircho Spassov and the then minister of the interior, Angel Tsanev, both cropped up during the investigations. They had diverted considerable funds with the help of dummies; in the course of the investigation those dummies confidently identified their abettors. General Radoulov, who was in charge of the investigation, informed Grigor Shopov, the then deputy minister of the interior. He in turn told Todor Zhivkov on the phone and they made a strictly confidential appointment at the Central Committee. There was no one else in the office, even the secretary was ordered to leave. Todor Zhivkov met him in prison. Having heard the report on Mircho Spassov and Angel Tsanev's deeds, Todor Zhivkov said: 'Look! Keep this absolutely secret for two or three months because those two are villains and I cannot save you if they decide to get you out of the way. I need time to arrange their removal.'

And indeed, in two months' time Angel Tsanev was dismissed. Mircho Spassov was also relieved of his duty, but he took another appointment as chief of department at the Central Committee. Obviously Todor Zhivkov did not have the courage to kick him out; that happened much later.

The late 1970s saw the formation of a network around the Cultural and Historical Heritage Foundation with the then deputy minister of the interior, Zhivko Popov, as the key figure. Mircho Spassov and Lyudmila Zhivkova placed complete trust in Popov. In this case too, Mircho Spassov's role as a chief organizer and abettor was covered up at the trial held later on against Zhivko Popov and his group. Spassov's name was still mentioned with terror. Popov was tried on charges of gross embezzlement of money and gold.

For a long time Mircho Spassov remained the chief henchman of the system. Todor Zhivkov placed him in charge of all operations connected with the ousting of political adversaries by legal proceedings of special character. Mircho Spassov played a well-known role in the foiling of the pro-Chinese plot involving Ivan Todorov Gorounya, Tsolo Krastev, General Tsviatko Anev and other conspirators who, in 1965, intended to stage a coup with the help of the military police company in Sofia. The plot fell through when the conspirators contacted certain military and civilian personnel whom they hoped to involve in the coup. It is to these people that the leads of betrayal can be followed. Mircho Spassov organized their surveillance, telephone tapping and active counteractions.

One should not forget that in the mid 1960s the fierce methods of retribution with the enemy were still dominant. Even in prison the would-be conspirators were under special surveillance.

Mircho Spassov was not averse to routine police operations. He aspired, however, to large-scale operations. In this respect Zhivkov trusted him unquestioningly.

At the end of the 1960s the wave of changes in Eastern Europe surged. New ideas of democratic socialism and market economy began to take shape. Hopes for change appeared. And yet the system and the level of 'real' socialism were far from ready for such changes. That is why the 1968 Prague Spring caused great anxiety in the East European capitals. They went ahead with large-scale operations to destabilize Czechoslovakia. Todor Zhivkov took the initiative; the Action Plan for Czechoslovakia and its implementation were assigned to his trusted man, Mircho Spassov. He collected intelligence information from the agents in Prague and studied the political situation in the country.

The last years of his reign in the security services were full of hysterical fits of intoxication and sadism.

Back to the ubiquitous chief of Department A.

The trusted people of Tsar Boris such as Architect Yordan Sevov, adviser to the Tsar, and definately a German spy, Genchev and Loulchev, told the People's Court that the chief of Department A, Geshev, had been one of the confidants of the palace. Genchev added that when it had to be decided whether the appointment of a high-ranking person was appropriate, the Tsar advised him to consult Geshev himself.

During the interrogation of another high-ranking policeman at the time, Manyu Nachev, he deposed that in the case of major crackdowns he had asked Geshev about the informer. The latter, however, either said nothing or revealed names which, when checked turned out to be completely uninvolved in such actions. Nachev had sent a report on the matter to the director of the police who had also refused to discuss it or had said that he would immediately order Geshev to report, which never happened. Despite this and despite the many changes of cabinets and their respective superiors, Geshev had remained irreplaceable. After Germany invaded Bulgaria during World War II, all chiefs of state security in the police, as well as the directors, were Gestapo agents. Much less experienced and merited people than Geshev were appointed State Security chiefs. He, however, was never appointed as such by the palace, even though after the capture of a group of underground activists parachuted to Bulgaria, Geshev was put forward for appointment as chief of State Security.

The investigations in connection with the People's Court trials identified all German spies in the Bulgarian police, but Geshev's name did not figure among them.

Two options remain: either he was a remarkable patriot or he worked for the British Secret Intelligence Service. The first option is hardly plausible because a great policeman cannot be sentimental on a patriotic basis. The British connection is better motivated. It is possible that Tsar Boris III, who always sympathized with the island empire, was aware of that connection. This explains why the monarch tacitly patronized Geshev and appreciated his professionalism but deliberately kept him away from the highest posts in the security services in order to deflect the attention of the Gestapo.

There is one more fact which confirms this assumption. Alexander Sankov, chief inspector at the National Police Force headquarters at the time of the armed anti-fascist resistance, evidently had a list of plants in the partisan units: he needed it to divert the counterinsurgency effort. These agents were, however, a monopoly of Geshev. Obviously, Sankov received the list from Geshev, who did not make this gesture to a newly appointed officer just by chance; the two of them were very close and since they were not related, they were presumably both involved in the British connection. Moreover there is no evidence of Sankov being connected with the Gestapo.

After 9 September 1944 the organs of the investigative authorities were helpless to gather information about Geshev and Sankov or even to trace the route of their escape, although information was available on all other senior police officers. Accordingly we can see further confirmation of the supposition that, as people of the Intelligence Service, they had escaped the country with the help of English spies.

At the end of August and the beginning of September 1944 the advance of the Soviet forces wreaked havoc in the state and political structure of the kingdom of Bulgaria. The secret services and most of all Department A were also in confusion. Getting ready to escape, the officers naturally resorted to their only real asset: the spy network in the Communist party.

This is how it happened according to eyewitness accounts:

> My name is Vesselina Nikolova Gesheva, 40 years old, born in the town of Silistry, resident of Sofia, Bulgaria, Eastern Orthodox, married, no criminal record, literate. I testify as follows:
>
> For some time Geshev was very worried, even apathetic. He would not touch food, he stopped talking to me and was rude to me for no apparent reason. This continued until 8 September 1944. In the morning we went to the tram stop. He usually went to work by car and saw me to the first tram. He did not return for lunch. I forgot to mention that there was an air raid alert that morning; I usually went to the Knyazhevo bomb shelter while he went to the woods. He had put on his overcoat at my insistence and, when he returned, he had left it at headquarters. That worried me and I kept asking him why he didn't bring his coat home. I even asked him whether he intended to leave me. On the 8th, in the afternoon, so that I wouldn't suspect anything, he sent one of his young operatives at around five in the afternoon to bring me his coat in a suitcase and the boy told me that Geshev would return later. The agent, whose name I do not know, was accompanied by Geshev's typist – now a secretary – Zhenya Stoyanova, who gave me 11,000 leva. I burst into

tears, assuming that he would never come back, but Zhenya assured me that he had only told her to give me the money and to tell me that he'd be back in the evening and that was all she knew. Recently, Mrs Zhenya Stoyanova worked for the Central Department at 9 Veliko Turnovo Street. Geshev did come back, smoking. No sooner had he stepped in when he told me he had to hurry on some business. He wouldn't have dinner. He was dressed in a light grey suit, hatless, in black shoes and he hadn't shaved for two or three days. He looked frightful. I asked him where he was going. His usual answer to such questions was, 'Don't you ever dare to ask me where I'm going when my job is involved.' I asked him whether he would come back. He replied 'Yes'. I asked him in case he didn't, who he was leaving me for. Instead of answering my question, he told me not to annoy him and threatened to shoot me and himself. I became scared and stopped asking him questions – all this took five or six minutes. I begged to see him off, but he wouldn't let me do this either. That was the last I saw of him, he tossed 6,000 or 7,000 leva to me before he left and he hasn't turned up since then. The next morning I didn't go to work because the traffic was blocked. I went on Sunday but there was nothing to do. I reported for work at 13 Murphy Street, where my office had been evacuated. On Monday I heard the announcement on the radio and went to work from where, together with my colleagues, we went to police headquarters to get our new safe conducts. Since then I haven't left the headquarters.

I want to reiterate that Geshev treated me very rudely even though we have been married for just a couple of months. To him women were only good for kitchen work. He could barely stand my company and kept sending me to the kitchen because he was convinced women were fools.

In Knyazhevo I've seen a young man going upstairs; an agent, called Dimitrov, who had grown up in an orphanage. I've often seen him talking with Geshev, usually in the morning, before he went to work. Geshev rarely travelled by tram. He usually drove to the headquarters together with Mr Pramatarov.

I wrote the above with my own hand. Vesselina Gesheva.

Gesheva's interrogation was conducted on 18 September 1944, just a couple of days after the establishment of the new government.

Here is what Andrei Pramatarov, chief of Department B at the police headquarters, confessed when he was questioned:

On the 6 and 7 of September, I was summoned to the Ministry of War by the police director Sava Koutsarov. He told me not to worry because the government had contacted and was negotiating with Marshal Tolbukhin and that they would come to some agreement. I returned to headquarters and told Geshev and Lyuben Dimitrov. Nevertheless, on the orders of Sava Koutsarov, military uniforms and rucksacks were brought in and I got one. Koutsarov must have contacted the military who had sent over these outfits because they were handed out by the then chief of the procurement department, Atanas Malinkov. On 8 September, despite Koutsarov's assurances, I decided to leave for Plovdiv where my brother-in-law lived. I left together with my brother, the then inspector Vassil Tsankov, Bogomil Krasnarev, Vesselin, the agents Todor Dermonski and Mircho Kikiridov, a friend of mine who was at that time staying with me. When we drove past the police headquarters, we saw Geshev and Lyuben Dimitrov standing at the gate. They asked us where we were going and when I told them that I was bound for Plovdiv, they decided to join us. They overtook us at the station with Geshev telling us that we had better travel separately on the train. We arrived in Plovdiv at six in the morning. The square in front of the station was crowded and we managed to slip into the city unnoticed. We had breakfast together in a café opposite the Hotel Paris. Then Geshev sent one of his agents to the provincial police headquarters to check what was going on. The agent returned and reported that the headquarters was deserted and that a sentry was posted. Then we decided to disperse and to meet again at four in the afternoon at the same place. I went there at the appointed hour but no one else turned up. I was staying with my brother-in-law and I returned to his house and we decided that I would leave for Svilengrad together with my brother and Mr Kikiridov. Since then, I haven't seen either Geshev or Dimitrov. Later on I learned in prison from Radoslav Mindizov that Mincho Hristov Mitev, a former inspector of the intelligence division [tracking down communists in the army], had told him that he had been sent to Italy to look for Geshev and Pavlov. He also told him that Sasho Pavlov and Sankov were there, but not Geshev. In 1947 I learned from Assen Bogdanov, ex-police commandant in Sofia, that while at large, he had met a friend of his, an ex-pilot, who had told him, that when he had been to Istanbul on business, he had met and talked with Geshev. I reported this to the then chief of state security, Stefan Bogdanov, identifying the pilot whose name has since slipped my mind. In prison I learned from Yanko Kalchev, former intelligence division team chief, that when we were in Plovdiv (9 September 1944), he had also been there, and, as he stood on the road to Svilengrad, he incidentally stopped a car in which he saw Ivan Fichev, uniformed, the driver, Nikola Geshev and Lyuben Dimitrov. He wanted to get in the car but they refused, saying there was no room for him. Kalchev had told this to Dobrin Venev Tsonev, Bogomil Krasnarev and Kosta Belchev. I also remember that at first he claimed that I had also been in the car, but when he learned later on that I had been somewhere else, he changed his story, asserting that Lyuben Dimitrov looked like me. In the past before 9 September the following police officers were close aides of Nikola Geshev: Peter 'Baritone' Dimitrov, his team chief Ivan Veshev, (another team) agent Lazar Sharenkov and, closest of all, Lyuben Dimitrov, who served under him as an inspector. Peperov and Veshev are dead and I don't know what has happened to Sharenkov. I also remember that he was friendly with agent Stoyan Stoyanov.

In his capacity as chief of Department A, Nikola Geshev was completely secretive. There were desks lining the walls of his office and he didn't confide in anyone. He never washed and changed his clothes once in six months and used to sleep at headquarters. His agents said he used to have sex with women who must have been as unwashed as him. Together with his above-mentioned aides he had lunch and dinner at the 'Wine cellar' and then they would go back to headquarters. Recently, in the summer of 1944, he married a passport office clerk. She was very plain. I do not know his brothers. His sister, whom I don't know either, was notorious as a fallen woman.

Concerning Geshev's and Dimitrov's escape, I believe the two of them must have been shot when they tried to cross the border because, as Popivanov – a friend of Dimitrov – said, otherwise they should have let their families hear from them, especially Dimitrov, who had children whom he adored. The drivers at police headquarters worked in shifts. I don't remember a particular driver to have been assigned to Pavlov, the chief of state security, or of any other chief. When necessary, they usually sent the duty driver for me. The prisoner Blagoy, an ex-driver at police headquarters, who is now in Sofia prison and works in the assembly shop, can supply further details on the matter.

I know the following about Pavel Pavlov and Alexander Sankov: on the 6 September, they came to the headquarters to seek visas for Germany. They were granted such visas. Later on, when I was sentenced, I learned here in prison that they didn't travel by train but drove to Skopje and from there retreated together with the Germans to Vienna. From there they left for Italy. I also learned that Sankov, together with his cousin, a journalist, left for Buenos Aires, where a relative of theirs who owned a jeweller's shop employed them. I remember hearing this from the prisoner Radoslav Mihailov who has been released. Mindizob told me that he had also learned of this in prison from Stancho Hristov Mitev, his friend and former colleague who visited him.

Alexander Sankov, newly appointed agent, was assigned to my department. He wasn't a good operative and wanted to be a boss because he had studied law. After Pavel Pavlov was appointed chief of State Security, Sankov was immediately promoted as chief inspector of State Security. Pavel Pavlov and Alexander Sankov decided to 'fix' the State Security personnel, and I was their main target. They wanted to replace me with a friend of theirs, claiming that I hadn't studied law and didn't speak foreign languages. The first thing they did was to establish an inspectorate headed by Nikola Geshev. They staffed it with close and trusted aides: Vassil Tsankov, Gencho Savakov, Milcho Angelov, Konstantine Gigov and Tsonyo Tsonev. The above inspectors were sent on Geshev's instructions to the provinces as state security inspectors. Thus Tsankov was sent to Skopje, Savakov to Stara Zagora, Angelov to Trun, Gigov to Pirdop and Tsonev to Kolarovgrad. They were supervised by Sankov who in turn reported to Geshev and Pavlov. Pavlov was at the root of the ill-feeling and intrigue against me: he resented my failure to report everything about the operation of the department to him. This was because my aides and I were convinced that he was a British spy.

A further clue leading to Turkey, is contained in the report of agent Moutsi:

From police officers in prison I learned that around 5 September 1944 Geshev and other police officers, dressed in military uniforms, drove in a headquarter's truck to the Turkish border.

> In February or March 1945 I was detained at headquarters. In our cell there was a young Turk, a Romanian deserter from before 9 September 1944. The Turk told us that he had been sent into internal exile in the area of Parvomai, but after 9 September 1944 he escaped to Turkey as his brother-in-law lived in Istanbul. The latter, instead of harbouring him, handed him over to the police. He had spent several months in various camps in Anatolia.
>
> We asked him what kind of people were held in those camps. He replied that there were Bulgarians, Russians, Greeks, Germans and Jews. We asked him if he knew who the Bulgarians were. He replied that there were soldiers, an officer from Shoumen and civilians. I asked him about Geshev, giving him his description. He told me that there was such a person and they called him the 'Pope'. When he worked at headquarters, Geshev was nicknamed the Pope, because he had studied in Italy. My conversation with the Turk led me to believe that Geshev was in Turkey.
>
> Pavel Pavlov, chief of State Security, and Alexander Sankov, chief inspector of State Security, were inseparable and the latter would do everything the former ordered. At work they were very independent and self-confident because they were protégés of Architect Sevov, adviser to the Tsar.
>
> Several days before 9 September, 1944, they met and escaped to Vienna with the German transports. From Vienna they went over to Rome, where they met a rich Argentinian lady over whom Pavlov and Sankov fell out. The latter, together with his cousin and the Argentinian, left for Argentina. Pavlov stayed in Rome where he worked in central heating.
>
> The source of this information is an Italian lady who had arrived to visit her daughter, married to a Bulgarian.

Presumably, Andrei Pramatarov and the agent Moutsi were the last to provide a reliable indication that Geshev was in Turkey. It is natural that Geshev should seek refuge precisely there, in the Middle East, where the British Intelligence Service had a ramified spy network and he felt at home. It is across Turkey that a large number of Bulgarian *émigrés* escaped shortly before and after 9 September, 1944. The under-aged Bulgarian Tsar Simeon II, his mother Giovanna (the widow of Boris III) and the late monarch's sisters, stripped of their royal prerogatives after a relatively trouble-free referendum, arrived on Turkish territory in 1946. It is there that Geshev mysteriously disappeared. No Bulgarian has reported having met him in the flesh since then.

Numerous checks among the Bulgarian expatriates dispersed all over the world in Europe, Canada, the United States, Australia and Latin America, have found no trace, or even a rumour of his presence.

In late 1989 and early 1990, after Zhivkov's ousting, ambitious sensation seeker quite hastily and without any documentary proof, sought a connection between Zhivkov and Geshev. One of them, Alexander Alexandrov, published in the press exciting stories about Geshev surfacing in the Middle East and Latin America under the name of Michel Mansour, about his marriage and about chance encounters abroad between Bulgarians and the great policeman and so on. Without foundation in documented facts, however, these versions were remembered as mere dubious titbits of gossip.

The active tracking-down continued until 1962. The Bulgarian Intelligence Service even worked out a special tracing operation code-named 'The Ram', a misnomer for an intelligent and expert high-ranking cop. Probably negative emotions prevailed over realities in this case. A person who controlled the fates of so many people seems to have vanished into history without a trace.

Let us try to reconstruct his sudden and mysterious disappearance from the distance of time on the strength of the few facts available.

As is known, around 9 September, 1944 he managed to make his exit almost unknown. The last person with him was his personal driver who survived and served a seven-year sentence as a political prisoner. He remembered that around 8 September, Geshev unexpectedly called him and ordered him to drive off to Plovdiv (where they were to rendezvous with somebody). On the road to Svilengrad, some 100 kilometres to the east of Plovdiv, Geshev ordered him to stop and he got out. He gave the driver some Swiss francs and told him to drive back to Sofia, without looking back. That was all. 'He carried a small suitcase,' the driver recalled.

Why on the way to Svilengrad? He obviously planned to cross over into Turkey. Most probably he had his own underground passage across the border and could count on people who would lead him safely to Turkish territory. The last order he gave the driver not to look back, also suggests that he intended to do that.

Why didn't he escape with the withdrawing German forces? Geshev had been and remained a die-hard Anglophile. He detested the Germans; he openly called them barbarians and, whenever he could, he refused to cooperate with them.

In Turkey he obviously expected to get in touch with his future partners. The Turkish capital swarmed with foreign secret agents. Ankara and Istanbul were major centres of the intelligence services of all great powers, especially Britain and the United States. Germany was to be counted out, as he would have sought contact with her spies in a different way and place. The German secret service at that time retreated with the army through Vienna towards the borders of the German Reich. The other option was to seek contact with the Soviet Intelligence Service. But that was hardly likely because Soviet troops were to enter Bulgaria in a matter of days. A contact with the Russians would have also been achieved in a different way. (Colonel Nedev was a case in point.)

The most plausible theory is that Geshev was trying to contact the intelligence services of the Western Allies. We have no concrete evidence to suggest whether he succeeded or not.

More than 40 years have passed since then and many secrets have been disclosed. Major Soviet spies have infiltrated almost all the large intelligence services in the world. They, too, didn't have the slightest idea of such a person working for any service. A number of major western spies from this period also spoke out. Many archives and records in Britain, the Federal Republic of Germany and the USA are no longer classified. Almost all depositories of information about World War II are accessible to researches. And yet, nothing is know about Geshev.

What can this imply? Obviously, police officer Nikola Geshev was a figure that did not serve only local and *ad hoc* interests during World War II. He was an agent complying with the rules of political espionage: his agents infiltrated parties and movements so that decades later, they could carry out strategic missions in the highest places and state governing bodies. Such cases remain classified for a very long period of time. Neither people nor archives speak out after 50, 100 or even more years.

In such cases even the mastermind of this spy ring has to keep silent and remain obscure because it is through him that powerful outside agencies pull the strings of his finely woven network. Such are the rules of the big political and intelligence game, and the gifted Bulgarian policeman would appear to play by these rules. This is definitely evidenced by the fact that Geshev disappeared so completely and absolutely mysteriously. He did not surface in the *émigrés* circles. There are no traces and clues of his activity in foreign services which at that time impudently and almost openly operated against Bulgaria. There is every reason to assume that his experience and qualifications, his expertise ought to have been made use of.

My profound conviction concerning Geshev's fate is built on the principle of studying documents and eyewitness accounts, as well as on the logical comparison of events which took place much later but whose implied intent had no other explanation.

Two things can be considered proven with a great measure of certainty.

First, that Geshev is a British agent because of the direction and the destination of his escape. This is corroborated by the contacts of the detected British agents in Bulgaria during the 1941 to 1944 period, especially after the closure of the British diplomatic mission in Sofia. These agents operated in the Anglophile circles of Bulgarian middle class businessmen and merchants: Francis Baker, Vadim Pavlovich Grinevich, Eduard Mitrose, Charles Burg Andrews, Georgi (Yuri) Platnitsky, Eduard Mikhailovich Sokolovski, Mikhail Dimitrievich Skaklikov and others. An impressive number of these agents were recruited among the White Guard *émigrés* in Bulgaria.

Their contact channels in those years converged in the geographically nearest point with the most favourable conditions for instant contact: Istanbul.

The second circumstance is that the credible witnesses assert that Geshev escaped and was present in one and the same country: Turkey.

All fugitives at that time carried the same investment capital: information about a spy network. Those who didn't have such information invented it; not Geshev.

At that time Kim Philby was head of Secret Intelligence Service Section 9, covering the Soviet Union and the Balkans. According to his reminiscences, he studied closely the materials about the communist movement in Eastern Europe (1943–46).

Since the end of 1946, Kim Philby was the SIS chief of station in Turkey. In Istanbul he gathered information about Bulgaria from the fugitives. He would hardly miss the opportunity of a face-to-face meeting with Geshev. But there fate met Geshev with a double agent, who used his official status to work for the Soviet Intelligence Service. From that point on, Geshev and his personal agents' files could have travelled in one direction only: for the Soviet Union.

No tracing action has been taken there for things can be hushed up practically in perpetuity. This is corroborated by Stalin's orders to Chervenkov to suspend the operation of the commissions tracking down *agents provocateurs* in the Bulgarian Communist Party.

There are further facts, but this is not the right time to disclose them. This version, however, confronts historians and researchers with a lot of questions.

Dramatic events began in Bulgaria at that time. The social and political ideals of the Bulgarian people were served under the sign of revolutionary impatience, enthusiasm and Bolshevik fervour. With time, however, the enthusiasm cooled down. The invisible tentacles of self-seeking, enrichment and a go-getting scramble for the top enmeshed society. Spite and sordid ambitions were rife with the opening opportunities for top jobs and promotion. The new government built its authority on hatred and persecuted and repressed the people who had controlled the wealth and the power of Bulgaria. History inexorably teaches us that when a government sows the seeds of hatred and vengeance, it will inevitably reap the fruit of hatred and vengeance. The until-recently wealthy Bulgarians or those who had managed to educate themselves, the better and the more talented people among the emerging party cadres, had to lie low before the club-brandishing militants who hoisted the flag of the 'sanctified' and 'justified' revolutionary violence. Human history inexorably proves that every idea vested with power turns into violence,

New government and ideals are not always chosen by the people. They are often brought on bayonet points by military violence. Thus the thundering war machine on the roads of Europe brought in early September 1944 a radical political change in Bulgaria. More than four decades had to pass before the Bulgarian people could realize that a government can do everything with bayonets except sit on them. By the way, these were the last words I managed to exchange with Todor Zhivkov in a short conversation a day before his retirement when he asked, 'Still, why do people reject socialism?'

Obviously, 45 years after the Communist party had come to power with the decisive help of the Soviet army, as party historians themselves admit, even the veteran party leader and head of state of Bulgaria had his doubts. The pendulum of history had swung back within 45 years.

2. Towards the Top

It is difficult to write about Todor Zhivkov just a couple of months after his ousting. Every viewpoint will be biased and emotionally vulnerable, and will arouse suspicion of self-interest or dubious morals.

On the one hand, I am motivated by the fact that I have to write today and now, when the distance of time will not have softened or ironed out my impressions of the people and circumstances. I must write about Zhivkov and his time for yet another reason; at present the Balkan arrogance and immorality towards the deposed leader has reached such proportions that one can hardly remain indifferent, especially if one has been 'backstage' of the great events, in the nerve centre of the ousted party leadership. Otherwise, we would be completely overwhelmed by the spectacle of hypocrisy, treachery and apostasy which has been running high in Bulgaria since November 1989.

People who until yesterday were showered with generous honours, titles and bounties are now trying to pass themselves off as opponents, heroes and even victims of Zhivkov. There was talk of 100,000 repressed communists, about plots and murders. Even Pencho Koubadinski, until recently a veteran Politburo member and close friend of Zhivkov, who wouldn't be employed even as a doorman by anybody else, is trying to pose as a hero. Next he will be telling us that his expensive safaris in Africa were an organized rebellion against Todor Zhivkov.

The floods of new labels including authoritarian regime, autocratic dictatorship, leader of the nomenclature, crafty intriguer and political speculator, have come forth as an expression of the journalists' unleashed speculation. They dismiss every reminder of the 35-year Zhivkov regime in a small, but still European country with a long and involved political history.

Somebody once said that everything in Bulgaria should be taken with a pinch of salt. We cannot expect a better historical destiny while we do not realize or learn to identify the real interests of those who speak and pledge in the name of the people. As long as we fail to recognize this, we will be deceived in our hopes and dreams of a more humane and prosperous society. That is why, with respect to many opinions and assessments about Todor Zhivkov, the phrase 'take it with a pinch of salt' will be an understatement.

There is a lot of shrewd reckoning in this drive to shower abuse, to lay the blame and the responsibility on a single person. To some this is an attempt to cover up their own guilt. How many people have been hiding for decades behind Todor Zhivkov's back? Why shouldn't they keep hiding there? All the more so now given recent events. Now, when everything has collapsed or is still crumbling, the blame has to be pinned on somebody; as always, the largest target is the handiest.

To others, this is a form of self-assertion. Is there a political figure in Bulgaria's post-liberation history who has not met with a similar fate? Death alone has saved a few of them from castigation, hatred, physical abuse or ridicule. Only a few political leaders of Bulgaria have never been imprisoned. The Turkish invasion and the ensuing five centuries of domination wiped out the medieval Bulgarian aristocracy which had led Bulgaria through the vicissitudes of a volatile history.

After the 1878 liberation, the young state found itself without a political élite, without ethics in the affairs of state and without political manners. Partisanship, corruption and intrigue increased and base political morals burdened society, especially in social and political strategy.

The methods are familiar: toadyism, fear and time-serving until the trap clicks and the man at the top gets caught in it. The ensuing mass 'heroism' and vengeance sometimes results in a savage delirium. Then it is the turn of the next one. The specific historical situation in which a person had worked and the conditions under which he had made his decisions are often ignored. If a political leader is taken out of this context, he can easily appear as a nonentity, as someone who was only capable of blunders and crimes or, as a professor of mine used to say, 'If we ignore the specific historical situation, we must blame the Pechenegs for not having built socialism.'

Certainly, the times and the conditions cannot justify a politician if he does not live up to his duty and morals, which are also the product of a specific age and, quite often, they turn from universally acceptable norms into an individual notion justifying self-interest.

In politics there are such categories as 'once' and 'for ever'. There are no perennial truths. The labels 'villain' or 'hero' are inapplicable in judging a historical personality, by his deeds. Such evaluations should always be nuanced and balanced.

In 1946, the Bulgarian people voted for a republic. For more than four decades the monarchy seemed alien to the ethics and the political values of the people.

The idea of a good monarch and of monarchy as a fair institution in the conditions of rife political machinations in the Balkans is now revived. It is seen as capable of maintaining law and order and of protecting the nation's interests, or at least the newly-established 'Enlightenment Monarchist Society' promotes it in this way.

Marx says that 'people themselves make their history but they do not make it of their own free will, or in the conditions of their choice, but under established, fixed and inherited circumstances.' That is why when passing judgment and writing on Todor Zhivkov, one should bear in mind that he was the product, the pillar and the victim of precisely those circumstances which produced the system. This system will weigh heavily on the memory of succeeding generations long after its demolition.

Full and abridged versions of Todor Zhivkov's biography have been written and published on numerous occasions, whether the public needed it or not. Each biography opens up an opportunity to focus on some colour or shade; to compose a tune which will please those who call it. I will therefore limit myself to those facts necessary to enable us to grasp the salient parts of a person's character. Todor Zhivkov was born in Pravets on 7 September 1911. Some earlier biographies give the date as 1909, but in such cases even a man would compromise with truth in favour of the latter date. He jokes about being a Virgo, saying that he had been spared the passive feminine role of that sign of the zodiac but would not let anyone play an active role towards his sign; instead, he himself had often performed such an active role. After this ribald remark, he would always burst into complacent laughter.

All sorts of legends have been sought in his life. Rumour has it that he was Tsar Ferdinand's illegitimate son because of a resemblance to the monarch's famous Coburg nose. To some gullible people that was the only explanation of the fact that he managed to stay at the top for 35 years without having the blue Bourbon or Orleans blood that ran in the veins of the Coburg dynasty. Rumours are spread about every long-serving head of state. They are an indispensable 'accessory' of every political career.

Todor Zhivkov inherited from his parents the valuable asset and the necessary condition for longevity: the health and psychological endurance of a long line of mountaineers. Even the hard political work and the relentless power struggles did not affect him.

Until the last years before his retirement he had a stable blood pressure of 130/170, and his pulse rate rarely exceeded 64 even in sustained exercise.

He had to have his little joke talking about his family. His favourite subject was his grandfather Vlado, who had lived to be 105. When some women passed by on their way to the fields, the villagers teased him, 'grandfather Vlado, just look at the women!' And he replied: 'Come on, lads, I'm no longer fit for that. If I were 90, it would make a great deal of difference!' It was from him that men in the family had inherited an early baldness. When the villagers asked him, 'Grandfather Vlado, what happened to your beard?' he used to tell a long and invented story about his travels to Constantinople where he worked as a builder. There he once fell into a lime pit and lost his hair which was a symbol of his masculinity.

Zhivkov was sometimes vain. He tried to hide the congenital baldness with an elaborate hair-style. When his hair turned grey, he regularly had it hennaed. In 1987, when shown the book on his daughter *Lyudmila Zhivkova. Life and Work (1942–1981). A Chronicle*, he looked intently at the first photograph showing him at the age of 30 with Lyudmila on his shoulders. He exclaimed with a nostalgic smile, 'Do you see how handsome I was?'

I don't think any well-known statesman has ever been immune to vanity. French playwright and actor Sasha Guitry says that 'vanity is often arrogance to others', but I never noticed any signs of arrogance in Zhivkov.

He came from an ordinary family which shared the common fate of our people. They tilled the land leased on a sharecrop basis. They were craftsmen and, like all Bulgarians, his parents wanted to see their children through school to save them from that curse – the daily toil in the fields.

Todor Zhivkov did not excel in his studies. His performance in high school was unconvincing and wavering. His relations say he completed his secondary education in Pavlikeni as a private pupil.

It would be interesting to find the source of his high school diploma, issued by Boys' High School No. 3 in Sofia, which appeared in the press after 10 November 1989. He enrolled to study law at Sofia University before 9 September 1944 but dropped out before the end of the first term. No record of his student days is preserved except his enrolling form.

Todor Zhivkov was conscripted belatedly into the Labour Service (1936–37). He often recalled the time when they went on strike and made the gypsy cook throw out the grub. The gypsy said, 'OK, but if they beat me, I'll give you away.' He often quipped, 'If they beat us, we'll own up.' He obviously meant to emphasize that a person can always yield to force.

He told another episode of his conscription to illustrate his resourcefulness. An officer walked up to a group of solders who had committed some minor offence to beat them. Todor Zhivkov was quick to make up his mind and he snapped out a command, 'Stand up! Attention!', after which he reported to the officer, thus defusing the conflict.

His biographies detail his admission to the communist party in 1932, his work at the State Printing Office, his participation in the Georgi Dimitrov defence campaign during the *Reichstag* fire trial, his dissent from the leftist sectarian course of the party and his suspension from party work. The revolutionary actions in which he was involved at that time are described with bombast, without reference to actual situations and people.

This is typical of the whole biography up to 1944. It lists numerous activities but they seem to go on self-contained, disconnected and aimless. That is why throughout his tenure 'sworn' and 'trusted' people whispered that his biography had been invented; it was a put-up job, and that he was actually Nikila Geshev's agent. That is how they accounted for Todor Zhivkov's close friendship with Mircho Spassov.

Many people secretly and eagerly looked into the facts of his life before 9 September 1944, into his mysterious visits to the villages of Duskot, Lissichevo, Govedartsi, to Sofia, the Balkan range and the partisan detachment which later became the Chavdar brigade. Needless to say, emphasis was always laid on the conspicuous inability of the police to identify and track him down.

Has Todor Zhivkov ever met Nikola Geshev? He has. This assertion is not based on interviews with and reminiscences of his colleagues and workers at the State Printing Office where he worked from 1929. He himself told me about it.

When Choudomir Alexandrov, Politburo member and secretary of the party's Central Committee, was dismissed from the Central Committee in July 1988 because of the disclosures concerning his wife and her kinship with former policemen, some veteran Central Committee members said: 'He is by far not the only one with such a background. What about Alexander Fol and his father who worked for Geshev.'

I told that to my colleagues in the office and only two or three hours later somebody had reported it to Todor Zhivkov. He called me at once. The conversation is reproduced below on the basis of notes in my note-pad.

'Have you said anything about Fol?'

'I have,' I replied. 'But when did they manage to tell you?'

'What do you know?'

'Comrade Zhivkov, I don't know anything special, actually. You know about the facts that were found back in the 1970s; about his father's connections with the palace, about his share in the censorship of communist books and newspapers and so on. Now they say that, apart from that, he worked for Geshev.'

Actually, the person in question was Nikolai Fol, the famous theatre director of the 1930s. His son, Alexander Fol, now a university professor of Thraceology, was for a long time the right-hand man of Lyudmila Zhivkova in his capacity as first secretary chairman of the Committee for Culture and minister of national education. The inquiry about his father was conducted precisely in connection with the appointments of his son to these high offices. There was much talk about Alexander Fol's 'suspicious' bourgeois background. This gifted scholar had many political enemies at the Central Committee who insisted on his dismissal from the state posts. But the professor was categorically endorsed by Lyudmila Zhivkova and, after her death in 1981, by her father.

Despite the frequent rumours about his imminent dismissal, Alexander Fol kept his education portfolio for a longer term than any of his predecessors since 1878. He was relieved of his duties when Georgi Atanassov, another historian, who had felt a strong antipathy to Alexander Fol since his university days, became prime minister.

Still, the latter retained his membership in the Central Committee – that is, in the upper crust of the 'nomenclature' – in Zhivkov's administrative reserve.

Several months before his ousting, he reappointed Alexander Fol as chief of cultural affairs. Zhivkov's downfall brought to an end the political career of the university professor, maliciously nicknamed 'the Courtier' by some of his colleagues.

Did Alexander Fol stand high in Zhivkov's favour by chance? This is hardly likely because in that same conversation about the father, Todor Zhivkov told me: 'I knew Nikolai Fol back in the 1930s. As an eminent playwright, at that time, he managed an amateur company at the National Theatre. He had announced a competition for the title role in Schiller's *William Tell*. At that time I was very keen on the theatre, and I entered the competition, reciting Hristo Smirnenski's poem *The Coal Miner*. I had a fit of stage fright during the recitation and I went home quite disheartened. In a week's time, however, I got word that I had been chosen to play William Tell. I was so grateful to Nikolai Fol.'

After a few moments silence Todor Zhivkov went on: 'As to Geshev, I knew him personally. I've been to his office. He was a very intelligent and cunning policeman. He interrogated me and said, "Now look, you're trying to be smart, but I know you are . . ."'

Again he said nothing for a while and then he added: 'After that he ordered them to beat me. They beat me three times, concentrating on the genitals. On the third time, the policeman who was escorting me said, "If you hold out this time too, the boss told us to let you go."' (This fact has never been mentioned and has been left out by the diligent biographer who never missed an opportunity to praise and glorify Todor Zhivkov.)

I asked him, 'What actually happened to Geshev?'

At once he answered curtly, 'He's dead. On the eve of 9 September 1944 a squad of Soviet paratroopers landed on the Turkish border and killed him!'

He said it categorically, defying all of Geshev's hunters who spent nearly 15 years trying to trace him. The version is implausible. At those troubled times a handful of Soviet scouts could hardly have located the smart policeman along the several hundred kilometre long Bulgarian–Turkish border. In addition, there was no reason at all to keep that operation secret until that particular day.

After 10 November 1989 the press carried some features claiming that Todor Zhivkov could not possibly have participated in the armed anti-fascist resistance in so many parts of the country within the brief span of time between 1941 and 1944. Moreover he never went underground: he put on plays, he moved openly and had his photo taken. The newspapers reproduced his safe-conduct under the assumed name of Ivan Dimitrov Tomov, issued by the Ministry of War, which allowed him to move freely throughout the country. Some people's suspicion was particularly aroused by the fact that the safe conduct was dated 14 April 1941, several months before the communist party decided to launch its armed struggle. Therefore, they claim, the party leadership had nothing to do with that document.

Notably, the real names of people and events in his biography usually give way to generalities such as 'the party promoted him', 'the party appointed him'. No real situations are described; only vague operations and phantoms instead of people.

In the autumn of 1943 he attended the conference of the Chavdar detachment in the Balkan range in his capacity as member of the party's provincial committee. At that time he 'left a clue': a wonderful photo showing him together with his mother, his wife – Dr Mara Maleeva – and little Lyudmila in the village of Govedartsi. He staged the plays *Khan Tatar*, *Ivanko*, *Dar Mornings*, *Three Chain Gangs*, and others all during that same period.

Everybody who has participated in the operation of headquarters and zones, and who has fought in partisan detachments, knows the secrecy, the time and the effort required by underground rendezvous, transfers, contacts and actions. At the same time, no formal trace has reached us from the 1941–44 period which would lead us to his underground activities. He moved openly and he was active organizing community-centre and theatrical performances in the village of Govedartsi.

There is yet another uncertain fact from those years, at the intersection of what are now Vassil Kolarov Street and Angel Kanchev Street, in Sofia. Todor Zhivkov and Misho Mishev (later secretary of the Central Committee) ran a small fish shop. They bought the merchandise from wholesalers.

How did they get capital to start that business? How did Zhivkov come to that partnership with Mishev? Documents available so far do not answer these questions.

How did Zhivkov travel from Govedartsi to the mountains via Sofia? As is known, the villages at the foot of the Balkan range were blockaded. It was particularly dangerous to pass across them because they were so close to Sofia. Still Zhivkov had no problems running the blockades, organizing a partisan movement and doing political work.

I have tried to interview survivors about his part in the Chavdar brigade battles. I asked them to describe his actual combat actions and part in battles or other operations. I received vague answers, hearsay and stories about miraculous escapes from battles and blockades.

In a conversation, I have heard Zhivkov himself say that in one battle his rifle hung fire and he failed to shoot at a gendarme who luckily didn't notice him. (Many years later, the famous Bulgarian fortuneteller Vanga reminded him of that episode.) He was proud of his actions and *sang-froid* in rescuing the Chavdar brigade from an utter defeat, and he used to say that he acted as decisively as Benkovsky. He took over, changed the tactics, contained the panic and kept the brigade combat capable. Witnesses, however, did not say anything definite.

Some Chavdar members asked themselves why the recruitment of new partisans in the area of Sofia, organized by Zhivkov early in the spring of 1944 ended with a crackdown and massacre of the defenceless, unarmed people. How did the notorious General Kocho Stoyanov, in charge of the encirclement, know the direction in which the large task force of the Chavdar detachment had to move to establish a free zone in Sredna Gora and the Rhodopi mountains? The instructions were brought to the detachment by Todor Zhivkov.

One of the Chavdar members, Kiril Milev, claimed that Todor Zhivkov and he had to rendezvous with an underground activist. The contact point was in front of what is now the Dimiter Blagoev cinema. 'We were the only two people who knew about that rendezvous. The police came to the rendezvous and arrested the underground activist. It was either I or him who had given away the rendezvous,' Milev asserted. 'Nobody else knew.'

Careful readers of Zhivkov's biography ask other questions, too. Why didn't the police learned of his 'unremitting' and various activities? Why didn't they have a file on him? Why wasn't he imprisoned and sent into internal exile? All the more so given that his participation in the headquarters of the First Insurgent Operative Zone and his contacts with the Chavdar detachment were so active that his false identity card could hardly have covered them up. At that time, as Zhivkov himself wrote in a 1945 autobiography, he successfully held the following positions of responsibility:he was secretary of the Youchbunar party district in Sofia, a member of the Sofia Provincial Committee of the party, in charge of the District Party branches, deputy commander of First Operative Insurgent Zone. There are eyewitnesses who claim that when he travelled to the Balkan mountains, he used the scheduled bus service and flashed a police identity card at the road-blocks. This evidence, as well as his encounters with Geshev, remain undisclosed or are left out for obvious reasons from his biographies.

His participation in the coup on 9 September 1944 has been repeatedly described, and it is no use dwelling on it. In a panegyric style, familiar before 10 November 1989, historians and biographers have been promoting the version of Zhivkov's leading role in the preparations and execution of the seizure of power in Sofia. In a private conversation, one of these biographers, the prominent expert on the history of socialist Bulgaria, Professor Dr Mito Issoussov, painted a different picture of Zhivkov's part in that operation: unproved presence at the insurgents' headquarters, a mysterious appearance only after the end of the decisive actions, and an equally mysterious disappearance for nearly a day after that watershed.

Interestingly enough, on 10 September 1944, Todor Zhivkov went straight to the police headquarters and, together with Mircho Spassov, was among the first to get hold of the police archives. They also organized the arrest of police operatives. Todor Zhivkov did not like to recall that period. He avoided talking about his connections with Mircho Spassov at that time, when both of them worked for a time in the newly established National Police Force.

An investigation was instituted in 1946 to attempt to verify Zhivkov's connections with Geshev and to collect evidence of his alleged activity as a British spy. The investigation was code-named 'Hedgehog' after the supposed alias under which Zhivkov worked for Geshev. Notably that operation started as early as 1946, when the Stalinist-style personality cult had not yet surged in the country. The showtrial against the top-ranking functionary Traicho Kostov was far away. Files on Communists and leaders began to be compiled much later, in 1949, after the aforementioned trial. What were the grounds for investigating Zhivkov? There were obviously reasonable doubts, as it was too early to speak of a spy mania in 1946 and Zhivkov was second secretary of the party's Provincial Committee at that time.

Colonel Mourdjev, subsequently chief of the counter-intelligence service, was in charge of the investigation. It is hardly coincidental that later on, in his capacity as chief of State Security Department 2, he took over the tracing of Geshev in 1951. That operation, as we have already mentioned, was code-named Ram. The two investigations clearly had a lot of leads in common, since one and the same officer was put in charge of both. The following text is taken from a memorandum, approved by Colonel Mourdev, chief of State Security Department 2, on 23 July 1951, concerning 'the initiation of a tracing procedure for Nikola Geschev':

> In July 1947 an investigation was instituted to trace one Nikola Hristov Geshev. The said investigation was conducted by Division E of Department 7 at that time.
>
> The investigation in question was transferred to the Department in March 1951.
>
> Throughout the length of his police service, he worked against the party, taking personal charge of the largest number of *agents provocateurs*.
>
> Immediately after 9 September 1944 Geshev went underground. There is evidence that he is now abroad, but to date the service has been unable to acquire reliable information on Geshev's whereabouts.
>
> PROPOSAL
>
> In view of the above and of the fact that so far we have not been authorized to conduct the above tracing procedure, your permission to assign the same to Team B-2 of Division 1.

Zhivkov often thought of Colonel Mourdjev until on 24 July 1989, over morning coffee with his office advisors, it was reported that the recently retired General Mourdjev had died.

Zhivkov remembered how he had been investigated at that time. The same Mourdjev had even gone to his wife, Mara Maleeva, and asked her, 'Are you sure that you know that man well?' She had given him a strongly-worded reply and had turned him out. Zhivkov continued: 'I knew that they were investigating me as a British spy. I had a trusted man in State Security who told me, "Comrade Zhivkov, we are investigating you, but if it comes to arresting you, I'll warn you." (At that time, in 1952, Todor Zhivkov was already secretary of the Central Committee.) I told him not to do such a thing whatever happened and to carry out his bosses' orders, even if it came to an arrest.'

At that time (1950–52) commissions were appointed throughout the country on the orders of the party chief Vulko Chervenkov to seek incriminating evidence about people who had collaborated with the police. Intriguing articles have appeared in the Bulgarian press about these commissions since 10 November 1989.

Yet another big question arises at this point. When Vulko Chervenkov met Stalin in 1952, the latter ordered him to halt the operation of the commissions tracking down police plants in the Communist party.

Why? What had happened? What could those commissions have discovered? Unpalatable facts or facts already known to Stalin and to the Soviet secret service? Is there any way to account for Stalin's move? It was certainly not an act of humanism because the communist dictator was notorious for his obsession with the struggle against 'the class enemy', against 'spies and traitors'. One way or another, the commissions halted their inquiries: Mourdjev had his hands tied.

The fate of Operation Hedgehog was sealed in 1956. Under the orders of the minister of the interior, a directive was promulgated that the collected material should not be read. All investigative records compiled up to now were stacked in the central heating boiler room of the Ministry of the Interior.

By a decision of the Politburo, headed by Todor Zhivkov, they were incinerated. The motivation was to calm and stabilize the work and the life of the cadres. In the same tolerant spirit, Mourdjev was not punished, but he remained under Todor Zhivkov's sustained control.

Operation Ram was abandoned around 1960. It disappeared among the unsolved files. According to the last tip-offs, Geshev was in Brazil and Argentina. Inquiries were made to no avail. It seemed that 'the Ram' would leave at ease the conscience of many people. All the more so now that the police archives, as well as the investigative records and materials gathered between 1944 and 1956, had been destroyed.

The fate of these archives troubled many people, Zhivkov included. In recent years, at public meetings, he often recalled facetiously that episode of his life.

It was evidently a disturbing subject for him. At plenums and sessions, Zhivkov tried to crack jokes about being one of Geshev's men and a British spy. On one particular 8 December, marked in Bulgaria as Day of University Students, when as usual he delivered a speech before select undergraduates, he once again laughingly claimed to have seen the investigative records on his alleged spying for the British. During the last year of his political career Zhivkov dropped such half-ironic, half-serious hints even more often. Over morning coffee with his advisors that thought seemed to be preying on his mind. He kept explaining and going back to the past. In any case, to him that wasn't just a minor episode; this dark side of his life psychologically determined a line of conduct which found expression in a clearly manifested anxiety and repeated explanations. On 13 January 1990, nearly three months after the ousting of the former head of state and first party leader, the *Otechestven Front* newspaper carried an article intriguingly headlined 'Has Todor Zhivkov been an *agent provocateur*?' The author Alexander Alexandrov quoted Georgi Chankov, a former party functionary, as saying that Todor Zhivkov's above mentioned safe-conduct under the false name of Ivan Tomov, dated April 1941, was not 'the work of the party' because the party leadership didn't start procuring such safe conducts until much later. The author also refers to his interviews with Zhivkov's printer colleagues, the late Ivan Knizh and Makedonski, who claimed that 'he had met Geshev in the office of the State Printing House director.'

Alexander Alexandrov, however, has had some more interesting interviews. Most probably a career intelligence man, Alexandrov met in Argentina with Geshev's former assistant, Alexander Sankov. The latter confirmed Geshev's intention to escape to Turkey, as well as his sudden disappearance around 9 September 1944.

Further on, the ex-policeman and now *émigré* told Alexandrov the following: 'Once, when Geshev was out of town, Dr Delius, the Abver chief of station in Bulgaria, whose real name was Otto Wagner, came to see me. A police agent was with me. I immediately dismissed him so that I could welcome the distinguished guest. I wasn't on friendly terms with the Germans. I realized that he knew where Geshev had gone and that was why he had come to see me. I said I was ready to help him if I could. The doctor showed me some photographs and asked me point blank what I thought about the two men in them. They were Geshev's agents, who posed as communists but actually informed on us to the communist leaders. I had my doubts about the one who worked at the State Printing Office; I thought Delius would get into trouble with him. I explained to him how he had been recruited and that later on he had helped us to eliminate a dangerous communist leader.'

Sankov then told Alexandrov that 'that young peasant' was called Tomov, (Todor Zhivkov). Delius showed great interest in him and 'took him to a weekend house near Knyazhevo where he recruited him as a German spy . . .'

Once, when he was in a good mood, Sankov confided to Alexandrov, 'Young man, Bulgaria is ruled by one of Geshev's men! You'll see where he'll land the country.'

According to the author of the article, information about Todor Zhivkov's role as a police plant had also come from Italy. A former senior state security officer, General G. Gochev, had told him he had better give up his inquiry.

Alexandrov also refers to the interrogations of the chief of State Security Counterintelligence Department B, Andrei Pramatarov and of another member of the same department, Assen Topalov. The two of them claimed to have seen Todor Zhivkov enter Geshev's office on various occasions. Alexandrov's other assumptions are to the same effect. He mentions the disturbance and disappearance of part of the police archives immediately after 9 September 1944 when Todor Zhivkov, holding the rank of Lieutenant-colonel, served briefly as chief of the national police force. In other words, he is suspected of having done his best to destroy all evidence of hidden *provocateur* activity.

A little later, the newspaper *Rabotnichesko Delo* carried another article by Alexandrov. The daily newspaper reproduced his letter sent to the Civil Committee of Enquiry into Corruption and Abuse of Power under the heading 'Traces of Todor Zhivkov's Betrayal'. The letter quotes numerous testimonies about Zhivkov's *provocateur* activity. However, the statements quoted by Alexander Alexandrov could not subsequently be corroborated and his article remained without evidential force.

Almost at the same time *Otechestven Front* ran Ivan Gerassimov's note 'The Contribution: T. Zhivkov and the Anti-Fascist Resistance', which also called into question the authenticity of his underground activity in the 1941–44 period. Among other things, the author mentioned a photograph of Todor Zhivkov taken in the summer of 1943, showing him carrying a fowling piece in the company of a notorious fascist and a staff officer from the Ministry of War. The ex-minister, Roussi Hristozov, expressed his doubts in the newspaper *Vecherni Novini*. Along with the assumption that in September 1944 Todor Zhivkov, Mircho Spassov and others destroyed part of the police archives, he also quoted the well-known party functionary Raiko Damyanov as assuming that Zhivkov was at the bottom of the major crackdowns on the party's Sofia District Committee in the autumn of 1934.

I myself have heard from the veteran Communist and longtime chairman of the Auditing Commission at the Central Committee of the Bulgarian Communist Party, Yordan Katrandjiev, that immediately after 9 September 1944, many communists wanted to work at the National Police Force Headquarters. A couple of months later, however, they left the coveted posts and took party appointments or other positions of responsibility. 'When our commission had to look through some police files later on, names had been cut out with a razor blade in the *provocateurs*' lists,' Katrandjiev claimed.

There is hardly anything surprising in this case, or any grounds for far-reaching moral conclusions, for invocations of conscience and duty. World history shows that police plants appeared invariably in all conspiratorial movements with political objectives. The same applies to the Communist party of Bulgaria after World War I. With his skills and talents Geshev takes special credit for this. He himself sometimes hinted that he controlled almost two-thirds of the communist leadership. He often boasted, with reason, that he was better versed in Marxism than a number of party theoreticians. On this basis he could defeat all ideological arguments of the detained communists and crush them, not only physically but morally also, thus creating conditions for possible recruitment.

Did he handle Todor Zhivkov in that way, too? No specific picture of their relationship can be reconstructed on the basis of the evidence cited above. None of this evidence is corroborated by documents and it is, therefore, only logical to question its reliability.

This writer's original clue was Zhivkov's own admissions that he had met Geshev and the related nasty memory of physical torture. Further on, however, my interest was rewarded by several documentary proofs.

One of them concerns a marginal note in a British diplomatic report from Bulgaria, which was sent from Sofia to London through secret channels in the spring of 1953. The diplomat tried to characterize the more promising people in Bulgarian politics and singles out the ambitions and the aggressive push of Todor Zhivkov who, at that time, was already at the top of the party. The diplomat emphasized in his report that in future Zhivkov must be watched very closely.

Three other documents, for the time being, are the only conclusive evidence of contact between Zhivkov and Geshev. It turned out that the police archives contained almost no documentary trace of the former-head of state and party leader. Only three records of Todor Zhivkov's interrogations dated 24 January, 6 March 1934 and 14 February 1935 have survived, as if by a miracle. All records were written in Zhivkov's own hand and were countersigned by the respective police officer in charge.

The first interrogation, held on 24 January 1934 came after Zhivkov was detained in one of the Workers' Party clubs, which was a legal form of the Communist party. After a list of biographical and professional data, Zhivkov testifies that he happened to be in the said club quite by chance.

All records show that Zhivkov replied very cleverly and managed to cover up every fact which could be used against him.

A month and a half later, on 6 March 1934, Zhivkov was again interrogated by Geshev himself. This is evident from Geshev's two signatures at the beginning and end of the record.

Obviously that interrogation was more thorough-going. After the routine biographical data, the dialogue focuses on the communist N.P. Yanchev. Zhivkov did not deny knowing him but claimed that he did not know him well. He didn't know he was a member of the Communist party and he did his best to convince Geshev that he had nothing to do with the activity of the communist in question. Further on, the record makes it clear, that Zhivkov had been detained after a search of the Workers' Party Club. He admitted that he was a member of the Print Workers' Union and that one year before he had been a member of the National Liberal Youth Organization thanks to which the National Liberal, Sariev had helped him find a job at the State Printing Office.

This interrogation took place only months before Zhivkov's promotion to a position of responsibility in the party. In the aforementioned autobiography dated 17 December 1945, published in Volume 24 of his *Selected Works*, Zhivkov himself writes on page 505: 'By the end of 1934 I became secretary of the Third Party District and member of the Regional Committee in Sofia. During those years (1932–35), I headed the operative bureau organizing street actions.' On the other hand, his meeting with Geshev took place only months before the major crackdown on the Sofia Regional Committee of the party in the autumn of 1934. Raiko Damyanov, secretary of the Committee since 1935, Boris Taskov, Boris Blagoev and other prominent party figures at that time, blame Todor Zhivkov for the crackdown. They lay the blame for other crackdowns in 1935 to him also. Because of that, according to the same communist functionaries, Zhivkov was expelled from the party. He himself writes in his autobiography that in the spring of 1935 he was dismissed from the Sofia Regional Party Committee, but attributes it to his dissent from the ultra-sectarian leadership of the party. The people who worked with him at that time, however, say he was expelled because of his *provocateur* actions.

As the minutes of the meetings of the Sofia Regional Party Committee at that time have been lost, we must resort to a logical juxtaposition of facts and situations. Here is another quotation from Zhivkov's 1945 autobiography:

'In March 1935, I was assigned to organize ultra-leftist action in Sofia in connection with a public police meeting of the head of the public force, Popzlatev, which couldn't but fail.'

He admits the failure of an action organized by him but does not list the reasons for this failure.

The last surviving record of Zhivkov's interrogation is a little unusual from the point of view of the typical police pedantry. It is dated 14 February, 1935 which means Zhivkov was at the police headquarters after the major crackdowns on the Regional Party Committee and immediately before the failure of the action he organized. The investigating magistrate who conducted the interrogation did not sign the record – a curious fact which cannot be attributed to negligence. As in the other two records, Zhivkov wrote down his evidence in his own hand. After the familiar biographical data, we read: 'In the past I was a member of the Bulgarian Graphic Union until 19 May 1934 when it was disbanded. I was also a member of the Vrancha – a Youth Agrarian Union. I have never been a member of any communist organization nor have I spoken from communist rostrums . . . I have not participated in the organization of communist rostrums in the factories in Bulgaria and Rasheev . . .'

Returning to the autobiography from which we have already quoted more than once:

'I have been in police custody several times: in 1935 I was given the third degree, probably as a result of *provocateur* betrayal. I assess my conduct in police custody as good.'

It is hardly likely, however, that 'this third degree' at the police station in 1935 would go carelessly unsigned by the investigating magistrate. Let us not blame Zhivkov that it is in this record rather than in the one dated 6 March, 1934 that he admits to his membership in non-communist youth organizations – a fact which is omitted in his autobiography. Immediately after 9 September, 1944 a start towards the top was only possible with a totally unblemished past political record.

All documents give us grounds only to build an hypothesis, rather than a conclusive allegation. Otherwise we will be biased in understanding a rigorously documented truth. What is more, isolated facts could in this way be used against any functionary who has fallen into the hands of the police.

A serious charge such as being an *agent provocateur* has to be supported by facts and documentary proof. Without them it would be immoral to confuse assumptions and proven truths.

The biographers say nothing about the way Todor Zhivkov was nominated and elected secretary of the Regional Committee of the party in September 1944, candidate member of the Central Committee in 1945, and first secretary of the City Party Organization in January 1948. For three years of party work that was a huge leap indeed. A little later, Zhivkov held the leadership of the Sofia Executive Council and of the city branch of the Fatherland Front. We should bear in mind that for a middle-ranking party functionary at the time, that was an impressive career. Which were the forces behind him? At that time, much higher-ranking leaders were in the capital: members of the Politburo, of the formerly underground party, the commanders of zones, headquarters and detachments, people who were famous throughout the country. Here were also the members of the party leadership in exile, who had arrived from Moscow and who had the complete confidence of the Soviet leaders. Morever, most of them were well-educated veteran revolutionaries experienced in politics. There was a large choice of fiercely competing cadres. But let us assume that he had the accomplishment of a leader and good fortune which, as far as his political career was concerned, betrayed him only in early November 1989. There was something more; Todor Zhivkov, as he later proved, had an extraordinary instinct for power and was the first among the incumbent leaders to realize the enormous significance of the Sofia Party Organization as a stepping stone to a big political career. He entrenched himself in that organization, got a foothold at all its levels and, having thus secured his rear, he made his decisive coup in April 1956.

In January 1950, Todor Zhivkov was elected secretary and alternative member of the Politburo. In June 1951, he was already a full Politburo member. He was successively in charge of agriculture, organizational matters and ideological work and, as such, he amassed experience in various different areas of party work.

In 1954 he was already a key figure in the secretariat of the party's Central Committee. That role became indisputable after his election as first secretary of the Central Committee.

In these years Todor Zhivkov was the right-hand man and major supporter of Vulko Chervenkov. The latter steadily endorsed him and, in the end, Zhivkov's coup caused his political death.

Todor Zhivkov did not like Georgi Dimitrov. He often told me that the personality cult in Bulgaria had actually started with Dimitrov's arrival; that he had brought managerial structure to Bulgaria, that he had transplanted all orders and directives of Stalin, that he had used Stalinist methods and style of work and favoritism. Zhivkov retained this hatred until the end of his political career. He never visited Dimitrov's birth place, the village of Kovachevtsi. When in June 1982 Bulgaria celebrated the hundredth anniversary of Georgi Dimitrov's birth, Zhivkov almost demonstratively sent the National Assembly chairman, Stanko Todorov, to the great festivities in the village of Kovachevtsi. In 1989, on Zhivkov's insistence, an attempt was made to rename the Dimitrov Young Communist League into the Bulgarian Young Communist League, thus formally eliminating the presence of Dimitrov's name in that organization.

One should bear in mind the fact that Zhivkov worked in extremely hard years. In the 1944–50 period a wave of revolutionary terror and violence surged. The old state apparatus was completely replaced and the monarchy was abolished. The opposition parties were repressed; terror reigned in the party ranks and it culminated in the 1949 trial against Traicho Kostov.

The people were intoxicated by the fact that the property and the real estate of the rich one per cent of the population would be expropriated so that the other ninety-nine per cent could live well.

What a great delusion! We paid a very high price for extending nationalization to the property that was earned which, as a matter of fact, bred entrepreneurship and initiative. I consider that collectivization of property was the most terrible invention of Marxism which has been taking a heavy toll on the people for more than a century and a half. The brutal dispossession had a dire and irreparable effect on material production, on public mentality and on personal ethics. The natural interpersonal relationships were disrupted, the yardstick of 'who is better' disappeared. People lost the mainstay, the 'value' of their work. In place of work acknowledged under the conditions of competition, with the market as the impartial judge, personal worth came to be weighed by treachery, hypocrisy, and toadyism as the ways to rise and to get a share of the cake.

Bulgaria was not spared the drama of nationalization in 1947 and of the land collectivization in 1950. Todor Zhivkov was an active organizer and promoter of this policy. He was in the front ranks of the party; a middle-aged generation which was the power base of the leadership in those years.

Todor Zhivkov also implemented the policy line which had been imposed to eliminate the organizational secretary of the Central Committee and prime minister Traicho Kostov, and his team in the party and the state. For his part, however, Kostov had blessed the crackdown on the leader of the agrarian party, Nikola Petkov. The Nikola Petkov case records contain no evidence of any connections with the western Allies' services. The charges of a coup conspiracy sound ludicrous at a time when Soviet troops were deployed in great strength in Bulgaria. According to the investigators' findings, the opposition headed at that time by Nikola Petkov, was armed with twelve fowling pieces, six carabines, eight revolvers and knives. Citing this information, Professor Mito Issoussov used to say that this was only part of Pencho Koubadisnki's hunting equipment for the African safaris.

After Nikola Petkov, the revolution devoured more of its children. It was the turn of Traicho Kostov. Our historians have traced the origin of that trial to the late 1940s. Its background concerns the relations with the Soviet Union; according to the studies, between 1945 and 1948, the economic relations between Bulgaria and the Soviet Union were beset by problems arising from the attitude of the state bodies towards Bulgaria. The trade negotiations between the two countries took as long as two and a half months: from 4 January 1945 to 17–18 March 1945. The negotiations lasted so long because the Soviet representatives offered Soviet cotton at a price of 350 leva, while they were only prepared to pay 220 leva for the Bulgarian tobacco – the price of cotton thus proved unjustifiably higher than that of tobacco. As a result of this, the relations between the two states became somewhat strained. On all these matters Traicho Kostov took a firm stand, as evident from one of his letters to Dimitrov who was then in Moscow and, later on, from some of his statements before Soviet officials.

Another dispute arose over the Soviet army's upkeep in Bulgaria. According to historians, Soviet troops entered Bulgaria in September 1944 and, until the end of the war, Bulgaria spent 23,500 million leva on their upkeep, while the country's national budget totalled only 48,000 million leva. Needless to say, this adversely affected the Bulgarian economy.

At Traicho Kostov's suggestion, Georgi Dimitrov repeatedly raised with Stalin the question of the Soviet forces upkeep. In the end, Moscow decided to review the matter in favour of Bulgaria. Traicho Kostov was one of the people who rightly sought economic relations on equal terms between the two states. Stalin relented, but his vindictive character could not tolerate the intractable Bulgarian leader. At that time the Kremlin contemplated a last battle against all 'native communists' – party functionaries who during World War II fought in the anti-fascist resistance in their countries. They were to be replaced by 'emigrants' from the Soviet Union who were to bring to their respective countries obedience and the Stalinist model of socialism. That was how a whole series of showtrials on trumped-up spying charges were planned against many native Communists in the peoples' democracies.

In Hungary their victim was Laszlo Rajk. In Bulgaria the choice fell on Traicho Kostov.

After the adoption of the State Secrets Act in October 1948, the directive that no information on the condition of Bulgaria's economy was to be made available to any foreign diplomat provided the occasion for the repressions against him on 7 December 1948 at one of the meetings of the Bulgarian delegation which had arrived in Moscow to coordinate the documents for the Fifth Party Congress. Stalin went over to Traicho Kostov, took off his spectacles, insulted him personally and accused him of being insincere to the Soviet Union. Traicho Kostov's case was aggravated by the fact that the Yugoslav government took a similar stand to his. In Yugoslavia, at the end of 1947, many differences arose with the Soviet advisors in the Yugoslav army and the Yugoslav economic ministries. A directive went out to withhold economic information from the Soviet representative in Yugoslavia.

Later on, the investigation against Traicho Kostov focused on an attempt to prove his 'connection' with the British representatives in Bulgaria, and with the British Intelligence Service, with Yugoslavia and the Yugoslav leadership. In August 1949 Traicho Kostov was arrested. On 20 September there followed the arrest of an enormous group of functionaries, including Traicho Kostov's wife and the entire team who worked with him before and after 9 September 1944 Ivan Maslarov and Nikola Pavlov. After his release from prison in 1956, Pavlov recalled:

> For a long time during the investigation I adopted the tactical trick of proving that the entire Politburo, the Council of Ministers, all deputy-ministers and the entire state apparatus were involved in that conspiracy, and I compiled a list of 160 people. Everybody realized the absurdity of my statement. All the more so, given that after Traicho Kostov's arrest, the number of advisors at the security services had increased from 4 to 14. The Soviet Intelligence had immediately dispatched General Chernov to Bulgaria in connection with the investigation against Traicho Kostov.

Todor Zhivkov witnessed all that but prudently kept silent about it. Worse yet, everybody else kept silent too. Zhivkov attended the July 1949 plenum of the Central Committee at which Vassil Kolarov read out his second report of accusations against Traicho Kostov and thus emerged as the person in charge of the political preparations for the trial. Presumably, the future head of state and first party leader attentively listened to Vulko Chervenkov's report too. In it Chervenkov mentioned that he had discussed mainly the Traicho Kostov problem at three meetings with Stalin between March and May 1949.

It was more than clear to Zhivkov that everything was lost, that Kostov's case was doomed. He therefore dutifully voted in favour of the plenum's resolutions.

The investigation raised the question why Traicho Kostov alone had survived the 1942 trial against the Central Committee when all the rest had been executed. His possible contacts with Nikola Geshev were also investigated.

According to the party archieves, however, Kostov alone did not make a confession to the police. Besides, in that trial, he was not charged with involvement in the Communist party's military organization, while Anton Ivanov, Peter Bogdanov and Nikola Vaptsarov were all investigated and convicted of involvement in the military organization, the military centre and the organization of the armed resistance in Bulgaria. Traicho Kostov was convicted only of his activities as political secretary of the Central Committee. Therefore, there is room for both doubt and vindication.

Other circumstances intervene. One of the brothers Balan, Svetoslav Balan (son of the famous Academician Balan), who served as Tsar Boris III's advisor several years before that trial, reminisced in his memoirs:

> At the time of the investigation Traicho Kostov's wife Lyuba came to see me and told me 'Mr Balan, my husband and you used to be classmates at Boys' High School No. 3. You shared the same desk, and you knew him very well. You probably know that he is under investigation. I beg you to intervene in the investigation and the trial with a view to his rescue.

Several days later, during a horse-ride with Tsar Boris III, Balan managed to have a *tête-à-tête* with him. He told him, 'Your Majesty, the accused Traicho Kostov is an excellent Bulgarian, a highly accomplished person who worked for our parliament after World War I as a shorthand typist. He was my classmate, the best student in our high school. Bulgaria will benefit if he is spared.' Boris answered him, 'Mr Balan, you know that I have never interceded for communists in Bulgaria with our judicial authorities.'

Several days after that conversation, however, Boris' orderly passed by Balan's office at the palace and told him, 'Mr Balan, his

Majesty decided to grant your request.' That was in all probability the truth about Traicho Kostov's life sentence issued in the 1942 trial. Seven years later, however, Stalin and Kolarov were far from the thought of sparing one of their own, who had been spared by the monarch. Actually, the trial was only a forceful illustration of the situation in Bulgaria.

Terror engulfed the country. The camps in Belene, Nozharevo and elsewhere operated at full capacity. The prisons were crowded with oppositionists who, too, had struggled against fascism. Any non-conformism and talent was punished. Many artists were repressed. It was the 'golden age' of the anonymous denunciations; the 'faithful' and 'us' were in fashion.

Mediocre people, who lacked intellectual ideas and ambitions, moved in for decades. In those years Bulgaria was the distorting mirror of Stalinism. Its social and political panorama reflected the tragedy of the Russian people – with a typically Bulgarian difference, personalizing and dwarfing it. That was the time of 'primary accumulation' of power and privileges through service and settling accounts.

I think that it was precisely then that duality struck roots in Todor Zhivkov's conduct and action.

As a function of the system, he was treacherous, calculating and unscrupulous for the sake of power. Outside the social role he had to play, Zhivkov was a liberal, kind-hearted, accessible, jolly good fellow. But is there any one of us who has not developed this duality due to Stalinism and the system of socialism? Zhivkov, therefore, was the creation of this system, even when he started for its top.

Let us return to the documents which preserve the pace of his hectic political life.

Obviously, Todor Zhivkov was way above the average level of the ruling élite between 1950 and 1956. The documents show that he became a key figure at the all-powerful secretariat and the multipurpose right-hand man of chief Vulko Chervenkov.

In just a couple of days in early February 1951, Zhivkov received a heap of 'directives' from Chervenkov.

Of course, not everything went smoothly between them. But even then Zhivkov had an enviable skill to skirt round confrontations. The following details a further episode which he recounted at a meeting with the first secretaries of the party's regional committees at the Boyana Residence on 22 March 1989.

What was the situation after the April 1956 plenum of the party's Central Committee? The situation then was very grave. I spoke at the Central Committee about the organization which had been set up to counteract the negative phenomena of that period. Our conclusion was that agriculture would have the worst and most disastrous effect on the development of the country. We, the Secretariat – I was in charge of it – managed to submit a memorandum to the Politburo about the serious situation in the countryside. Certainly, the memorandum did not sound that alarmist or otherwise it could not be reported. Vulko Chervenkov agreed and nominated a commission headed by me to elaborate the agriculture problem and to consider it at the Politburo and from there, at a plenum of the party's Central Committee.

We worked out a proposal. I sent it to him in Euxinograd. He used to spend the summers there. Soon after that he called me in connection with our proposal. Our meeting was attended by the Soviet ambassador, Bodrov. He started scolding me in the presence of Bodrov: 'You want to divide the party's Central Committee over this report.' He was very nervous. I told him, 'Comrade Chervenkov, I do not quite understand why you level these accusations at me. This is the work of the commission approved by the Politburo. You determined its composition. We submit these proposals.' But he did not agree with me and said, 'I don't want you to work on the commission any more. Hand it over to Chankov and he will handle these matters.'

I went back and told Chankov. He took over the commission and submitted half-hearted measures to the Politburo. But Chervenkov did not go along with these cosmetics either. Then riots broke out and so on. I later tried to find out, when Khrushchev arrived, whether Bodrov had briefed the Central Committee of the Soviet Union Communist party about this conversation. They told me that he had.

In the summer of 1950, the waves of the personality cult shattered the artists' party branch. Todor Zhivkov took an uncompromising stand stamping the great Bulgarian painter Alexander Zhendov as an agent of a foreign intelligence. 'Maybe you owe the party a definite answer: who stands behind you? If the party and the Central Committee do not stand behind you then who does? Which espionage services, if any, which enemy, if any? Who drives you and directs you? When will you tell it? You must tell the party. Everything else is of the devil.'

That was the formal accusation of the party, formulated by Todor Zhivkov on the pages of *Rabotnichesko Delo* on 19 February 1950.

A style which needed no commentary: 'Once you are not with us, you are against us.' A style which slowly and methodically led the party to a collective suicide and turned it into a caste whose sole concern was to keep its power and privileges. We should not forget, however, that the year was 1950 and a further three years had to pass before Stalin's death. The ideological dogmatism, the political obscurantism and the pathetic hate for 'the class enemy' were widespread in the Soviet Union and the peoples' democracies. The annihilation of 'the enemy, carrying a party membership card' was in fashion.

When the international communist movement started to recover after Stalin's death, the Twentieth Congress of the Soviet Union Communist Party made its shocking disclosures. In Bulgaria, the Congress decisions were implemented with hesitation and ambiguity. Vulko Chervenkov obviously was unable to anticipate the proportions of the initiated process or to grasp its essence, and he opted for political mimicry even though he himself had attended the Congress as head of the Bulgarian delegation. (Todor Zhivkov was not included in the delegation.)

After Stalin's death there were timid attempts in Bulgaria to criticize the personality cult in the style of Khrushchev. At the January 1954 plenum, Chervenkov resigned his post as general secretary but actually retained his leading position in the Politburo. After the sixth party congress in 1954, the question of electing a first secretary came to the fore. The choice was limited to two candidates: Raiko Damyanov and Todor Zhivkov. With the support of one of the powerful figures in the Politburo, Georgi Chankov, Todor Zhivkov got the job. The post, however, was still nominal. Vulko Chervenkov continued to play a key role in the leadership in his capacity as prime minister and was in charge of the Politburo work.

As is known, the report at the April 1956 plenum should have been delivered by Chervenkov. He, however, drafted a report containing only general evaluations and conclusions, while Moscow urged for a report castigating the personality cult. Chervenkov obviously continued to believe that he would get away with cosmetic changes, a bit of subdued criticism and harmless labels. Besides, deep down he probably resisted the decisions of the Twentieth Soviet Union Communist Party Congress, its conclusions and guidelines; the categorical break with Stalinism. Chervenkov was one of the most inveterate Stalinists in the international communist movement. The fact remains, however, that he laid himself open to a direct attack. (More than 30 years later, history repeated itself: the Soviet Union took decisions which proved too sweeping to be put into practice by Todor Zhivkov's political capabilities and he found himself defenceless against a surging wave of radicalism.)

The Soviet government was not happy with the slow pace of reform in Bulgaria. The year was already 1956. Three years had passed since Stalin's death but precious little was being done in Bulgaria to support Khrushchev's campaign. The Soviet leader became impatient and started looking for a substitute for Chervenkov. The vibrant first secretary of the Central Committee caught his eye. It is difficult to say whether Zhivkov first received Soviet support and then started to conspire with like-minded people or *vice versa* to bring about Chervenkov's downfall. The telephone calls he made were person-to-person or were put through the Soviet embassy. One way or another, Zhivkov himself decided the circle of people he could rely on. They included authoritative figures such as Georgi Damyanov, Politburo member and chairman of the Presidium of the National Assembly; Dimitar Ganev, secretary of the Bulgarian Communist Party Central Committee; Encho Staykov, Politburo member. Zhivkov raised the matter with Ganev and Staykov during a hunt. They knew which way the wind was blowing and the two of them promised him their support. Zhivkov talked with Damyanov in the latter's National Assembly office. 'I went there,' he recalled, 'and in a matter of ten minutes I outlined the plan for action. Damyanov stood up and started pacing the room. He did not say anything for around 20 minutes and I got rather nervous. Finally he just said "OK", and the April plenum thus got the green light.'

Todor Zhivkov began writing a report which he cleared with the Soviet ambassador, Prikhodov. Undeniably he acted fast and resolutely.

There was nothing sensational in this report. It was a compilation of assessments and formulations, far less politically keen than Khrushchev's report to the Twentieth Congress. But at that plenum, held from 2 to 6 April 1956, which subsequently gained such notoriety, Zhivkov laid the first solid foundations of his rule. That was how the famous 'April Line' in the party's policy was born, and it was invariably associated with his name and assessed as a turning point in history.

Todor Zhivkov was nevertheless cautious. He needed the plenum's undivided support. He obviously knew how to present himself in the party conclave as a 'pope' accommodating all colours and shades. To some he was mediocre, which meant tractable; to others he had done great services to the party. To others Zhivkov had done no service to the party which meant that they were guaranteed a long political life.

It seems that the minutes of the April plenum have been deliberately lost, so that Chervenkov's ousting could not be reconstructed. One of the authors of Todor Zhivkov's 1981 biography asked whether such minutes were available. Todor Zhivkov, smiling and friendly until that moment, frowned and sharply replied, 'There were no minutes. Everything that happened at the plenum was written down in its decisions and published in the newspapers.'

Todor Zhivkov made three calls to Moscow during the four days of the April plenum. Two of his conversations were with Khrushchev. The Soviet leader insisted that Chervenkov be dismissed from all state posts. The third call was with V.I.Molotov. His close ties with Chervenkov in the years of World War II modified the situation. Molotov managed to persuade Khrushchev of the need for 'leniency'. Zhivkov was instructed accordingly.

Chervenkov was relieved of his post as prime minister but remained deputy prime minister until 1961. A year later, when Zhivkov finally consolidated his position, Chervenkov was dismissed from the Politburo and expelled from the party. He paid for underrating Zhivkov and for his illusory conviction that state power was stronger than party power.

Even at that early stage, Todor Zhivkov proved skilled in the art of achieving the possible and the real in politics, and did not appear with a set of intellectual political illusions and ambitions. The criticism at the plenum was measured and no member of the former leadership was purged. Zhivkov diplomatically showed respect for its members up to the point when they began to get in the way by their actions or inaction.

Even though the April plenum is not a topical subject now, it started Todor Zhivkov's 35-year long domination of Bulgarian political and state life, and it marks an important period in Bulgaria's contemporary history. The brutal political and physical supression and elimination of political opponents gave way to new, more flexible actions and forms of totalitarian rule. With time, with the build-up of formulations and experience, Todor Zhivkov's policy took its particular shape. Indecisive and at times contradictory, it still played a positive role in the life of the country. This role, however, was performed in a limited political space: Stalin and Stalinism were things of the past, its hangovers lingered, and the interests of the socialist countries' bloc led by the Soviet Union lay ahead.

And yet, the foundations were laid, laboriously and painfully. Several days before his arrest in January 1990, Todor Zhivkov sensed the danger of a court trial and said; 'I can surrender them everything and forget about it, but I will not give them the April plenum and its deeds. I will fight for it.'

This was maybe the last desperate gesture of a politician who had never felt the bitterness of the slightest defeat in his political struggles.

3. The Pillar

When Todor Zhivkov assumed the leadership in 1956, he inherited the personality cult and a system which in those years could only be improved, but was unable to acquire human face. What had he gained through his experience in the twelve years since 1944 when he had risen through all levels of party leadership? He had shed any moral unease at trampling the rights of those who thought differently, but had acquired the knowledge that power had to be 'won, not received', a phrase he would often repeat. Of all those who sealed his fate at the meeting of 9 November 1989, Zhivkov had been the only one to have experienced all the secret moves of the power struggle. All the rest had been political extras who had received their leading posts from him and with his blessing.

As part of the system and practice of rule, the following convictions and formulations had become deep-rooted in those years:

- collectivization and liquidation of the political and economic freedom of all workers, peasants and artisans.
- a prioritized development of heavy industry.
- a stepping up of the class struggle which even in the period of peaceful coexistence acquired acute political, economic and ideological forms.
- revolutionary vigilance and a greater role for the state and security organs in the struggle against the surrounding capitalist world.

These postulates bred hostility, intolerance and hypersensitivity in the struggle against the least signs of unorthodox thinking.

Combined with the philosophy and ethics of the times, the foundations of the totalitarian system were laid in Bulgaria. The principles on which it was based found their political and organizational motivation. Thus the fortress's foundations were cemented as an unshakable bastion against every intellectual and political attack.

A. Autorkhanou, a conscientious researcher of Stalinism, as well as a Russian professor and dissident, defined in his book, *The Technology of Power*, the key principles of the totalitarian system.

The first calls for an all-embracing communist party wielding full control. The entire state structure – politics, the economy and culture – must subscribe to a uniform style of party leadership. Nothing should escape the party's vision – no man, no object, not time or space.

The second principle is to select people capable of implementing this party line and endowed with two characteristics: fanatical loyalty and organizing talent. The top man, even if he were a genius, could not be physically present everywhere. He only assigns the policies. The bureaucrats and officials are the instruments who implement them.

The third principle is to recognize only initiatives which effectively reproduce 'the general line' – the so-called 'creative initiatives'.

A fourth and very important principle is that of discipline whereby 'I' is replaced by 'we' as an expression of a readiness for self-sacrifice in the name of the party and the ideal.

Like Avtorkhanov we too could ask how many were able to pass the test of these principles? The talented and the restless gave way to the true party functionaries who could not care less about what happened to 'the idea'. What mattered was their hold on power which from the means had become an end in itself.

After 1956 and the dethronement of Stalin's cult there appeared symptoms of hesitation as to the means and forms of party leadership and rule. This was also felt in the international communist and workers' movement.

The dramatic events in Hungary in 1956 fuelled these processes. 'A strong man' had to be found for every single socialist state to protect the power and the interests of those who remained in government after Stalin.

The Bulgarian society was ready to find its 'strong' leader of 'a new type'. The taste of power and privileges had gained a new devotee. Despite some critical remarks levelled at Todor Zhivkov at the April plenum, at those top tiers, the Politburo and the Central Committee; it was considered that he had the best qualities of a party leader: dynamic and energetic, quick thinking and flexible. More and more people were becoming convinced that he was the right man despite his lack of education and erudition.

In the fast pace of those years, experience and manoeuvrability in party work remained the prime qualities for a rapid rise.

And indeed, even at the first post-April plenum meetings with the party cadres of the city of Sofia, Todor Zhivkov demonstrated an ability to master the petty bourgeois element and the champions of absolute democracy.

Gradual progress within the framework of the law and Communist party principles were the boundaries set by the April policy to contain the energy of society. The struggle against 'loose petty bourgeois morality', against 'the disruptors of party discipline' and anti-party manifestations was raised to the rank of political norm. In the wake of the events in Hungary the surviving opposition and its maturing heirs lifted up their heads. 'The suspicious elements' kept under surveillance – Nikola Petkov's opposition, the handful of monarchists, the Social Democrats – who had been hit by the nationalization in 1947 were subjected to a wave of repression which continued, by ebb and flow, until 1960.

During Todor Zhivkov's first meetings with members of the Union of Artists and Writers, the matter of individual responsibility for the repressions during the period of the cult was raised. Zhivkov recalled this as one of the difficult periods in his political biography:

> I had to parry the attacks of these meetings, to threaten to unclassify State Security files and reveal who had been behind the persecution of various artists. This cowed quite a few people and the meetings passed successfully, although with difficulty.

By the next party plenum in September 1956, Zhivkov had become the master of the situation. The plenum displayed his ability to devise policies that would appeal to people who until recently had been his adversaries. Repressed Communists, people who had been tormented and insulted at concentration camps and prisons sat side by side at the plenum and in government with their political enemies who had ordered their trials and imprisonment. Three successive ministers of the interior – Anton Yogov, Georgi Tsankov and Roussi Hristozov – and those who had prosecuted Communists worked calmly together.

One should admit that Todor Zhivkov did not persecute his personal political opponents within the party nor their descendants as long as they personally did not revolt. He knew them, remembered them and watched their actions and moves, but he never administered any judicial or administrative sanctions against them. The removal from a responsible post was compensated by a high pension or another harmless job, which secured them a high standard of living and public status. He was afraid that the consequences of the repressions might hinder his career. When he learned in 1962 of the atrocities of the forced labour camps near Lovetch and Scravena, he immediately ordered an investigation, followed by their closure.

I think that it was precisely with this that he succeeded to lull the vigilance of his opponents. Even during those years he managed to display his unifying and organizing talent.

'April nuclei' began to take shape at all tiers of control of life in Bulgaria. An 'entire April generation' joined the party. By 1960 the cadre in the regional and district party committees had been replaced by a selection process that weeded out potential political rivals such as Raiko Damyanov and Anton Yugov from the main party organizations.

The 'April generation' took over the leadership of the Komsomol, the state and economic apparatus, the army and security forces, the artistic unions. It permeated all spheres of life and took hold over all threads of power.

The platform for the struggle against the cult hypnotized and tied the hands of Todor Zhivkov's opponents. He personified the change in the party and anybody who dared to oppose him was labelled 'a surviving Stalinist' and supporter of the cult. This miraculously effective formula for the ousting of the inconvenient and the doubters found much use over many years.

The Komsomol Congress of 1957 provided yet another telling example of Zhivkov's style of work. Among the Congress's official guests were Todor Zhivkov and Vulko Chervenkov. When the latter was announced, the delegates gave him a standing ovation and started chanting: 'BCP, BCP' (Bulgarian Communist Party). During the intervals the party instructors made their rounds among the delegates and told them how to conduct themselves and who to applaud. Thus the then first secretary Alexander Dimitrov was removed for his failure properly to assess the situation. The star of Ivan Abadjiev rose, until then an unknown first secretary of the Komsomol from Stara Zagora, who was destined for higher posts in the central party organs, and ultimately became a candidate-member of the Politburo.

Curiously, in the symbols, the vocabulary and the day-to-day affairs of the totalitarian system many plain categories such as political interests, political struggles and the consolidation of power came to be replaced by terms such as 'line', 'continuity' and 'renovation'. These terms actually masked the same political and personal interests – the struggle for and consolidation of power and personal position.

Todor Zhivkov lacked outright political opponents in the first post-April plenum years of his affirmation. Politburo members had been close associates of Chervenkov, and others were marred by their career in compromised agencies and active involvement in the personality cult. Anton Yugov, a member of the Politburo and chairman of the Council of Ministers, had behind him a long party career and a successful spell as minister of the interior. But his active part in the campaign against Tito made him politically inconvenient in the light of Khrushchev's new policy towards Yugoslavia. Yugov's demise in 1962 therefore failed to surprise anyone.

All in all, by the end of 1962 Todor Zhivkov had totally eliminated all his previous rivals or potentially dangerous opponents who had strong connections and influence in the party. To his credit this took him nearly six years, whereas in Stalinist times he would have needed but a few months of unscrupulous moves.

At the end of 1962, he already held in his hands both party and state power – the beginning of 30 years of carefree rule over the country.

To some 'carefree' might seem an overstatement, but several things determined my choice of adjective. The economic or political groundwork for the emergence of an opposition which might have poisoned the atmosphere of the all-powerful ruler was conspicuously lacking. Power seemed to be an eternal godsend.

There was also the particular structure of power; the fact that the top man had his hands on the armed forces leadership, the party and state apparatus, the repressive structures and the media. How could such unlimited power be used? This depended greatly on chance; on the intellectual and moral qualities of the person at the top of the party and state affairs.

Still, it would be historically untrue to describe Todor Zhivkov as the sole motivating force in his struggle to consolidate his power.

He was far from alone in this struggle. In fact, throughout the 1960s, there were social groups and interests which supported his position as an autocrat.

The dilemma of the 1950s, following Stalin's death, had been whether to reject outright the Stalinist model of leadership and rule (for which neither the domestic nor the international conditions were right) or, without altering the essence, to seek an enlightened monarch capable of controlling these processes. History was yet to propose before the Communist parties the theoretical and practical task of completely uprooting Stalinism. That is why Zhivkov championed a policy which combated the most monstrous sides of Stalinism – murder, terror and forced labour camps – but this was a far cry from a policy which could alter the system as a whole. It was not until the late 1980s that the radical developments in the Soviet Union forced the issue of power in Bulgaria; as a choice of further socioeconomic development and as a recognition of the appearance of reform-minded movements.

But at the time when Todor Zhivkov rose to power, the historical task had been different: to ensure a controllable rejection of the Stalinist methods of rule while preserving the system's advantages instilled from its very conception in the 1930s. The political mentality of the party did not reject the system, but only the personality who had caused its deformities.

On principle a communist party contains quite diverse social groups and interests who, on their own, are too weak morally and materially to defend their interests. Out of necessity they invent one-party rule as a defender of supraclass interests, essentially the interests of an entire nation and society. As an extra safeguard they want to see at the top of such a party a strong personality wielding unlimited power.

The formation of the privileged caste of the so-called active fighters against fascism and capitalism has been a telling case in point. Ever since his status was instituted in 1959 right up to Zhivkov's ousting in November 1989, they grumbled against him, they contested portions of his biography and developed an appetite for internecine intrigues. But as soon as anyone questioned their privileges and power, they fell back on Zhivkov as their rightful leader. It was this stratagem that provided one of the social mainstays of the top party and state leader. He regularly and purposefully increased their perks and, in return, 'the active fighters' gave him their support. For that reason alone, they do not have the historical right to judge him today. To gain public acceptance alongside the rest of the political and social forces, they must first return their apartments, villas, incomes, their and their children's diplomas – and backdated.

Did Todor Zhivkov have any political opponents?

My assessment is that during the 35 years of his rule, he did not have any real political opponents. I am leaving aside the repressed representatives of former parties and the isolated cases of individual resistance. What was more, protest was naive and laughable, in the form of jokes, leaflets and threats.

Yet he never had any real opponents within the party and state. Or, if there were any, they were not rallied behind any different programme. They were rather people who envied his position, guided by the belief that they would do much better if they were in his shoes. I once heard the former top-level party functionary Todor Prahov, who had been sent hastily by Zhivkov into oblivion on a lavish retirement pension, say, 'I have no need for money or property. I only wish I was back on top to show them how to wield power.'

The military plot against Zhivkov in the mid-1960s, which has lately become a central topic was another telling example. It involved several dozens of generals, officers and famous partisan commanders voicing unhappiness with their careers after 9 September 1944.

A leading civilian in the plot was Ivan Todorv-Gorunya, an active figure on the Central Committee, backed by General Tsviatko Anev, the military commandant of Sofia (newly promoted to the party leadership).

Ideologically, the plot was prompted by Khrushchev's downfall, which led the plotters to expect a similar change at the top. Yet Todor Zhivkov was not behaving at all like a leader about to be replaced.

The plotters' platform, if it could properly be called so, was a mixture of Maoism and Stalinism. They claimed that Bulgaria was turning bourgeois, and charged Todor Zhivkov with betraying the 'communist ideal' among other things. They had distributed in advance among themselves such key posts as the defence ministry, the general staff and even the premiership. In other words they had been driven by a lust for power and personal ambitions, rather than by any ideals.

Their plans fell through after they sought to co-opt, among others, the then city commandant for the Ministry of the Interior,

General Dimitar Georgiev and the head of the Military Academy, General Velko Palin, who leaked their intentions. The original plan had been to disable the security guards with the help of one of the army companies in the capital during a plenum of the Central Committee, and there and then demand the removal of Todor Zhivkov.

Alerted, the State Security organs put some 200 people on their tail. That operation was crowned when a 'bug' was attached to the peaked cap of one of the coup's engineers – General Anev. This had been done during a specially convened conference at the Ministry of the Interior. During the two-hour meeting, intelligence operatives placed the pickup in the cockade with the antenna leads hidden under the hatband. Ironically, soon after the meeting, General Anev told one confidant, 'I'll be damned if they are not beginning to smell something. That I was summoned to that meeting is worrying me.'

This in fact was the first sentence recorded by his surveillants. From then on the sensitive ear of State Security recorded every word uttered by the general and helped compile the fat volume of state evidence.

Gradually, the plot was unravelled. The participants were tried and sentenced to various prison terms. Their political and judiciary downfall was orchestrated by three people: Dobri Djourov, Velko Palin and Mircho Spassov.

To dispel any doubts that the generals' and officers' platform had lacked a modern model or an ideological backbone, suffice it to quote from the surveillance and wiretap reports, which were submitted for Todor Zhivkov's eyes only.

> On 26 December 1965, General Dinov (assigned to carry out the armed attack and take control of the plenum) and Mavrodiev concluded in a conversation that Ivan Assen Georgiev, the man executed as an American spy, had been the first person to set out against Khrushchev. On his way to the firing squad he had said, "I tried to save the world from Khrushchev."
>
> On 13 January 1966, Dinov and Mavrodiev agreed that State Security and the Ministry of the Interior were rife with scum. They had very few of their own people there. They contemplated the return to power of Chervenkov and Yugov in Bulgaria and Malenkov, Voroshilov and Molotov in the Soviet Union, after which things would revert to normal.

> On 17 January 1966 discussing the Habana conference of Communist and Workers Parties, Dinov says that it had demonstrated how right the Chinese were and how completely isolated the Soviet delegation and their policy had been. The Chinese had received the support of many parties. He wished their policy would be adopted by the majority of the parties, so that the Communist party of the Soviet Union would have to backtrack at its Twenty-third Congress. Otherwise, it would be even further isolated and the entire communist movement would back China. Dinov mentioned that it was time for Brezhnev to go.

None of the plotters served a full sentence. Within a few years all were released. Some of the officers did not even cross the threshold of prison cells, but were merely demoted.

Notably, not a single person was sentenced to death on political charges during the entire rule of Zhivkov – quite an important fact against the background of the political excesses in Hungary, Czechoslovakia, Poland and Romania within the same timespan. Among the many reasons was Zhivkov's skillful trouble-shooting and damage control, which deteriorated only from the mid 1980s onward.

Many people now accuse him of suppression. But if Zhivkov did indeed suppress the top-level cadre, the suppression of all public and political initiative in the nation was the work of the entire party. This is inherent to any dictatorship. The social and economic nature of the Stalinist model creates its own most horrible weapon: its dictatorship is made invulnerable by the lack of economic independence on the part of its citizens. And this is particularly valid for a country such as Bulgaria, which has all the conditions for private agriculture and craft. Every opposition dies in embryo because it lacks a nourishing medium, an economic base on which to build politically self-confident personalities.

Todor Zhivkov used this ready-made model to perpetuate his personal power. Politically he supported the original system and introduced only cosmetic changes which were far from adequate to meet the nation's future needs.

Did he see the shortcomings of the system and its injustices? In my numerous meetings with him and during my work with him (1974–89), I have never heard from anyone else such condemning and categorical assessments of the shortcomings of our system as I did from him. This allowed me to preserve my own critical manner and style of work. During the 15 years of my contacts with him, I have submitted to him many memos and reports in which I made it a point to write the truth; no other leader gave me as much courage to criticize as did Todor Zhivkov. What was dangerous was to vent such issues behind his back. Then manoeuvres, intrigues and slander were put into action by other interested people and institutions.

I never heard of anyone getting into trouble for acting in good faith, for criticizing or making proposals through Zhivkov. To accept or turn down such proposals was his personal choice, but they were never invitations for trouble. The worst that could befall one was an end to his official career. Many close friends of mine asked me: 'You have this confidence and complete access to him. Why don't you ask for a promotion?'

The truth was that he was an excellent judge of people; who would be suitable for public posts and who would serve better out of the limelight. I shall give an example: I was an aide to the general secretary when the then minister of economy, Stoyan Ovcharov (who rose to that rank after only two years of close association with Zhivkov) had to present in Parliament the annual plan for the country's development. I had a heart-to-heart talk with him some time before that: 'You are a young minister and besides you are not responsible for the present state because you are a newcomer. You have to show that our economy is in disarray. We are facing a bad crisis. Everything points in that direction. That is your only chance to survive, to show what an inheritance has been dumped in your lap.' I was completely taken aback because he asked me: 'How will I criticize the April policy?' Although he was the author of several documents on an economic reform, he failed during his brief tenure to do away with the myopia and hesitation. The upshot was one more deception, one more cover-up of alarming objective indicators which should have been presented before the entire nation. I cannot imagine why the leaders of that government always took the wrong steps. I doubt if they have even one paper to show, which has been presented to the Politburo, to a plenum of the Central Committee or to the National Assembly, in which they warned that the country was facing harsh difficulties or proposed any radical changes or solutions which somebody had rejected. To table such a document did involve a certain risk, of course, but it had never been a physical or political risk. The only thing they would have risked was to lose points in their career.

The truth was that Todor Zhivkov hated to deal with bright individuals on the Politburo or the Council of Ministers, especially if they displayed signs of restlessness and disobedience and could therefore disrupt the reigning tranquillity. Reading the minutes of the Politburo sessions, you will see how its members competed with the most shameless flattery to a point where one outdid the rest by saying, 'We are fortunate to be breathing the same air as Comrade Todor Zhivkov.'

The Politburo style was attuned to Zhivkov's theoretical and political ambitions, his personal mentality and idiosyncracies.

It was therefore viewed as very bad manners for a Politburo member, a secretary of the Central Committee or a minister to push publicly an idea or programme of his own even within the ministry itself or in any other restricted area of activity. This was punished as lack of discipline, as adventurism and bossiness. Another rule was that any public speech had to mention the April line and Zhivkov's role at least a couple of times. After the 'announced' restructuring he began to 'scold' and to want his name mentioned not more than once in speeches and reports.

Was Todor Zhivkov a dictator?

On the surface, he was. He was at the top of a dictatorship which he himself personified. In the long run, all decisions in the state were made only after his approval.

However, he was only dangerous for those who would challenge the pattern of his authority at the top. He handled them without gloves. But who could think that in the conditions of single party rule, power could be handed over to another party functionary, let alone voluntarily, for example, to Pencho Kubadinski, Stanko Todorov, or to some of the younger members? Would it have made any difference? None at all. Only certain circles of party or state cadres would have been forced out. What would follow would have been inevitably the same: orders, speeches, letters and so on, which would not have changed the system an inch.

That is why Todor Zhivkov realized that those around him could only be pretenders and not reformers within their own party platform.

As to the cadres at other levels where he had contacts with ordinary people, citizens and artists; he behaved to them in a markedly different way. He demanded and tolerated criticism and dissatisfaction from them. They could raise much more dangerous questions without fearing for their careers. This can be confirmed by hundreds and thousands of people who he received and whom he gave a hearing to. After their complaints about the mess in the country, he would take ruthless and uncompromising measures.

For their part, his entourage had chosen for themselves the role and the posture of cringing lackeys. I do not know of anyone making him angry just because they wouldn't fawn on him.

On one occasion around 1976, in the reserve of Beli Iskar (outside the town of Ihtiman), Todor Zhivkov had gone hunting with his closest associates. The company sat down to watch the television news. One of the stories was about the opening of an exhibition and contained quite a long excerpt from the opening speech of Svetlin Roussev. Not once in that speech did Roussev mention the April line or Todor Zhivkov's name. Zhivkov was riled at 'these intellectuals who think too much of themselves.' Obligingly, 'the pearl in the shah's crown', the poet Georgi Djagarov, who was then vice-president of the State Council, added: 'You are right, Comrade Zhivkov. They must acknowledge the hand that feeds them and kiss it.' After 10 November 1989, in the well-polished style of political hypocrisy, Djagarov would demonstratively throw away his party membership card. In one of the 'confessions' to the press, he would recollect how hard it had been for him to endure the suffocating atmosphere around Zhivkov and how much he had fought to save the ethics of creative individuality.

It was also dangerous to come out with an attention-grabbing report or speech in Zhivkov's presence. He was left unsatisfied, and would make the point with evaluations such as 'empty theorization' and 'remote abstraction'. Usually several people closely watched the statements and public appearances of the top-echelon leaders and reported whether they had followed the rules of the game. This was one of the ways to create intrigues and to eliminate all contenders for a place in Zhivkov's closest circle.

The normal mechanism of making decisions was as follows: prior to raising an important issue before the Politburo, Todor Zhivkov would gather the inner circle of confidants. During the last years these were Milko Balev, Grisha Filipov, Dimitar Stoyanov and, at times, Yordan Yotov, who was considered an honest but inexperienced comrade. From outside the Central

Committee apparatus those most closely involved were Dobri Djourov and Pencho Koubadisnki. Only after the 'inner circle' adopted a position, would the issue be tabled before the full Politburo.

Todor Zhivkov most closely watched the current prime minister and the number two man in the party – people potentially capable of holding a position of their own. He usually got tired and disenchanted with these people very quickly because of their failure to 'put into practice and carry out' his reforming plans and because they were normally the prime target of intrigue. Zhivkov had strong personal reservations, too, because he saw them as the top contenders for his post.

There was only one proper action: anything was all right if it was passed through the general secretary himself. A brilliant model in this respect was Grisha Filipov with whom I worked for a couple of years. Anything he did had to be sanctioned by Todor Zhivkov.

There were, of course, instances of disobedience. A March 1989 report by trade union chairman Peter Dyulgerov expounded the need for independent unions. Afterwards, in both a 21 April speech to mark Lenin's anniversary and a nationwide May Day address, he omitted any mention of 'the line' and 'the name'. He was at once reported by a rival of his. Zhivkov became angry, several people added grist to his mill and publicly disavowed Dyulgerov, who was subsequently isolated and branded a traitor. Only a prolonged illness saved him from an ignominious dismissal from his post.

Todor Zhivkov never personally encouraged a cult of his own personality. This was done by the people surrounding him in the top echelon of the state and the party. They needed an idol to disguise their personal interests, amorality and mercenary motives. The dividends from the glorification of Zhivkov were in the form of posts and privileges. Zhivkov was rather the product than the cause of this overpraising. Especially dangerous was the new generation of politicians who had risen through the Komsomol ranks. The older generation of leaders had their own images, positions, ambitions and biographies. The new generation was diligent, clever and ready for any compromises. It was capable of anything but honest work and thinking. Nor would it be true to explain all developments in the country by Todor Zhivkov's personal qualities alone. Many competed to serve him, to slander and to weave intrigues against their rivals.

As Bernard Shaw once remarked: 'Kings are not born but are the product of mass hallucinations.' Or, as noted in the foreword to Marx's *Das Kapital*, 'One should not hold a person responsible for the conditions that produced him, no matter how much he tries to rise above them.'

Zhivkov's efforts to stay abreast of the latest ideas on science and government are undeniable. His reliable instinct told him that to survive at the top, he would have to recognize the new prospects. A fruit of this understanding was that Zhivkov gradually freed himself from the leading cadres in the economy and science who held their posts not because of knowledge and talent but as a reward for their past political activities.

In 1963 Zhivkov first pointed to the need for new forms of economic planning and management. The culmination of this search was the July 1968 plenum, after which people started talking about markets, profits, competition and independent producers. But the events in Czechoslovakia and the overall situation in the world cancelled out these frail steps and they froze the hopes for reforms in embryo. It is a fact, however, that in the 1960s, 1970s and 1980s, Bulgarian theoreticians were not burdened with restrictions which were as heavy as were imposed in the other socialist states. No scholars were punished for their research or discoveries. Instead they plotted and laid dogmatic traps for each other.

The detailed chronicles of Todor Zhivkov's times will save me the efforts to accompany my thoughts with quotations and references to his deeds. In his works, in his speeches delivered at plenums and congresses, and in his lectures, we find a passion to invent and discover new laws and to seek 'scientific' contributions.

Many articles today hint arrogantly that his secondary education had not been all that successful. I think that deep down Zhivkov had a complex which never left him at peace. This was the complex of intellectual inferiority; that the others were better educated and informed than he was. That is why Zhivkov sought to prove his competence and erudition by all means. This was cleverly used by many people who communicated through 'scientific terms' with him, proposed ideas and wanted money to implement them. Many of them were conscientious, they just sought the support of their leader, of the top man. Todor Zhivkov had an inate talent and intelligence which allowed him to grasp things very quickly. This was supplemented with a phenomenal memory. He quickly found his way into the core of complex reports, to evaluate whether a proposal had something to offer as part of the general policy. He quickly recalled figures, difficult scientific terms and categories.

There is something quite positive in the fact that numerous working groups were created around Todor Zhivkov, to prepare material and formulations on various issues. As a rule these groups included the top experts from the respective sphere. I personally have taken part in them. Usually the idea for a problem's solution was formulated by Zhivkov. After that the working group withdrew in isolation – most often to Pancherevo near Sofia. It is not true that Todor Zhivkov's decisions were usually made at the spur of the moment. But the work of the experts was often reduced to intrigues and struggles on the one issue of who would be recognized and awarded (not materially though) for the effort. Such personal bickering very often sidetracked the good ideas. Just as often the outcome was predetermined by a particular quotation from Todor Zhivkov, since nobody wanted to confront his practicality or definite opinion. In Zhivkov's 35 year rule no stone was unturned in Bulgaria's social affairs which had not been the result of detailed instructions from Zhivkov himself. This practically ruled out the existence of any public criticism because he took everything as a personal offence.

Over the years, he acquired the feeling of infallibility and painful touchiness. Combined with his unlimited power, this certainly led towards degeneration in the party and in the atmosphere of the state. But that sort of atmosphere was useful to the people with unlimited amorality and cynicism. There were quite a few such people around Zhivkov.

Was Todor Zhivkov a convinced communist? This question may sound strange but I believe that he had never been a convinced communist. He merely used the existing party machine and communist ideology as a means to stay in power.

Todor Zhivkov saw the inefficiency of public ownership and often asked: 'Well, what did we achieve by abolishing private ownership? What did we offer in return? We cannot find a substitute to private ownership.'

Yet he defended state ownership.

Or he used to say: 'Well, what did we achieve by abolishing religion? What did we give the people in return? Religion at least teaches them not to steal. And we cannot teach them even that much.'

Yet he defended the communist ideology.

When in a good mood he used to say: 'Who was the person who fooled us in to signing up for socialist study circles? Look what came out of socialism.' He used to laugh loudly, then add, 'We were young and gullible then,' and he laughed again.

Yet he zealously defended the system of socialism.

It is a wonder that towards the people with whom he worked most closely, he always maintained a delicate decorum. I have never heard him raise his voice or insult someone. He never voiced outright displeasure with his speech writers, but repeatedly said, 'OK, OK. It will have to be evolved further but for starters it will do.' He had the talent to encourage, to create a cheerful atmosphere, to joke with himself and with those around him over failures and successes.

By nature he was benevolent. As long as his power was not threatened, he was more than good-natured. As all dictators, whose second nature is mistrust and touchiness, he had gradually surrounded himself with loneliness. Indicatively, after the death of his wife Mara Maleeva, his New Year's Eves usually followed a similar pattern: his next of kin would arrive an hour before midnight, would spend an hour exchanging presents and good wishes, after which Zhivkov would be left alone. He watched television until two or three in the morning and then went to bed. His working day was rarely shorter than eight or ten hours.

He knew how to start a conversation with anyone. He quickly found his way into the intimate human problems of those with whom he talked and remembered facts and details about a huge number of people. I mention this because I have observed scores and hundreds of leaders who liked to put on airs and ignore and crush the people around them, without caring the least that they were live human beings, sore at heart.

His willpower, dilligence and efficiency were most impressive. I do not remember him postponing business meetings for personal reasons, unless of an utmost serious nature. His hunting trips were with people with whom he could have business conversations or people he was to work jointly with in the future. In essence they also followed a schedule. When hunting, he displayed interest in the development of the reserve and forestry and he met the people working on the reserve. Once, in the autumn of 1988, in the Karamoush Reserve he told me: 'Young man, when I go, they might deny me everything, except one thing: thanks to these reserves, I increased Bulgaria's wildlife more than twice and kept these regions ecologically clean. The way things are going, there will be nothing left for the ones after us.' He pensively added, 'I was never much for hunting. I started doing it after my wife's death when I was left on my own.'

Indeed, in his personal life, he lived isolated, within his family. He did not like holidays and days off because of the forced inactivity. His annual vacations also passed with numerous meetings and talks, as if he were afraid to remain free of work for a couple of days. I have watched his pleasure and ease of communicating with the common people around the guards, the waiters and the gardeners. He did not do it out of protocol or politeness. He never made them feel lowly. Whenever possible, he invited them to a meal, and confided to them highly personal matters.

But he had the natural gift to fight for his power by all ways and means. And he did not stop at anything, even the lowliest work, so long as it fortified the base he was standing on.

His morning banter with the waitresses would contain questions such as who drank the most coffee at work (which member of the Politburo and the Secretariat); who drank it with whom; who was whose pal; what they had talked about and so on. He highly valued information of all kinds. A Western journalist who had met him wrote:

> 'I have rarely in my life met a politician who so carefully listens and absorbs what he hears. He obviously knew well that one of the mainstays of power is the completeness of information.'

By nine in the morning he would gather his aides and review the press, the newsletters, the latest rumours and jokes. Then he would compare this to official reports through the party, state and special channels. For 35 years his duty was to protect and support the system because he held the rights and the responsibilities. Zhivkov was the sole unrestricted recipient of diplomatic and intelligence reports and reports on the domestic situation. He also read all this information by himself until late in the evening. He collected all kinds of personal and business information about the people surrounding him.

In this aspect he was much aided by the people who slandered each other. He loved to oppose the people around him. He did not like them to be friends or to have anything else but business contacts. That was also how he decided on who was to be appointed in the party and government bodies. He usually put next to the leader a person who had had close working relations with him so that they would not end up fighting. As a result they would spend much of their time together, then go to Zhivkov and talk behind the other's back; Zhivkov revelled in this.

Scholars have long noted how the Machiavellian ideas fit perfectly the Stalinist dictatorial regimes. Maybe because they combine an European and an Asian line, which produces a unique crossbreed. Many have cited Maurice Jollie's famous book *Conversation between Machiavelli and Montesquieu in Hell*, where Machiavelli teaches the legislator Montesquieu to:

- separate politics from morals.
- place power and shrewdness above the law.
- paralyse individual intelligence.
- delude the nation through his outer appearance
- agree to freedom only under the threat of terror
- keep the country ignorant of world events and the capital, ignorant of events in the countryside.
- turn the instruments of thought into instruments of power.
- mercilessly perform executions without trial and to order the resettlement of people.
- demand endless praise for each of his actions
- personally teach others about the history of his rule.
- use police as a mainstay of the regime
- have trusted followers whom he awards with different decorations and trinkets.
- promote the cult towards the usurper to the level of religion.
- create a void around himself, and thus make himself irreplaceable.
- weaken public opinion until it sinks into apathy.
- imprint his name everywhere and always, just as the drops of water leave an imprint on the granite rock.
- make use of the advantage of turning people into informers.
- rule society through its vices.
- speak as little as possible.
- avoid revealing his thoughts.
- alter the real meaning of words.

Every single line above seems to illustrate magnificently the style of a leader in a classic totalitarian system. And Todor Zhivkov was precisely such a leader.

Put into action, these 'rules of leadership' maintained a unique atmosphere which was defended at the system's apex and was devolved further to each and every unit of society and level of government.

One needed a lot of energy and skills in order to survive in such conditions. I, myself, seemed to have picked one of the best paths to survival. Avoiding endless 'ambushes' in the corridors of power which I was not good at because of my frequent bouts of nerves, I opted for the principle of bringing every conflict with a stronger opponent in the hierarchy out in the open. As soon as I sensed that someone had sown the seed of mistrust and hesitation, I would raise hell on some matter of principle and engage in an open conflict with my stronger rival in his and Zhivkov's presence.

This shocked the adversary because in this country struggles are usually waged behind the scenes. He was transfixed by the fact that he would in all cases lose more than I, the ordinary aide. Curiously, Zhivkov never reproached me for such conduct, often witnessed by other colleagues of mine. Bringing such conflict into the limelight of the hierarchy saved me from any backstabs.

Zhivkov loved to collect compromising material which he used as soon as the situation allowed. He could wait for years or strike with lightening speed.

Georgi Vutev is a case in point. A former secret service officer, in the late 1970s and early 1980s he was deputy minister of foreign trade in charge of personnel. With his combative and audacious conduct he had managed to scare the security organs with his party connections and *vice versa* – to scare the party cadres with his 'special' status at the special services. Actually he was a personal friend and close confidant of Milko Balev, who was then at the peak of his power: a Politburo member, secretary of the Central Committee in charge of the work of the Secretariat, and at the same time Zhivkov's chief of staff – an almost untouchable person of the general secretary's *alter ego*.

As deputy minister of foreign trade, Vutev, a brutal man, had given Georgi Sergiev, a Bulgarian-born West German, the exclusive rights to market Bulgarian white-brined cheese in that country. Sergiev bought thousands of tons of cheese each year. Vutev received a kickback, out of which he bought expensive presents for those in power: pianos, cars, jewellery, cassette players and videos for their offspring. He had reached such impudence that he threatened and surveilled people, and collected information which he then reported to Milko Balev. He also appointed his relatives and close friends to foreign posts. As a person, Vutev was actually nothing more than a comic figure, but he made up for this with a lot of hatred against the people he worked with. He presented himself as one of Todor Zhivkov's men and, on his behalf, gave promises, allocated posts and evaluated personnel.

For many years he poisoned the atmosphere at the Ministry of Foreign Trade and challenged the ethics of many honest people with his power which was supported from the highest places. But after a series of formal complaints from the communists, in 1983 Zhivkov ordered a secret investigation. The investigation was carried out by General Todor Radoulov, at that time deputy head of a department at the party's Central Committee in charge of the work of the Ministry of the Interior. He revealed several instances of corruption and reported them to Todor Zhivkov, along with the conclusion that Vutev was a dishonest and corrupt leader. Zhivkov did not believe the facts at first and said that they were the result of Andrei Loukanov's intrigue (he was then deputy prime minister). But he locked the report in his safe without telling anyone.

It was not until 1985 that I witnessed a conversation in Zhivkov's office when one visitor found the courage openly to say the truth about Georgi Vutev. Todor Zhivkov was highly alarmed, called the chief of one of the counter-intelligence divisions of the Ministry of Interior and assigned him to carry out an investigation without informing the minister of the interior, Dimitar Stoyanov, who was a personal friend of Milko Balev's. The operation was to be carried out in complete secrecy without the knowledge of the heads of the Ministry of the Interior (except Grigor Shopov, the first deputy minister at the time). A special group was set up to carry out the painstaking fact-finding mission abroad and in the country. The risk was enormous, because Vutev had informers at all levels of State Security.

The group had nearly wound up its case after unearthing evidence involving one of Vutev's confidants, Dimitar Popov, also known as Count Cianno, a representative stationed abroad. Popov's arrest at Sofia Airport was prevented when his flight from

Berlin crashed off the runway, near the village of Krivina.

The work continued and facts were found providing evidence of corruption and power abuse. On the eve of the thirteenth Party Congress in 1986, the investigation was in full gear.

The chief investigator reported the results in the presence of interior minister Dimitar Stoyanov and his deputy, Grigor Shopov. To his credit, he did not hesitate to call things by their proper names or to name the recipients of the expensive gifts and large sums of money. Here I want to underline that very often the officers of State Security have been the targets of unjustified criticism. Thousands of honest people work there night and day without public praise. They were the ones who averted many cases of arbitrariness, risking their jobs and preserving their dignity. In many cases their adversaries wielded a lot of power and had enough contacts and opportunities to launch a counterstrike. In a one-party system, one often did not know what might occur if one exposed a given person and from where he might expect the next blow.

Two days after the report, Todor Zhivkov fired Milko Balev from the post of chief of staff and in the process asked him a series of uncomfortable questions – How were the Japanese motorcycles bought for his sons? What kind of presents had he received?

But at the thirteenth Congress Zhivkov did not find the courage to dismiss Balev as a Politburo member and secretary of the Central Committee. Balev had been his longest serving aide and associate in the post-1956 power struggle and Zhivkov valued such services. As far as Vutev was concerned, he was arrested, tried and sentenced to 15 years in jail. His associates were penalized and removed from their jobs.

So much for the charges that Zhivkov abetted corruption. He received many signals from the watchdog agencies and ordered immediate investigation and actions. Zhivkov sent to prison for 12 years his fellow partisan and chief of the security service UBO General Penchev, for corruption in connection with the allocation of housing. He fired his personal aide, Tinko Vodenicharov, because he had accepted presents from improper people. Zhivko Popov, a friend of the family and of Lyudmila Zhivkova, received a sentence of 20 years for corruption and abuse of power. Zhivkov's personal pilot, General Evstatiev, committed suicide after Zhivkov had ordered an investigation into his affairs. He fired a bodyguard for overcharging on a car sale. He fired his personal typist because she had appropriated cognac and cigarettes from his entertainment stock.

He shied away from anything which could pin him down. It is a little known fact that when he was mayor and first secretary of Sofia and, later on, as a high-ranking party and state official, he was offered for sale nationalized mansions, previously owned by the Goubedelnikovs, the Chepranshikovs and other rich and famous families. He, however, flatly refused and all his life lived in state-owned flats and weekend-houses.

Zhivkov was not infatuated with wealth, despite the poverty of his youth. In this his peasant nature clearly failed him and he surprisingly demonstrated a lack of any small-mindedness. Todor Zhivkov had no love for money or objects. To him power mattered more than anything. Besides, he had unlimited access to luxurious residences and villas throughout Bulgaria. Yet he did not accumulate wealth. It is a proven fact that Zhivkov had no personal villa or apartment, no car or any sort of real estate. For his 35-year long rule, he received many presents on different occasions – jubilees and holidays, in the Boyana Residence Zhivkov made a museum where he sent these objects: carpets, crystal glass, paintings, silverware, silver and gold artefacts. I remember the occasion when Mikhail Gorbachev sent him an expensively ornamented tea-urn which Zhivkov did not even wish to see. When his secretary tried to make him take a look at it at least once, he replied: 'He did not send it to me. He sent it to the chair I occupy. Why do you think he did not send you one?' And he refused to see it.

Experts say that this collection of Todor Zhivkov's gifts is worth hundreds of millions. The gold articles alone weigh around ten kilogrammes. If he had wanted to become rich, all this could have vanished without a trace in a couple of decades.

By the end of his political career, in about 1986, he began building a weekend house for his children. He was one of the few who, having had UBO build their houses, waived the 20 per cent discount on the construction costs and paid as much as the next man.

He was very moderate in his personal habits. He ate moderately. When he was at the Central Committee he usually had lunch at a small table which they covered with a table cloth. His menu very often consisted of bread, cheese, olives, tomatoes, sausages and other savouries. He refrained from overeating. Even when he was out hunting, he ate once a day, at lunch or at supper-time. He rarely drank or smoked.

As a hereditary peasant, however, he hated prodigality. He gave his granddaughter 600 leva pocket money per month and it was funny that he counted the money twice or thrice. And just to be on the safe side, he asked his secretary to count it once again. He also helped his relatives, his brothers and sisters with small sums of money. Or when an acquaintance from his home town came to complain about one thing or another, he took out money and gave freely.

I learned a curious fact in 1980. We were hunting in the Tsar's reserve in Bistritsa with several other people. I learned from the security chief at the time, General Kashev, that Zhivkov actually covered all the expenses for the hunting and had bills for everything. Later, I learned from his personal physician that he did the same for medicines: he paid for them and took the bills, even though as a fighter against fascism and capitalism he was legally entitled to receive them free of charge. When he was arrested in 1990, he presented these bills to the magistrates and they could not hide their surprise.

I do not want to seem naive, but I do believe that the talk going on about his billions in Swiss banks are inventions of a fantasy and a result of the well-known Bulgarian maxim to heap all accusations on a loser.

I recall one occasion shortly before his downfall. One of his aides reported a letter with an appeal from one of his comrades-in-arms to be given 1,000 square metres of land for the construction of a country house. He had not heard well and asked: 'How much? A thousand metres? What does she need it for? All she and I need are two metres of land. She is as old as me.'

It was then that he said: 'Boys, I own nothing, neither a house, nor furniture . . . I have one blanket to cover me with when I die. I also have some saved money, but very little. My children have an apartment, a villa and a car each.'

I think that Zhivkov was telling the truth. Some people might say that these appartments and villas are quite large and luxurious. However, let all of you try to imagine being in his place: for 35 years of absolute power, imagine what he could have done for himself and for his children.

Listing these facts I don't want to evoke soppy sentiment. There is just one point I would like to make: these are facts which can be checked by anyone who wishes. I just wonder what would happen if everyone's past was so thoroughly investigated for 30 or 40 years into the past? If what they had built, bought and arranged was checked in the way that Todor Zhivkov is being checked now? Perhaps everybody should go through this treatment. They should be made to declare their income and expenses and be prosecuted to the full extent of the law if they cannot account for any discrepancy. Only then can we apply a reliable standard to people and their actions, and to the high-sounding declarations that pour in from all sides. Then we will hear fewer lies. In some cases, it will be as quiet as a graveyard.

The truth is, however, that with respect to his children Todor Zhivkov made the greatest mistakes of all. We could have forgiven him everything but not this lack of principle, especially when he began to promote his son Vladimir to the top of the state and the party. This fatherly bias acquired drastic dimensions.

Vladimir Zhivkov had no ambitions. Unlike his sister he had never wanted to have power. He drank a lot and found himself in unsuitable company and circumstances.

These lapses were diligently concealed from his father and the politicians proposed another 'therapy' – a political career. Especially insistent were Milko Balev and Georgi Yordanov, who persuaded him that his son could make a good political career.

One occasion, in particular, became widely known. Vladimir Zhivkov had been co-opted by the National Assembly to replace the late Politburo member and member of Parliament from an electoral region in Mihailovgrad, Ivan Mihailov. In the evening before his first meeting with the electorate, the young Zhivkov had had too much to drink and the meeting failed to take place. A second one was arranged and the people accompanying him, received strict orders to keep the son from drinking even if they had to use physical force.

They came back radiant: 'Everything passed perfectly well. They welcomed him with bread and salt.'

Todor Zhivkov expressed doubt: 'That much? You have gone too far with the preliminary "preparations". I doubt that they will welcome him so.'

But they insisted: 'They adore him, Comrade Zhivkov. They really do!'

I think that such toleration of his son was the last straw and made every honest communist feel insulted and humiliated.

Nikola Geshev: the photo circulated for his capture after 9 September 1944.

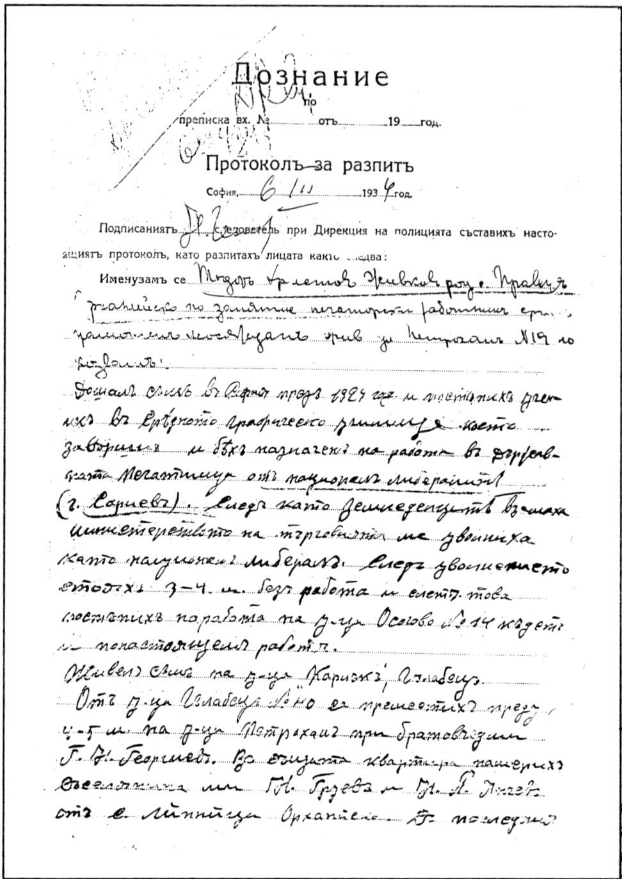

Дознание
по
преписка вх. № .... отъ .... 19.... год.

Протоколъ за разпитъ

София, 6 III 1936 год.

Подписанията .... следователь при Дирекция на полицията съставихъ настоящиятъ протоколъ, като разпитахъ лицата както следва:

Именуазмъ се Тодоръ Христовъ Живковъ

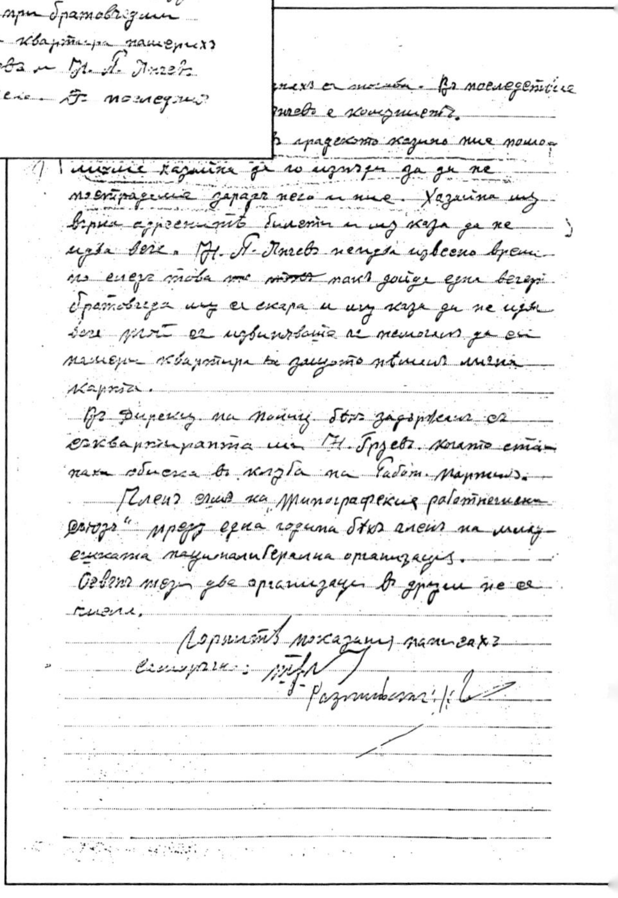

Police investigation papers in connection with Todor Zhivkov: the investigation of 6 March 1936 was conducted by Nikola Geshev himself.

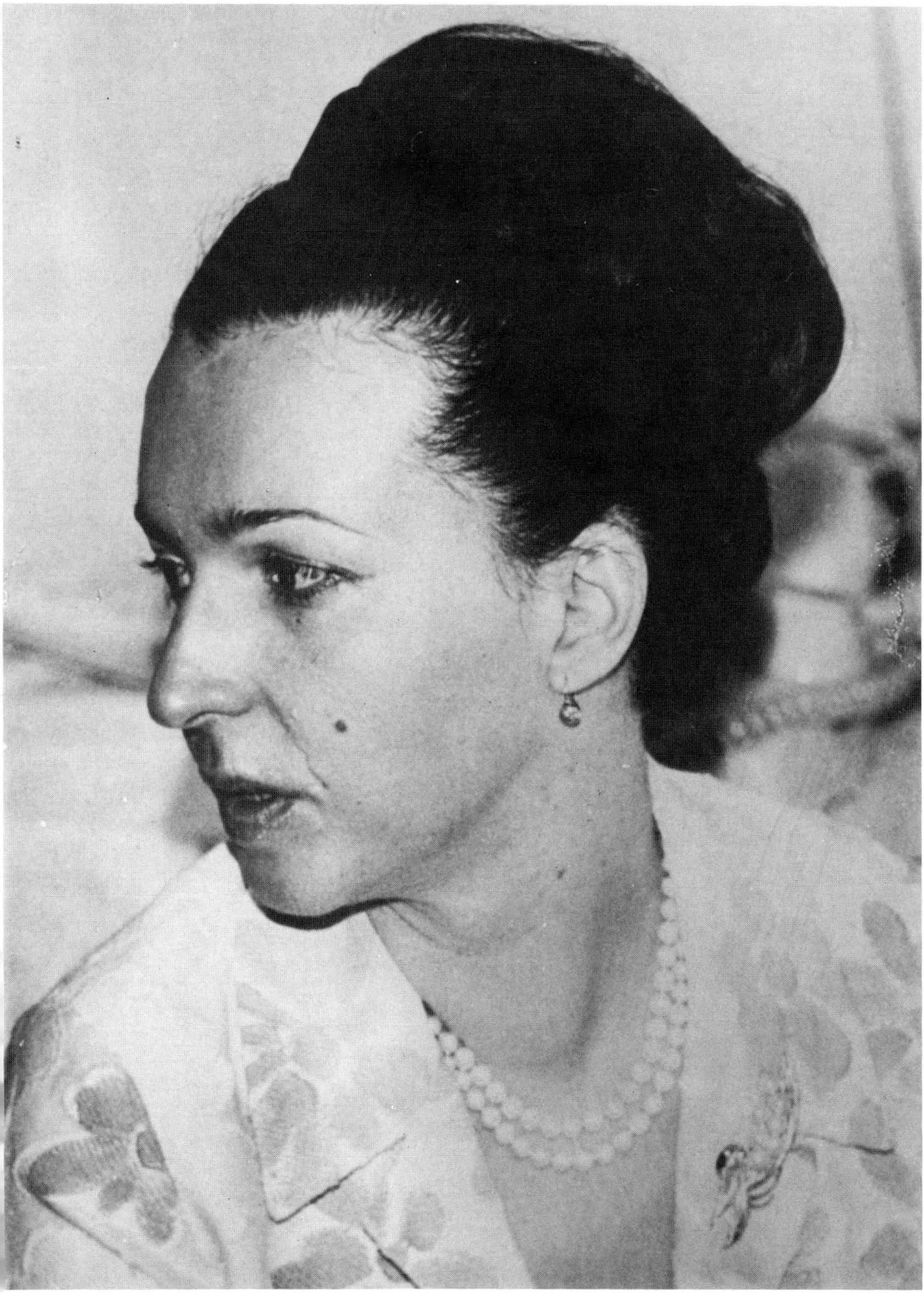

Lyudmila Zhivkova in conversation.

Above: Todor Zhivkov and Leonid Brezhnev: hunting at the Volden Reserve, Bulgaria, September 1973.

Left: Todor Zhivkov and Mikhail Gorbachov: a cordial and brotherly welcome.

Todor Zhivkov could not stand the slightest hint of criticism about his children. He was awfully touchy on this subject. He persecuted most of all those who offended him personally or a member of his family. He could forgive and forget a political mistake, but for offences of that kind he forgave nobody and persecuted them with revenge and anger. Even an honest attempt to tell him the truth about his children was unacceptable. This consequently led to a strong political reaction on the part of the Bulgarian public which he failed to understand until the end of his rule.

On the whole, only a few people could afford to bring him bad news. Consequently this intolerance towards unpleasant information became the style of the entire Politburo. That is why he was often misled and, more precisely, cheated.

I have witnessed reports by people responsible for one or another party sector. They skipped and toned down the negative facts in their reports and dwelled on the successes. They knew what Todor Zhivkov wanted to hear and what he did not. He personally tried to hear nothing which could lead to negative emotions or moods. It was as if he had a safe, egoistical mechanism of a biological nature.

When he had formulated a given idea, he asked questions but only listened to the answers he wanted to hear. He did not like to hear considerations and arguments about other decisions, different from the ones he had accepted. He always wanted the initiative and the idea to be his work and was permanently ruled by this power-loving egocentrism.

My appointment to his cabinet coincided with the beginning of the plans for the introduction of the shareholding principle in the organization of the country's economy. On principle, there is little one can say against shareholding. But for the improvement of Bulgaria's economic conditions it was nothing short of an abstraction. Experts helped us feed the computer data on the 100 biggest factories in the country, which accounted for more than 75 per cent of the country's industrial output. The figures showed that a large part of them were unprofitable; we could therefore not consider introducing shareholding companies, to cure Bulgaria's unfavourable economic condition. I reported to him. He listened to what I had to say and asked dryly, 'OK, what else is there?' signifying that the conversation was over. I left confused. After this, in all of his speeches, Zhivkov began to mention the 'magical' shareholding principle in the Bulgarian economy and about the workers' shareholding.

What were the actual roots of his egotism and uncompromising attitude, of this faith in his personal capabilities and ideological infallibility?

Maybe it was due to his 35-year long rule, a period free of dramatic events, a period one could say, of political stability and comparatively steady economic development. I do not want to dwell on the figures but, until 1984, Bulgaria had not experienced any negative trends in its economic development. But this was maturing and acquiring destructive dimensions. The symptoms were at hand, but no one wanted to see them or analyze them. Least of all Zhivkov who until then was only glorified and praised.

There was something else, of course. Zhivkov's 35-year rule was supported by two main pillars – the armed forces and the repressions which acquired different hues and forms over the period, as well as the support and trust that came from the Soviet leadership. These two groups acted flawlessly and permanently formed his conviction that in all critical situations he would manage to remain at the top. As time went by, this feeling of security and lack of personal criticism pushed him to the edge of a kind of mania of infallibility, of absolute self-confidence, to the belief that all his ideas and actions in the management of the country were on time, original and correct, that it was 'the others' who failed to implement his well-thought-out ideas.

Let us take a look at the two pillars of his regime.

The security organs and the repressive apparatus are the base of power in a totalitarian system. In different periods of Bulgaria's history after 9 September 1944, these organs stood over the state and party. The State Security Department until 1956 worked openly and unrestrictedly against party and state leaders of all ranks. Terror then could freely take all forms and uncontrollable dimensions. It was in such a way, that a given dictatorship began to implant mass fear the roots of which lay in the foundations of the system and which hourly infiltrated the public's lifestyle. If it could not generate fear or if at a given moment this fear disappeared, then the dictatorship was dead. In our country this fear did not begin to be overcome until as late as 1987, under the influence of developments in the Soviet Union. Todor Zhivkov could not understand this and continued to believe that he was standing on solid ground, and that the system continued to create fear and respect for his rule.

For 35 years Todor Zhivkov worked alone and let no one take a look at the work of the army and the security organs. The people who supported the system and led the armed forces were Army General Dobri Djourov, Colonel General Velko Palin and Mircho Spassov. It was they that clamped down on the previously mentioned plot and threw hundreds of officers out of the army and the Ministry of Interior in 1966 and 1967. Mircho Spassov was deputy minister at the Ministry of the interior for almost 20 years. He was entrusted with the operational field work and reported directly to Todor Zhivkov. Spassov was in fact the man who replaced the ministers of the interior and had practical control over the entire ministry.

After 1956 a change took place in the system. The party and state now stood over the security apparatus and the repressions were carried out only against people who actively demonstrated their dissatisfactions. The forms of work became more covert. For example, the department which kept taps on top level personnel was conspiratorially called the 'Department for Struggle against Anti-party Manifestations' within the Sixth Division of State Security. This department had a separate account, separate files and informers, and a free hand with respect to top party and state leaders. (The department was closed down after 10 November 1989, along with the entire Sixth Division.)

This structure was under the control of Mircho Spassov and, after his dismissal, of Deputy Minister Grigor Shopov, an honest and modest man.

The information acquired by this department was destined for Zhivkov alone. The rest of the members of the top party leadership had heard about but knew nothing of the structure and organization of this department. When former minister of the interior Angel Tsanev on his own account disobeyed the principles of 'the game' and interfered in the wiretapping of Politburo members, he was immediately removed. This and other actions on his part made Zhivkov begin to doubt his loyalty. Such a person could therefore no longer be in charge of security and represent one of the pillars of the system and be its 'first man'.

Zhivkov used to find solid support in the security organs and their technical capabilities, and wide network of informers. The pillar did not crack until the layers themselves shifted and the entire structure tottered. Until that moment its famous files were intensively updated because they outlined the portrait of the entire society.

Those were not really operative files. The field agents collected data on everyone who was of interest in a particular sphere. The data was accumulated without effort, because every service, enterprise, theatre or artistic union knew who the state security person in charge of them was. The people who liked to talk behind each other's backs mutually slandered each other. They disclosed intimate sides of their lives and discredited their rivals in connection with books, roles and films. In many cases it was precisely thanks to these 'files' that State Security found out about cases of corruption, abuse and heavy conflicts. The range of action of the security organs was wide indeed – from the clearing up of civil conflicts to surveillance and struggle against Todor Zhivkov's opponents.

The following top secret memorandum concerns a request from a pop singer to Todor Zhivkov and illustrates how the system solved intrigues:

> In his appeal X raises the question that he and his close associate from 'H' pop group have been subjected to blackmail over the past several years, which not only interfered with their work, but also left them in a situation of absolute insecurity.
>
> The inquiry into the matter has revealed that:
>
> The information from M.P.A of the city of Plovdiv and K.L.L of the city of Sofia and other sources make it plain that ——— and ——— had amoral relations of a homosexual nature. In connection with this, action has been undertaken to separate ——— from ——— and to aid his development and growth as an adequate person and artist———

Usually such cases followed careful directions from the top through the party sections and state organs on the procedure of action and the solution of the problem.

The following text from a top secret memorandum concerning Stoyan Mihailov Mirchev illustrates another product of the system which carefully watches out for political enemies.

On 24 November 1987, Stoyan Mihailov, secretary of the Bulgarian Communist Party's Central Committee, in a conversation with friends and research workers, spoke about the different aspects of party policy in their restructuring.

In connection with the punishment of four professors at Sofia University he declared that the actions against them had been incorrect and hasty. He expressed the agreement with his friends that the situation which had ensued from the enforcement of punishments could have unforeseeable consequences.

He complained that he had recently been left out of events. He expected his removal as secretary of the Central Committee of the Bulgarian Communist Party quite soon, due to his objections over some of the formulations and practical steps connected with the course of restructuring.

He was the sole person from the party leadership to have expressed his disapproval of Todor Zhivkov's report of January 1987 on the restructuring in the Soviet Union and its reflection in Bulgaria. He did not agree with the decision on the new administrative and territorial division of the country.

According to Stoyan Mihailov, the forthcoming National Bulgarian Communist Party Conference would not make any decisions and it was hardly the right time for its holding.

In a conversation with Svetlin Roussev on 1 February 1988, Stoyan Mihailov congratulated Roussev on the opening of his latest exhibition and expressed his satisfaction with the work of the editor-in-chief of the *Narodna Kultura* newspaper who had permitted a reproduction of a Svetlin Roussev painting to be printed on one of its pages.

From the conversation on 6 November 1988, between Stoyan Mihailov and Svetlana Sharenkova, a research worker at the Institute of Sociology with the Bulgarian Academy of Sciences, it became clear that Stoyan Mihailov had known beforehand from Sharenkova about the founding of the Club in Support of Restructuring and Glasnost in Bulgaria, and on 6 November was informed by her about it and the members of its elected leadership.

The mass wiretaps were both a myth and a reality. A myth, because the people working in all state and party organs did not dare talk openly over the phone from their offices and even from their homes. They were seized by the pathological syndrome of supersecrecy and reassurance. For them the well-known phrase 'This is not something that can be discussed over the telephone' did not signify a desire to preserve an intimate secret, but a warning lest the person at the other end might 'drop' something which could have unpredictable political consequences.

To have tapped the phones of dozens of people and servicemen was, of course, technically impossible. The wiretaps affected only those people who created a serious and grounded interest by their actions and conduct.

Technology to control a greater number of conversations was later introduced, but the recording mechanisms were tuned only when they registered preassigned words. Despite the equipment, the recruitment of agents was of major importance. I see today, in the front ranks of the opposition, people who had previously been working as State Security agents and who, with their present display of anti-communism and extremism want to ease their conscience, rather than do something for Bulgaria.

Here is a case in point. A rather controversial television star of the moment asked for a flat to meet his creative and housing requirements. The request was referred to Todor Zhivkov. He objected: 'Why should I solve the problem?' But then he was told that 'the star' in question had been a long-serving secret agent of State Security Department 6 operating under the alias of 'D'. According to Agent B, Agent D had prospects and accomplishments for sweeping actions. Of course, he received the flat.

One inevitably recalls the aphorism that ever since anonymous reports replaced duels, the number of victims rose.

The second pillar of Todor Zhivkov's personal rule was the support he had from the Soviet leadership. There has never been an East European leader who knew so well how to balance his conduct before all top leaders of the Soviet Union.

The support he received way back at the April 1956 plenum, as he fought to remove his political enemies, taught him that in Bulgaria's history after 1878 there had been very few and very brief periods when something had been decided without the Soviet Union.

Zhivkov did not like 'excursions' in to the past, but with a flash of historical insight he had grasped that Bulgaria was connected with the Northern colossus by geopolitical fate. That is why he zealously controlled the political channel of ties with the Soviet Union.

Nobody had the right to work closer with the Soviet representatives in the country or in Moscow. Nobody was to gain more confidence and support from the Kremlin than him. Those who had not understood that, soon experienced his political rage. The people closest to him had sensed this peculiarity in his conduct which was most strongly expressed in the form of fear from the pro-Soviet plots. Many people used this as the strongest weapon against their political opponents. It was enough to convince him that a Politburo member or a secretary of the Central Committee had had close ties with Soviet Embassy officials or Kremlin leaders in order to get that person fired. This weapon was especially strong in the hands of Milko Balev. Such insinuations led to the sacking from the Politburo of Alexander Lilov and Choudomir Alexandrov. Andrei Loukanov and the secretary of the Central Committee, Dimitar Stanishev, were kept under close watch for their exceptionally close working relations with Moscow.

While Brezhnev was in power, Zhivkov had no problems with those who wanted to attack him from the rear, through Moscow. He had such a clear-cut personal friendship with the Soviet leader that all letters which Brezhnev received from complaining Communists requesting help and measures against Zhivkov were returned to Bulgaria and personally handed over to Zhivkov. The authors were left in a degrading position and were often penalized. But after Brezhnev this confidence decreased and Zhivkov was no longer so sure of how he stood with the Soviet leadership – an uncertainty which troubled him and made him suspicious.

Had Zhivkov made for himself a categorical historical decision concerning which road of development Bulgaria should embark upon? My personal view, subjective though it is, is that he proceeded from the existing political realities; to seek every opportunity to bow to the East while keeping an eye on the West. Though not well versed in history, Zhivkov grasped the consequences of Bulgaria's location as a crossroads between East and West. Bulgaria's geographical location and its historical fate as a door towards the Orient predetermined its becoming a battlefield of diametrically opposed internal political forces. Zhivkov understood this reality and tried to find some sort of acceptable balance between the Orient and Occident, but he was tripped by the internal and international structures which the system of socialism had bred and developed while it ruled the country.

Domestically, until 1956 the political structure had been entirely built on the Stalinist model. The structures and their method of functioning reflected the social and political stratification of society – a party and administrative apparatus with its own interests, an army and organs of security, state-owned property with the monopolistic and absolute rule of the party in the taking of political decisions.

On the international level, the Warsaw Treaty was built within a strictly defined framework of relationships. Each national decision was viewed from the point of view of the military and political alliance of the member states. Any search for individual ways and models of development was entirely ruled out. It is empty fantasy and hypocrisy to claim that Zhivkov, or anyone else, could have changed the bone structure of this political organism. The attempts in Hungary in 1956, in Czechoslovakia in 1968 and in Poland in 1980–81, as well as other events of which there is sufficient evidence, point to the fact that the attempts for radical changes were utopic. To claim anything else is sheer demagoguery.

In the Warsaw Treaty countries, use of terms such as market, profit, profitability, independence and decentralization were sufficient cause for academic repression. At least, in Bulgaria, they were made part of the propaganda vocabulary, albeit empty of their real meaning. In Bulgaria, Todor Zhivkov tried hard to break out of the political deadlock with the help of pseudo-revolutionary phrases and scientific formulations which solved nothing, but at least created the impression that Bulgaria was pursuing a modern lifestyle and had successfully overcome the Stalinist dogmas.

Zhivkov constantly sought new ideas in the West and unsuccessfully attempted to graft them on Balkan soil. Nothing resulted, because he was careful not to swerve away from the official Soviet line. That is why Zhivkov adapted himself quite successfully to every new Soviet leader. He had a sixth sense when working with them and sought intimacy and ties with their closest associates, their families included. He could not have survived so long otherwise. It was their 'blessing' that had won him the battle for power at the April 1956 plenum and the Khrushchevian halo of a fighter against the personality cult.

He highly valued Khrushchev, but admitted that he, too, had received a 'drubbing' from the Soviet leader who, in the last years of his reign, had grown fond of the word *dubinka* (flogging cane).

He succeeded in achieving especially close and friendly relations with Brezhnev. The long period of their joint work allowed Zhivkov to win the unlimited confidence of the Soviet leader. One way he achieved this was by infiltrating the Brezhnev family. A lady diplomat at the Bulgarian embassy in Moscow, Milka Kalinova, succeeded in winning the friendship of Brezhnev's daughter, Galina, his son Yuri and Yuri's wife, whom she showered with expensive presents – fur coats, jewellery, vacations in Bulgaria – all paid for by the UBO. Kalinova received inside information about forthcoming changes, which she conveyed directly to Zhivkov, making him the most well-informed person in Bulgaria about everything which was going on in the Soviet Union.

After the July 1968 plenum, whose decisions (brilliant and bold by the standards of that time) were eclipsed by the events in Czechoslovakia, Todor Zhivkov made one more attempt to draw the attention of the Soviet leadership to the global problems of socialism.

In the early 1970s, he was mesmerized by his visit to Japan. He visited scores of factories and institutes, he saw and realized how hopelessly backward Bulgaria was in science and technology. From Japan he wrote Brezhnev a strongly worded letter raising the inevitable problems which would arise if they ignored what was going on. On its way back from Japan the delegation was received by Brezhnev who gave Zhivkov a long and angry lecture: 'You, Todor, have realized only one thing and one side of capitalism, but you haven't seen the other, the one of exploitation, unemployment, and so on.'

There is plenty of evidence of the brutal actions of both systems which in those years ran an arms race and spared no effort to undermine each other by all possible means. That was the time of the Vietnam War, of US military intervention in all parts of the planet. International relations were characterized by suspicion, deviousness and the escalation of mistrust and outwitting. In that situation it was unthinkable to give the go ahead to a dangerous political and economic experiment based on pluralism and private property. I have heard Todor Zhivkov praise the economic programme and the economic management experiment in Czechoslovakia which were devised by Professor Ota Sik. What he did not approve was the premature renunciation of the party's leading role. Later, comparing Gorbachev's perestroika with the reforms in Czechoslovakia, he openly blamed the Soviet government for failing to realize what socialism needed: a change in the basic production relations. Not to allow a couple of papers to make a fuss but to introduce a market economy with real prices, taxes and wages. 'That was much better planned in Czechoslovakia in 1968,' he said in connection with the preparations for his last visit to the Soviet Union. 'Everything else is demagogic and idle talk.'

But let us go back to that time.

Todor Zhivkov headed a delegation and was the only East European leader with Dubcek and Krigel to sign a sweeping programme and treaty on cooperation for the following 20 years. It happened in April, four months before 21 August. Czech researchers believe that the decision to invade was made on 3 August, when the top leaders of the socialist countries met in Bratislava. Others say the decision was made in July.

At that time the Czech leaders ruled out the possibility of an invasion. Tito did not believe it either and, when he visited Czechoslovakia, he assured the Czech leaders that there was no such risk. Information was gathered from all intelligence sources, the prime targets being Krigel and Dubcek. Even their personal doctors were recruited as informers and reported on their intimations.

What has been kept secret even to date?

The first plan for the invasion of Czechoslovakia was drawn up much earlier. It was worked out by Brezhnev, and the outline was sent to the top leaders for coordination as early as May 1968.

TOP SECRET
SINGLE COPY
PLAN FOR THE CONDUCT OF OPERATION 'X'

I. The Political Situation in Czechoslovakia

After the January Plenum of the Communist Party of Czechoslovakia (KSC), the Zionist, revisionist and counterrevolutionary elements in Czechoslovakia launched an all-out offensive against socialism, against the KSC and the authorities of the dictatorship of the proletariat. Their main objective is to detach

Czechoslovakia from the socialist community and to orient it towards the West.

The threat posed by the extremist and counterrevolutionary offensive is clear to the sound forces in the Czechoslovak republic and above all to its vanguard, the working class, which is resolved to defend the socialist conquests under the leadership of the KSC.

The Czechoslovak People's Army is not affected by the revisionist plague and the State Security authorities resolutely fufil their duties, even though they are deprived of operative command and are denigrated.

The Communist Party of Czechoslovakia is not defeated and has enough strength which, if organized and spearheaded by authoritative leaders, will manage to halt the offensive of the reaction and will normalize the situation in the country.

The revisionist and counterrevolutionary forces, as a result of persistent subversion, have managed to entrench themselves in the mass media and the cultural unions. After the January plenum they managed to capture new important positions in the Central Committee of the KSC, the government, Parliament and the National Front which gave them an opportunity to take the initiative. Realizing that overt anti-socialist and anti-Soviet activity would not work on Czechoslovak soil, they adopted 'silent counterrevolution' tactics, screening their activity behind demagogic slogans of friendship with the Soviet Union and the other socialist countries.

At present the revisionist and counterrevolutionary elements in Czechoslovakia have no real chance to carry out substantive and political changes. That is why they seek to demoralize the party and to take over the state apparatus.

The situation in Czechoslovakia necessitates action to restore the KSC's leading role and to normalize the situation in the country.

II. Purpose of the Operation

To consolidate the leadership of the KSC by purging it from all right wing revisionist elements who push the country towards the West.

By raising the party's leading role, the new leadership should carry out the necessary actions in an atmosphere of friendship with the Soviet Union and the other socialist countries.

III. Political Actions

Before the operative plan is put into effect, it is necessary to carry out certain political actions to create the appropriate political and psychological conditions in the country, needed to secure mass support for the further actions of the new leadership.

These actions could be:

1. To have the radio broadcast and the newspapers publish appeals and letters from the workers' militia.
2. To organize street demonstrations of individual workers' militia detachments.
3. To have individual party branches produce resolutions, letters, appeals, etc., demonstrating their resolve to defend the ideals of the party and the acquisitions of socialism.
4. To have individual party branches stage street protests, hold demonstrations and meetings, rallies, etc.

The press and the radio in the socialist countries should provide detailed coverage of these actions of the sound communist forces, thus giving them moral support.

IV. Operative Plan of Action

1. On the night of the appointed date the major enemy and Zionist elements should be isolated and overpowered on behalf of the new leadership.
2. On that same night, the radio stations in Prague, Bratislava and Brno, the television station, the CTK news agency, the post office and the telegraph should be captured and the newspapers and the foreign correspondents' dispatches should be placed under the control of the new leadership.
3. The Ministry of National Defence and the Ministry of the Interior should be seized and all further actions that may have to be taken with respect to the army and the police, should originate from and on behalf of the leadership of these two ministries.
4. Special measures should be planned for the neutralization of the command personnel of some army units of which there is evidence that they may take action against the new leadership.
5. Measures should be taken to restrict the access of Czechoslovak citizens to the missions of the capitalist countries.
6. Measures should be taken to neutralize possible action on the part of foreigners staying in Czechoslovakia at that time.
7. Extra measures should be taken to safeguard the border

between Czechoslovakia and the Western countries.
8. On the night or on the following morning, the new leadership should issue an address to the Czechoslovak people to explain its actions as defence of socialist democracy and securing the implementation of a 'programme for action'.
9. On the following day the workers should be called to a rally and the workers' militia should hold a demonstration in Prague at which the speakers will explain the platform of the new leadership.
10. A Plenum of the Central Committee of the KSC should be convened at which the members of the new leadership should make speeches, forcefully denouncing the group of counter-revolutionary elements, including those in the Central Committee of the KSC, which under the banner of socialist democracy work for elimination of democracy and for the country's separation from the socialist camp. It should be moved at the plenum to expel some members of the Presidium and the Party's Central Committee.

V. Forces and Means
1. Sound political leaders should be found to take the lead and carry out the plan.
2. A group of senior officers from State Security, the National Defence, the Ministry of the Interior and the workers' militia should be enlisted in the leadership, and forces at their disposal should take charge of the practical fulfilment of the plan.
3. The principal forces on which the leadership will rely for the fulfilment of the plan are the workers' militia, State Security, the National Police Force and some army units.
4. A back-up plan should be worked out in case the first one fails or is betrayed, and it should involve the use of some units of the armed forces which the new leadership would have at its disposal.

VI. Active Measures
1. Leaflets in Czechoslovak should be circulated, and they should discuss the following points: socialist democracy is in danger; the reactionary elements push the country towards the West; the process of consolidation must continue by upgrading the role of the Communist Party and by defending the acquisitions of socialism.

2. Letters should be written to several undecided and now neutral members of the Central Committee of the KSC, who would be called to break with their indifference and to take the side of the sound forces, defending the cause of socialism and friendship with the Soviet Union.
3. Actions should be planned to discredit Krigel and his group as Western agents connected with the Zionist centres which make preparations for the break off of relations with the Soviet Union and for Czechoslovakia's orientation towards the West.
4. A leaflet in Czechoslovak should be circulated on behalf of the 'underground leadership' of the pro-nazi National Democratic Party demanding autonomy for the Sudetenland, the return of expatriated Germans and the holding of a referendum on the self-determination of the Sudetenland.
Note: Depending on the changing situation in Czechoslovakia, new actions may have to be carried out or the ones listed in the present plan may have to be revised accordingly.
22 May 1968.

These were the results of the decisions taken in Yalta and Potsdam. These decisions turned out to be too stringent and egoistically cut out for the East European nations.

How much time had to pass before we could realize what a long and perilous road was covered by the two military and political systems, so that such a plan of action could be viewed as an anachronism now?

Along with this, Zhivkov was famous for his solid stand in support of the Soviet line at all international meetings and forums. This increased Brezhnev's trust in him.

In 1968, for example, as developments in Czechoslovakia were maturing, Zhivkov was one of those who supported the use of force to nip in the bud the processes of democratization in this Central European state.

Zhivkov's reward, Brezhnev's complete trust, was used not only to stabilize his personal power, but to seek political, economic, military and even cultural benefits for Bulgaria.

The culmination of personal relations between Zhivkov and Brezhnev was between 1971 and 1974, when they met annually, went hunting together and held long conversations. Particularly important were their 1973 talks at the Voden Residence, when

Zhivkov succeeded in gaining remarkable political and economic benefits for Bulgaria.

First of all he neutralized the Soviet reaction on the Macedonian issue by convincing Brezhnev to enforce a tacit and neutral position on the controversy between Bulgaria and Yugoslavia. This was an important breakthrough in the traditional Russian and Soviet siding with Serbia and Yugoslavia. For a certain period of time, Belgrade lost a major supporter of its attacks on Sofia over the Macedonian issue. The research efforts of those Soviet historians and anthropologists who energetically supported the ideals of an independent Macedonian state seemed to disappear in thin air.

Besides, Zhivkov managed to obtain political and economic guarantees for the country's development. An important outcome of the talks was the correction of prices of Bulgaria's agricultural exports to the Soviet Union. Brezhnev agreed to offset the shortfall, by free aid to the tune of hundreds of millions of roubles annually.

Bulgaria reached an important agreement with the Soviet Union for the delivery of raw materials and energy products which by far exceeded its needs. During the oil crisis of the 1970s, Bulgaria bathed in a sea of Soviet petroleum, metal, timber, coal and cotton. Bulgarian exports to the Soviet Union meanwhile enjoyed fixed prices, ensuring on occasions a profit margin of 200 to 300 per cent. The personal agreements of the summit quickly reached the lower levels of ministers and general directors of economic enterprises. A cognac diplomacy was used to bribe Soviet partners into accepting shoddy goods for their 'seller's' market. Bulgaria's economic boom in the 1970s and early 1980s was therefore ensured by the flow of Soviet economic blood.

Bulgaria's privileges reached a drastic point when trainloads of Soviet goods had their freighting papers changed while crossing Bulgaria *en route* to the West. In fact, just by re-exporting Soviet petrochemicals, the Bulgarian chemicals industry was able to report a foreign exchange revenue of 800 million dollars (Bulgaria's total export today stands at around 1,800 million dollars).

Soviet diplomats in Bulgaria were thwarted in their attempts to end this plunder, since the agreements had been reached at the highest level possible – between Zhivkov and Brezhnev.

Some were even recalled from Bulgaria, on the tacit charges of 'trying to set the two general secretaries at odds.'

While the Soviet Union had succeeded in exporting its Stalinist model of socialism, one should not overlook the other side of the coin; Bulgaria would otherwise never have managed to achieve the national wealth and the living standards of the 1970s with its unproductive economic system in which the average daily work load was around four hours. Zhivkov had simply found a cosy nook under the mighty Soviet raw material umbrella. For a long time this 'nook' remained a rich gold vein.

In return Zhivkov gave something which the Soviet Union neither wanted nor needed: assurances that Bulgaria wanted to become its sixteenth republic. This Todor Zhivkov promised to Khrushchev and Brezhnev. He even tried to lull Gorbachev with such faithfulness.

Naturally, the Bulgarian leader was a mature enough politician to have realized the absurdity of such assurances on both national and international levels. Zhivkov flirted with Bulgaria's faithfulness, he flattered the egotism of the 'top man' at the Kremlin, and such emotionally coloured political utopias earned him the right-hand spot in all photographs, which preserved for posterity the historic meetings of the communist leaders.

But to his credit he never allowed the deployment of Soviet troops or armaments on Bulgarian territory. To buttress the economic agreements with Breznev, Zhivkov made certain he would be giving something in return. In July 1973 a document was adopted, entitled 'Guidelines for the Development of All-round Cooperation with the USSR'. It contained the entire ideological propaganda arsenal of totalitarian rules, but not even the slightest mention of what Bulgaria would actually be giving to the Soviets.

Two months afterwards Brezhnev was proclaimed 'Hero' of the People's Republic of Bulgaria. Most deservedly, in fact, although at that time we saw it as a personal move on Zhivkov's part, unaware that the country was profiting quite handsomely from Brezhnev's vanity.

Brezhnev's last years were particularly difficult. Zhivkov saw this and worried that Brezhnev had become just a toy in the system's mechanism. At their meetings, Brezhnev was coherent only in the first ten minutes after which his vacant look wandered around the room. After Zhivkov's report, Brezhnev would turn to

Chernenko and ask, 'Konstantin Ustinovich, is Todor saying the right things?' And Chernenko would reproduce verbatim what he had heard from the interpreter.

Around 1980 Zhivkov made a small revolt. He asked several high-ranking functionaries such as Chernenko and Ustinov: 'What are you waiting for? Don't you have somebody more appropriate for number one?' Chernenko had reported this to Brezhnev and, in his last years of power, Brezhnev's affections for Todor Zhivkov cooled off.

What use did Bulgaria make of the unique economic terms and privileges which it received from the Soviet Union?

Zhivkov and the people around him were overcome by a megalomania which made them believe that the economic policy was infallible and that the results were their own doing. Nobody wanted to face the truth that we were just a tick on the elephant's body. Nobody predicted that this elephant would fall ill.

Economists succumbed to the political dictate and decision-making. Bulgaria set out to build a structure more typical of much larger economies, based on vast raw material, human and financial resources. The country's investment policy sought to speed up the development of industries such as electronics, robotics, laser technology and heavy engineering. The squandering of capital into so many spheres slowed down and subsequently caused the sharp deterioration of Bulgaria's traditional economic sectors. Once a developed agrarian country, it suddenly faced the problem of feeding its own population. The 1970s and 1980s saw the construction of 16 electronic factories, and a single potato store.

It was true that with our electronic production we balanced the huge raw material supplies from the Soviet Union. The crisis surfaced when these sectors were no longer the coin of exchange in our mutual relations.

The determined implementation of Stalin's theory of prioritized industrial development caused lasting human, financial and ecological disproportions in Bulgaria's economy and market. Prestigous industries were kept alive with dollar injections. The Bulgarian economy no longer relied on the natural laws of development, but on external *ad hoc* factors. In economic history there is hardly one example to show that this is the right road to national prosperity.

Between 1975 and 1985 re-exports of Soviet raw materials and

OPEC petrodollars allowed Bulgaria to build industries which could only function normally if they swallowed between 2.5 billion (in 1975) and 4 billion dollars (after 1985) annually. The intoxication had become almost pathological. Nobody heard the sober-minded but timid voices of different experts predicting Bulgaria's ruin. To me, the most catastrophical consequence of the totalitarian regime in Bulgaria was the unsuitable economic structure implanted as an idea by Georgi Dimitrov at the Fifth Bulgarian Communist Party Congress in 1948, and which had found full practical realization by the 1970s.

Therefore, I found it largely inexplicable that after 10 November 1989 all responsibility was laid on two comparatively young figures in the last government: Stoyan Ovcharov, who was appointed minister of planning and the economy in 1987 and Petko Danchev, deputy prime minister for only a few months.

Ognyan Doynov and Grisha Filipov are also mentioned; surprisingly, the present chairman of the National Assembly Stanko Todorov, who was prime minister until 1981, is frequently omitted. With his well-known shy smile he evaded a critical query from an opposition reporter with the quip, 'But shops were full in those days.' True, but Stanko Todorov was one of those who caused their emptiness soon afterwards. I do not know of a single person from his cabinet to have ever doubted the major trends of Bulgaria's economic development.

It was precisely during the 1970s that Zhivkov's regime acquired its brilliance and vanity. The country had an active trade balance, the market was tranquil and the intelligentsia drew on the never failing cultural funds and was obedient. Security was in secure hands. Bulgaria created the impression of a blissful idyll. Zhivkov and his daughter, Lyudmila Zhivkova, were in their heyday of glory, honours and acknowledgements. Everybody sought their blessing: politicians, the military, actors, writers and musicians. An approving nod meant a career; raised eyebrows or a grimace of displeasure amounted to political or professional ruin. But Zhivkov himself was never the executor. Scores of volunteers rushed forward as hungry hyenas to struggle and drown the culprit and thus display loyalty and personal faithfulness.

In those years there were still enough perks to spread around: official Mercedes limos alone numbered over several hundred, not to mention the other makes. Scores of official villas appeared, hundreds of channels for the distribution of awards were created.

New, open and discreet forms of top party and state servicing appeared. A gross consumerist attitude emerged at all levels of state rule. Public property became increasingly unmanageable, defenceless against plunder and embezzlement.

Curiously, Zhivkov was not for a moment misled as to the true state of things; I will mention just one episode.

In 1984 Gorbachev came to power in the Soviet Union. In one conversation with Zhivkov the idea emerged that now was the time to take a firm stand and to speak out bravely and honestly about the most pressing problems. Thoughtfully, he concluded, 'That's right. This will also be a sort of investment for the future.'

Then, very briefly, he dictated a number of theses which would form the backbone of his message to Gorbachev. Zhivkov had earlier tried to raise some sharp political questions with Brezhnev but had been sharply ticked off. Now an opportunity was at hand to take 'a beneficial position'. The following excerpts were taken from that personal message:

> If our potential were given a chance to analyze events in our society, it would find good solutions and traditional approaches to the development of the socialist society. We, however, have never allowed it to do so. We are afraid of making mistakes. Some scientists may occasionally err. A mistake takes a mistake. But many of their findings are true. Then there is the problem of the appearance of relations and even entire social groups which are alien to socialism and which seriously deform our society.
>
> At present the complex of accumulated institutions and apparatus is so vast and decentralized that it swallows up more costs and social energy than socialism can afford. Worse yet, instead of helping the country's development, this apparatus is exhibiting a decidedly bureaucratic attitude.
>
> This apparatus has surrounded itself with an entire stratum, a self-reproducing social group whose interests and privileges would suffer from any programme for social development and change. That group's most powerful weapon is that it empties of content all decisions and transforms them into hollow slogans, into hundreds and thousands of bureaucratic documents which only fake change and action.
>
> Our political theory and practice had failed to create counterbalance to this dangerous phenomenon, but one of the obvious reasons for its development has been the indefensibly

> long delay of the restructuring and improvement of the socialist political system in line with the new circumstances. Especially important is the question of the social tension which has accumulated over the last decades and which puts to the test the leading role of the communist party.
>
> In general, the protest is directed not against socialism, but at the destruction of its principles; not against socialist rule, but against the inefficient methods of government; not against the communist parties, but against the mistakes in their policies.
>
> Hence the tasks and obligations of our parties: to guarantee the functioning of socialism free of deformities and arbitrariness, to restore the confidence in the laws of the socialist state, in socialist justice and control and in the electivity and replacement of cadres.

Several days later, having the final version of the letter, he dicated a postscript of sorts for our own consumption. I quote from my short-hand notes, 'What did the foregoing exposé to Gorbachev mean?'

Nobody can convince me that what I have said is wrong.

The Soviet Union is at the root of all the successes and failures of our socialist community. We do not deny this and have always underlined it. But when we talk of the Soviet Union as a major power in the development of the socialist countries, we cannot hide the real situation of things.

It is a fact that the Soviet Union is lagging behind in technology. And this has been taking place for more than just a few years; since after World War II.

The Soviet Union was the main supplier of equipment to all socialist states. But because of its failure to carry out a proper economic policy over the last decades, not only the Soviet Union but all of the socialist states have begun to lag behind. Take the former German Democratic Republic and Czechoslovakia, for example; even if there are valid reasons for the slow development of the rest of the socialist countries – Poland, Hungary, Romania and Bulgaria – there are none as far as the former two countries are concerned. The Soviet economy held back all the socialist countries, and continues to do so.

Therefore, the main obstacle before our development is the crying backwardness of the Soviet Union. I won't dwell on the reasons for this backwardness, but it is nevertheless a fact.

The Soviet experience, which we adopted after the victory of the revolution, is rooted in wrong economic principles. By repeating the Soviet example we created the conditions for the deformation of socialism in our countries.

How did Zhivkov–Gorbachev relations develop after that?

Piqued, the Soviet leader hinted that he 'would not be lectured.' It was not an arrogant show of personal insult, Gorbachev acted logically as the head of state of a superpower and the leader of the world's largest leading communist party. Todor Zhivkov regretted that indiscretion and wished he had raised the matter in a personal letter rather than in a formal document. He waited a while and began worrying that there was a lot of talk in the Soviet Union but nothing was done in earnest. He kept telling the same joke:

Question: 'Which Bulgarian town is named after Soviet perestroika?'

Answer: 'Batak.' (The reference was to the Turkish word for chaos and disorder.)

On several occasions Zhivkov told this joke in public. Some people hastened to 'tip off' Moscow that he was attacking perestroika in the Soviet Union.

One way or another, Zhivkov did not let himself be seen as 'waiting to be lectured'.

His dictated theses and restructuring concept took shape with the shortest possible delay and was adopted at the July 1987 plenum. While it has been completely forgotten now, objectively it contained many fundamental ideas which both now and in future will be fleshed out with tangible political and economic content. Let us recall that basically, that concept proceeded from equality and diversity of ownership, from the separation of the communist party from the state administration, from corporate self-management and municipal self-government, from new principles on pensions, banking, shareholding and so on. Practical work went ahead with the issue of Council of Ministers Decree No. 35, encouraging free enterprise and of Decree No. 56 on economic activity which is still in effect. Many ministries were closed down, many parasitic departments were eliminated.

This restructuring met with much resistance. This time, however, bureaucrats were really badly hit although they fought back and clung tightly to their positions.

The mighty pillars of a party leadership and rule, the departments of the Central Committee and of the regional and municipal committee were closed down. However, it is still too early for a historical assessment of these facts.

How did the Soviet Union react? The secretary of the Central Committee of the Soviet Union Communist Party, B. Medvedev arrived in Sofia. In a four-hour discussion he made it clear that Moscow was sceptical about what was going on in Bulgaria.

Todor Zhivkov had to go to Moscow in person and explain. He did so on 16 October 1987. The verbatim report of the Zhivkov–Gorbachev session of talks at the Kremlin, from which I have quoted below, will help us set aside, to some extent, the *ad hoc* considerations that dictate our assessment of one personality or another. The documentary evidence will be the most accurate and impartial medium of ideas about the future of socialism, without the political hypocrisy of formal declarations or the hollow fluency of propaganda statements.

Todor Zhivkov: Winding up, I would like to point out that we will both be able to move decisively ahead only if we manage to overcome bureaucratic centralism and the incumbent bureaucrats' apparatus. Wherever we go, we always run into that apparatus.

Take agriculture in this country. So far we have had five structures, five levels of management. Can a modern state, be it a socialist one, tolerate anything like that? That is why we are changing things there, and we think this is the right thing to do.

Now we are discussing the future of the National Assembly. Obviously, it will be a working corporation and its operation will incorporate in a new way elements of legislative, executive and supervisory power. Most important of all, it will remain the supreme body of power in this country, a body of people's self-government. I make this point, because one of our comrades, at conversations at the embassy, said that the National Assembly will be a presidential institution. That was his personal opinion and he should not have said it. For there will be a National Assembly in future too, and there will be a supreme executive and administrative body of power in the Council of Ministers. This body is more or less there, and it won't undergo any substantial changes.

But, you see, the problem of separating legislative and executive power in the conditions of socialist self-government of the people does not face Bulgaria alone. It is a common problem. We address it guided by the conviction that it cannot be entirely solved at present. Obviously, it is rather a problem of the future.

There is yet another question: about form and content. This is an exceedingly important question concerning the dialectic of our development. Judging by our own experience, we can't split form and content mechanically. In the 1960s we tried to introduce a new economic mechanism. We failed because we believed it was enough to change the content only. In the 1970s we again tried to do something to this effect. But the form once again stifled the content. In the early 1980s we made new steps. We can say that something came out of it. But basically, we failed again. Why? Because the political forms stifled and crushed everything.

Social form is not a wrapping of social content. It is above all a means to organize this content. No new content survives, if we don't reorganize its functioning; if the form is not changed accordingly. I wonder where and in what we are wrong in Bulgaria when we seek to change the form, and in this way attempt to organize the socialist content we have created?

Some people tell us that we are not ready because we are introducing new forms without having prepared the respective new content for them. This contention does not correspond to the actual state of affairs. Over the last few years, and especially during the last two and a half years, we have been purposefully working on the shaping of a new content. We have worked out, submitted to a nationwide discussion and already enforced a new labour code. We implement our formulations about associations as new types of economic structures, as a form of management of the self-managing economic organizations. We worked out a concept on the further development of the cooperative movement and so on. Thus we have a new content, on the basis of which this country has entered the initial stage of society's progress to a qualitatively new state. In all likelihood, these will be prolonged processes which will cover a period of at least 10 to 15 years.

There is one more thing. Changing the form inevitably affects some elements of the content. It is only logical that we should change, to some extent, the essence of the content too. But, as I have already observed, these are changes which assert the socialist character of both production relations and the political system in this country.

At this stage, new and old elements inevitably coexist. That is why we attach great importance to the problems concerning the promotion of new forms so as, for once, not to let the old ones stifle the new ones.

In changing the form, we encounter a number of difficulties. In a number of cases we are compelled to make some tactical concessions. For instance, we closed down a number of ministries, but we did not immediately dismiss their employees. We are handling very carefully the personnel which we are to dismiss from the party and the state apparatus. We plan to allow them to keep their previous salaries, but we won't be able to provide them with some of the privileges which have been available to them so far, such as cars and secretaries. There will be discontent, but we will fight it resolutely. On the other hand, we don't have such problems with the working class, the agricultural workers and the intelligentsia. They give us a different kind of problem. They arise when we want them to work in keeping with the new rights, obligations and responsibilities of the workforces. We will inevitably run into such problems in the allocation of socialist property for management and administration.

For both here and in the other spheres, we seek a new correlation between democracy and centralism. Essentially, we place the further development of centralization on an economic basis. To this end, we will be promoting the principle of contractual relations between the state and the self-managing economic organizations. As is known, we have established new banks. This is another form of centralization, of large scale centralization. This centralization, however, will be carried out not by administrative means and levers but through the national currency. This will allow us to exercise direct control over the development of the national economy and to control the market in this country by economic methods. You see, in both cases we are seeking to break up the administrative centralization and to replace it with an economic based centralization.

We will also introduce momentous changes in the sphere of the legal superstructure. There will also be changes in the intellectual sphere.

What problems do we have? We were seriously hit by the drought which has persisted for three consecutive years. This year with a planned national income growth of seven per cent, we will achieve five per cent at best. We also have problems with the material and technical supplies. We have run up debts. Two years ago I headed the Currency Commission with the Politburo. We managed to cut our debts down to 3,000 million dollars. After that the commission was taken over by the Council of

Ministers. I don't want to be misunderstood. I am not shifting the blame onto others, but under the circumstances by the end of the year our debt will reach 6,000 million dollars. Our assets total 1.5 thousand million. I once again took over the Currency Commission. By the end of the five year period, we will pay back another 1,000 million dollars. In this way, we will reduce our debts to 3,500 million dollars. We are taking decisive measures. Under the circumstances this is our only chance.

Concerning the relations between our two parties and peoples. As you mentioned, this is a special relationship of brotherly friendship and cooperation. It was this way under Stalin and Khrushchev, and under Brezhnev. After the April 1956 plenum this relationship materialized in all cells of the political body.

Now, in view of the new situation and the tasks we have set ourselves, we must outline additional measures for their development. We want new decisive steps to demonstrate how a giant country such as the Soviet Union and a small country such as ours can pursue their friendship and integration. This will have an enormous political and ideological significance both at home and abroad.

Talking of our relations, I cannot but note the fact that in the course of 30 years we have never given the Soviet Union any trouble. We will not give it any in the future either. We are perfectly well aware of what the Soviet Union is and what responsibility we have for the common cause of restructuring.

I absolutely agree that we have to get things straight between us. The information received must be *bona fide* and it must be correctly interpreted before it is reported to you. Here is an example with Comrade Honecker. During our talks he said nothing about the restructuring in the Soviet Union and in our countries, but in the car he asked why we had eliminated the Council of Ministers. I replied: 'Yes, we have eliminated the Council of Ministers, the Academy of Sciences, we are planning to eliminate the party, and we are negotiating with the patriarch to eliminate the Holy Synod, too. As to the Council of Ministers, we did eliminate it, but not the ministers. I introduced some of them to you at the welcoming ceremony and you met the rest at the dinner.'

Clearly, when such information is received and when it is misinterpreted and reported that way, the results may be monstrous.

Mikhail Gorbachev: I listened to your presentation attentively and with keen interest. We are indeed at a revolutionary stage, at a time when no rifle shots are fired, but when all that we do is extremely responsible. In its depth, scope and new forms of organization and management this is a revolutionary renewal. And once it is a revolution, you don't play at revolution. Revolution is an art. It is not something to be trifled with, as the classics of Marxism-Leninism emphasize. Slogans alone won't work. They must be translated into specific actions at each stage.

We accept your ideas about the objectives and tasks of restructuring with great satisfaction and understanding. We have always said that this is our common stand. I even think that Comrade Zhivkov can do more than we can. In my case, for example, they can say, 'he lays the blame on the previous leadership.' With you there is no such problem. Nobody can say: 'where were you, Comrade Zhivkov, during those 30 years? What have you done that needs restructuring now? The truth is that over these 30 years Bulgaria has achieved a lot, it has turned into a modern socialist state. If restructuring is needed now, it is not because of the faults and the stagnation, but because of the new tasks which socialism must tackle.

Concerning your elaboration on form and content. I think that this problem must be rationalized. We have already said as much in public, and I will say it in my report on the seventieth anniversary of the Great October Socialist Revolution. The more we stake on the command–administrative method, on directive leadership, the more tasks we set ourselves to achieve by these methods, the more the apparatus grows. This phenomenon is described in Parkinson's law.

Lenin categorically warned of the risks of red tape. He always pointed out that where there is bureaucracy, new tasks can only be carried out by setting up new units in the apparatus which are assigned these tasks. That is why I have a different formula for the form and content question. It is a question of overcoming the command–administrative method, the directive leadership. The main weapon against bureaucracy is democracy. We have no differences on this point, either.

Todor Zhivkov: We must also take into account Lenin's formulation about the struggle against the bureaucracy emerging under socialism. He raises these questions in 1919, in 1921 and in his last work.

Mikhail Gorbachev: We are also convinced that structural changes are needed. I will discuss some matters so that we can get straight on certain questions.

Let me start with the methods and rates of restructuring. At this stage we risk taking hasty action. I will share my experience. We can crush everything old at a blow. But we cannot create the new things at a blow. If we adopt such an approach, we'll end up with a void, with bedevilling difficulties, especially in the economy. We merged four ministries into two, but people still won't work. If we decide to eliminate everything, we may completely disorganize management. We both have the same plans, theoretical and political. They overlap to a large extent. Of course, we take into account the specific realities in each country. Our experience has convinced us of the importance of tactics for the fulfilment of our plans. For inappropriate tactics may 'undermine' the strategy. We are guided by the conviction that we face different tasks: long-term, medium-term, current and urgent ones. Our strategy is mapped out for a long historical period. That is why we start with those tasks whose solution brooks no delay. We must solve the food problem and the housing problem. If we do not do that, we will compromise the very idea of restructuring. A medium-term task is the retooling of the economy.

This is how the business of democracy stands now. We cannot delay the solution of this problem, but we must not rush it either. Now we must start on an experimental basis and then go ahead with changes. We may amend the constitution, too; but this will come much later. If we load all that on society, we will not achieve the desired result.

In this connection we started asking ourselves certain questions. We wondered, for instance, how it is possible to carry out restructuring both at the centre and at the local level without wide-ranging discussions in Bulgaria, how everything can change rightaway? This gave us a cause of fraternal worry. Then I decided to send over Comrade Medvedev.

Perhaps we don't get everything right, but we are afraid that if you fail, they will say 'See, they are copying the Soviet Union and that's where they land.' They can also blame us, 'Why are you misleading your friends?' Our sense of responsibility urges us to ask ourselves such questions. To some extent we have been sharing the experience of what is going on in Bulgaria. Is it possible to ignore the people and raise and decide such matters over their heads? Is it possible that all this should take place without glasnost and democratic mechanisms? This gives us a cause of fraternal worry.

The other question concerns the party, the thesis that it will not be 'the main agent of power'. In our country the party has also usurped the solution of economic tasks. In Leningrad I said that the regional party committees were handling economic problems, I spoke of the need to differentiate the functions. The Soviets are also not doing their job properly. Why is this so? Party cadres are not idlers. But some of the methods in the style of leadership which we now criticize have been created by ourselves. We have therefore not done our job properly.

We cannot wash our hands of it and blame the party. It is us and us alone who keep assembling party activists, who keep urging them and spurring them on: 'We must fulfil the plan for the year, for the five year period.'

What has to be done? We have to differentiate the functions of the party from those of the state. The party bodies must work by political methods and work on policy-making with the cadres.

Socialist society is built consciously, this process is spearheaded by a revolutionary party. That is why we are alarmed by the formulation that the party is no longer going to be the 'main agent of power'. The question arises as to how the development of socialist society is further to be directed.

Socialist pluralism and its components can only be organized by the party. A restructuring without the party, a democracy without the party, is impossible. We are worried by the appeal to divest the ruling party of its power, to revise the fundamental formulation about the party's leading role. When we talk of differentiating the functions of party and state, it is another question. It is possible to change the forms, the methods and the accents. As to the party's role, its place is in the vanguard.

We saw, by the way, how the party in Yugoslavia turned into a debating club. Now they are bickering there and they urge for getting down to brass tacks, but they can't go ahead with anything serious.

Of course, nobody here thinks that Comrade Todor Zhivkov wants to eliminate the Bulgarian Communist Party. We agree that the party must rid itself of extrinsic functions. When it is in power, these functions acquire a special character. The matter is debatable.

Why should, for example the secretary of the District Committee deal with the unloading of train-loads of coal? It is absolutely correct to put such things right. We have no differences with you on these matters.

We want the restructuring in Bulgaria and the Soviet Union to bring us even closer together. I accept with great pleasure your suggestion for still closer and businesslike cooperation in all spheres, to upgrade the cooperation and closeness of our two countries to a qualitatively new level. The Soviet Union's capabilities are growing. As early as this year, 38 per cent of our mechanical engineering output will be world class. We will persevere in our efforts in this field.

Information has reached us, however, that some of Comrade Zhivkov's closest aides favour turning Bulgaria into a 'mini Federal Republic of Germany', or a 'mini Japan'. Such hints have been dropped in conversation. These conversations worry us. Some people around you have pro-Western leanings. You must know about this. There are people among your closest aides who think that technologies should be taken from the Federal Republic of Germany, from the West. Such talks and leanings worry us. If there are people around you who are obsessed with a 'mini FRG' or a 'mini Japan', you should not keep them close to you any longer. Because all answers to your questions, all solutions to the tasks set must be sought in socialism and in its vigorous development. This is the right way to solve them.

Todor Zhivkov: Thank you for your candid tone, for your sincere comradely attitude.

The questions you discussed cannot be a cause of worry. I, however, have my doubts about the objectivity of the information you receive. Perhaps you should ask your embassy to reanalyze everything going on in this country. As far as I know, there are two or three clever comrades there who could do this. Not just inform you, but grasp the essence of the things we are getting under way there. Or maybe, actuated by go-getting motives, someone or some people in the highest echelon in our country are interested to present the state of affairs in such a way.

I have been informed, for example, that we have loaded it all on society quite unexpectedly. Is this true? I have already told you about our preparations. A long time ago, far before the July plenum, we raised and discussed the matter of cabinet changes. Before the plenum we adopted two major political declarations. One of them concerned the allocation of socialist property for management and administration, and the other concerned the transformation of the municipalities into self-governing communities of the population. They were released for nationwide discussion. That was how we prepared for the transfer of socialist property and for the country's territorial division.

In connection with the forthcoming national party conference, an election campaign is under way in the party. Is it possible, while holding this campaign, that we should not elect new municipal and regional party committees? This year we have to hold elections for local authorities. Is it possible under the circumstances to keep the old bodies of power and to leave the changes we've mapped out for after the elections? What I mean to say is that we are not rushing things. We are following the logic of the problems which have to be solved.

Mikhail Gorbachev: Think again about what you told me. You are reducing the number of district party and state officials. Those are the very people who made their way up under Comrade Zhivkov, who loyally worked for implementation of the party line.

Todor Zhivkov: I already noted that we are not stripping those people of political confidence. We are not dismissing them, we are not firing them because they bungled up their jobs. But there is nothing else we can do, once we have arrived at the need to establish new bodies of territorial administration.

We realize that this is a difficult and painful operation. That is why I treat the redundancies with care and consideration. But, as I have already said, we can't allow them their previous privileges. As is known, some of those people write anonymous complaints, and some are addressed to you. But this will not help them.

I would like briefly to discuss the question concerning the party's role as a leading and guiding force of socialist development, of the process of restructuring. At the July plenum we clearly and unequivocally set forth our stand; that the party can no longer be an echelon of state administration. This implies it must upgrade and strengthen its role as a political vanguard of the people and as a leading and guiding political force in our development.

Mikhail Gorbachev: If you mean to rid the party of certain extrinsic functions, I agree. But you raise the question about a separation of power between the party and the state.

Todor Zhivkov: Yes, we do not raise the question of ridding the party of its extrinsic functions of state administration, but of differentiating between the functions of party and state. It was not by chance that we reached this conclusion. At the time, when socialist rule was still being established in this country, Georgi Dimitrov raised the question of ridding the party of some extrinsic functions. This question was also raised by Vulko Chervenkov. We, too, raised it after the April plenum. If we did not achieve worthwhile results, it was due to the very way in which the question was formulated. The real point is not to redistribute once and for all the functions between party and state, but to eliminate the situation in which the party is also an echelon of state administration.

I will make no secret of the fact that I am surprised that there are people in this country who seek to divert Bulgaria from its socialist road of development, to turn it into some sort of 'mini Federal Republic of Germany' or 'mini Japan'. There are no grounds for such a thing – no technological, financial, let alone political grounds. Ten days ago the president of the Bulgarian National Bank came to see me. I raised the question about the attraction of Western capital and the partial repayment of credit in goods. That is why I asked him what amount of capital had been attracted to Bulgaria so far. The National Bank president told me that the foreign capital totalled 260 million dollars. That's all there is to it. Everything else is fiddlesticks.

Mikhail Gorbachev: I don't think this is invented.

I leave these pages without comment. I am not an historian, and they refer to a rather recent past which one should approach with a sense of historical proportion. Whoever possesses political culture, whoever knows the shattered theory of socialism, whoever does not labour under a partiality for the two leaders will be able to decide on his own the side in whose favour truth tips the balance. This question is rather addressed to myself: 'Doesn't one of the leaders elaborate quite a few of the ideas the practicability of which has been the aim of the ruling party and the opposition in Bulgaria since 10 November 1989?' I will refrain from an answer because it would inevitably have to address the views of the other leader. Or should I content myself with the trivial apologetic stand that every truth is specific, that everyone carries in his beliefs 'his own truth'? Such truths, however, may cause tragedies when they lead to historic U-turns with unforeseeable consequences or when they inflict suffering on the people.

I wonder whether the people realize how vain their leaders are. I also wonder when millions of people will stop their century-long swing from one political theory to another. Until then they will be the victims of experiments and intellectual and political ambitions, of people who transfer the chaos of their own minds into society, messing up the life of many generations. Let everyone find his own answer to these questions.

I, for one, would just clear up one fact. When Gorbachev reproached Zhivkov that some of his closest aides wanted to turn Bulgaria into a 'mini Federal Republic of Germany' or a 'mini Japan', the Soviet leader had in mind Ognian Doynov. At that time the latter was engaged in active and successful negotiations on signing lucrative long-term agreements with Japan and West Germany on the delivery of state of the art technologies for the major mechanical engineering plants in his country.

In this connection Zhivkov was simply curious that some people in positions of responsibility were pursuing their own policies against the national interests, that they not only leaked important information to Moscow, but even distorted it. But the matter here was rather delicate. Zhivkov could not use the powerful State Security surveillance and bugging teams against these people.

That is why he acted more carefully. Finding his way with characteristic practical ingenuity in such intricate situations, he acquired his own informers in Moscow, at the 'output end of the system'. Before long, he identified the schemers. Then Zhivkov lay in ambush and bided his time for the strike back.

The preparation for such a strike started with the State Security investigation of one of our ambassadors in a European capital. A number of his unlawful and legally punishable actions were proven: accepting gifts and bribes and suspicious connections with the 'higher echelon' people already targeted by Zhivkov.

Locking the records of the investigation in his office, Zhivkov said, 'Their time will come soon.' Time, however, caught up with him. The change on 10 November prevented the strike. Still, I wouldn't like to be in the place of those people, if Todor Zhivkov decides to speak out.

Obviously, Todor Zhivkov was the pillar of a system whose stability depended on many factors: factors incumbered with many political and ideological prejudices along the road of our development.

It is very easy now to ask, 'What were the communists doing all that time? They led the country to the point of crisis.' Seen from a narrow political aspect such a question might seem justified, but without an assessment of the actual correlation of forces, of the specific historical circumstances, we can never fully grasp the outlook and ethics of a politician and administration. I know that it is difficult to speak of ethics and honesty in politics as eternal categories. In politics what matters are the interests and this very often makes them incompatible with the rigid notions which are often used to describe human virtues and ethics. That is why Todor Zhivkov liked to say, 'Only history can one day judge us all.' I did not agree then, but today I am liable to agree that our contemporaries, burdened as they are with passion, emotion and unfulfilled ambitions, cannot be objective judges. It is very difficult to explain to a contemporary fired by political partisanship that the biggest number of blank spaces are to be found in the back pages of history.

People are impatient, they want change now. They won't be satisfied with historical criteria. What they want are Bavarian steaks, Swiss chocolate and French perfume. Their faces are turned towards the shiny shop windows of the West.

Within the strict canons of the alliance, which he more or less tried to follow in good faith, Zhivkov managed to play the 'Western trump' as well. A number of steps in the 1980s sought to make the country an intermediary in the technology transfer from the West to the Soviet Union. In itself, the idea was quite original. But developments in most recent years showed that the country was organizationally and economically unable to perform that role.

I have been present at meetings with Japanese and West German businessmen. I listened to Zhivkov talk during his contacts with Western business circles. There was a lot of ambition and goodwill in his words, but nothing connected with this was carried out competently. Zhivkov hesitated, made concessions with ideology, sought to bridge the gaps between socialism and capitalism, but the overall picture remained hazy. This can easily be explained. We were tied down politically, militarily and economically with the agreements among the CMEA and the Warsaw Treaty member states. A number of attempts to engage in more radical forms of economic cooperation were thus aborted.

A case in point was the idea to assign the giant heavy engineering project in Radomir to the Japanese corporation Kobe Steel. But the backers of the idea in the Politburo were labelled as 'pro-Western' and the partnership deal went instead with the works in Novokrematorsk in the USSR.

Despite all this, Zhivkov managed to play a game of 'double alliance' with the Federal Republic of Germany as well as the Soviet Union (in view of the fact that Bulgaria had been Germany's ally in both the two world wars) and to receive credit facilities on economic, rather than political terms. At these meetings with the Western business circles during the last years he promised that Bulgaria's economy would follow the principles of Western market economies and ownership. Zhivkov was especially close to the late Bavarian politician Franz-Josef Strauss, with whom he consulted on foreign policy matters before any decisions were made and even before he had informed Bulgaria's allies. Zhivkov relied greatly on these personal contacts which he figured to use in the future. But he was cautious too, because of people whom he described as 'swine who slander'.

He did not go any further than to declare actions of readiness to introduce a multisector economy, ownership and market. He was burdened by the economic doctrine and the prejudices of the old school, and by practices which had survived for more than four decades. Biologically and ideologically he belonged to the old school of Communists and he found it very difficult to break free from his die-hard convictions. Yet although his policy towards Western businessmen was hesitant, it was seen as a sign of law and order, albeit of a conservative brand. Western businessmen never refused to cooperate with Zhivkov and his team.

The economists who had to create the favourable conditions for the attraction of foreign capital by removing the archaic forms of state monopoly on foreign trade did not act on time. Zhivkov swore and raged that theirs was a 'totally criminal sphere on all levels', but took no action.

The people on the Politburo were a despairing sight: mediocre, dull and passive. The members of the Politburo and the Secretariat, ministers and members of Parliament led a good and calm life in the shadow of Todor Zhivkov. They received all the assignments 'from the top', coordinated all issues with him and under the guise of 'coordination' shifted their personal responsibility on to him. These people intuitively knew that in a one-party system passivity increased the odds of survival. The active, showy part of work and government could be left for Zhivkov. With his egotism and ruler's egocentrism 'the top man' took everything in his hands and this was an enormous error in principle. It tied him in personally with all the assets and liabilities of the system. Society was moving forward, deep structural changes occurred and the system which supported Zhivkov tried to adjust itself, but this was becoming increasingly difficult.

Slowly and irreversibly the people no longer wanted to live according to the system, yet the system was not ready for change. The outcome of this contradiction was to seek a scapegoat for the unresolvable conflict which society started to face. And there was only one choice on hand – Todor Zhivkov.

4. By the Laws of Beauty

I first met Lyudmila Zhivkova in the spring of 1976. In my capacity as advisor at the State Council I was assigned to participate in the implementation of the policy line of improving the structure of management of the ministries and departments in the intellectual sphere. The principles of the cybernetic approach were fundamental to the reform process.

Our contact was sporadic. I remember that very often my meetings with Lyudmila Zhivkova were in comic situations. She gathered teams of experts with whom she discussed the adopted approaches and patterns. They were talking about 'information technologies', 'processing, operative and control blocks', we 'subordinated', 'multiplied', and so on and so forth. I remember that during one discussion the then deputy chairman of the Committee for Culture and head of the Theatre State Corporation Pavel Pissarev, having realized the idea and demonstratively shuffling 'boxes and blocks' which was expected to produce some effect, said on leaving, 'Still, I think that the ingredients of success in the theatre were discovered 2,000 years ago by Aeschylus: to make good theatre, you need a good director and a good actor,' and he gave us a sneering look. He was right. We were then prey to 'scientific approaches'.

At that meeting Lyudmila Zhivkova plunged headlong in to the interpretational labyrinths of esoteric terms and categories, boldly mixing them up, but she could not be blamed for it. After all, she was a historian. Just like her father, she had a special liking for complicated quasi-scientific terms. He in politics and she in culture sought awe-inspiring 'code notions' which were supposed to provide a clue to the solution of all problems. The new 'concept' was immediately taken up by the mass media. It became not only the propaganda 'talk of the town', but also a semiotic sign for an entire political campaign.

We started seeing each other more often during our joint work in the summer of 1976. We were working out a Committee for

Culture programme for aesthetic education. A working group was set up, comprising many cultural and political figures.

When Lyudmila Zhivkova first addressed that working group, her words were a collection of quotations from Hegel, Marx and Berdyaev. She obviously wanted to impress us with her erudition and original thinking. In this case, however, the combination turned out to be unsuccessful.

At that meeting I suggested that we should not adopt an élitist approach to aesthetic education but seek the practical value of intellectual and moral training for the lifestyle and work of every individual. She supported me and started listening to what I was saying. She even told her father that I stood out at those meetings.

We established a close working relationship right from the start. She saw the profit motive ideas I propounded as proof of her views that creativity is inherent in every human being. People in our country could only benefit from a combination of the two points of view.

I sought the backing of Professor Elit Nikolov who had become director of the Institute for Culture. I suggested that we go together to Lyudmila Zhivkova and talk about the forthcoming Third Congress of Culture. We wanted the keynote report at the congress to focus on a single subject, the subject of man, his development and active part in the life of the country. Some time earlier, Elit Nikolov had elaborated at the State Council some very interesting sociological ideas on turning man into a criterion and basis of the entire pyramid of management units in the economy, politics and culture. He was very enthusiastic about the idea to establish in Bulgaria an organization similar to the one in Sweden to protect people from bureaucracy which, as he put it, 'sends people from pillar to post as if they were footballs.'

At the meeting, apart from the subject of man, we raised some other major problems facing culture. They suited her stance as a young and ambitious leader seeking expression and self-assertion. We did not get an answer at the meeting. She said she would think about it. And, indeed, she called us in a month's time and told us she approved of the idea and asked us to start work on the theses of the report. We were to get together in ten days' time to discuss them.

We first met at the Arbanassi Residence near Veliko Turnovo. Lyudmila Zhivkova loved that place. I also liked its ancient architecture which was in perfect harmony with the historical atmosphere of the area.

We started our first working discussions. She invariably focused on the ideas of aesthetic education and the awakening of the creative germ in every person. To her, this reasoning had an implied meaning, she was looking for something dormant which was yet to awake in the aesthetic beginnings of man. She repeatedly referred to the teachings of the Indian mahatmas and mentioned cosmic powers as well. I still had no experience working with her and I did not chime in because I could not understand a word of her impractical effusions. It was interesting to watch the local party bosses who, after several drinks, dozed off in their chairs and only from time to time volunteered some uncalled-for remark. After that we talked in private and admitted that we did not understand a thing. Wary, some of them hastened to add that 'we are not that learned for such things'. Still, it was bad manners to call into question her thoughts. Everyone was afraid to be sincere and accurate in his evaluations. Lyudmila Zhivkova had been lucky to reach the top at an auspicious historical period for her. At that time, the country was making steady progress and there were no signs of a crisis. Crowds swarmed around the Zhivkovs and tried to catch their eye. Now that I read and hear of the 'dissident' role of the intelligentsia and of everybody having fought against Zhivkov's totalitarianism, I have this to say: if someone put a face on the authoritarian regime and the obsequious atmosphere surrounding the Zhivkovs, it was certainly not the peasants and the workers, nor the party apparatchiks. There was no bourgeoisie either. Those were precisely people belonging to the so-called 'artistic-creative intelligentsia' who had smelt out the easy prey. The hypocrites, toadies and spongers who cringed before Zhivkova at that time were the single largest lot of that sort I have ever seen. One whispered that he could do 'something' for Bulgaria in Mexico and immediately got a business trip. Another said he had discovered some 'infinitely interesting' links between Indian and Bulgarian culture and was sent straightaway to work there. It was a prime time for the intelligentsia.

Ideas, books and exhibitions were promoted in inconceivable places in Europe, Asia, Africa and America. Among other things, weekend houses, flats and royalties were demanded and obtained for 'upgrading the world historical role' of Bulgaria! The poor

Bulgarian people! A large number of those artists later joined the forefront of the restructuring, of the 'struggle' against Todor Zhivkov and presented themselves as 'victims of repression and crackdowns'. They would slander, intrigue and waylay each other if only they could get in her good graces. They often suffered heart attacks and brain strokes out of envy and malice. How many kept clear of that sordid wave? Just a few, maybe.

After 10 November 1989, however, they declared in one voice that it was their right to speak on behalf of history and that it was they who now had to play a messianic role.

This should give the future political leaders of Bulgaria some food for thought. It seems to me that if a politician wants to succeed, he must seek a power base in the real structures of Bulgarian society, in the workers, peasants, scientists and engineers, even in the armed forces. Zhivkov father and daughter paid a high price for the illusion that they would find support precisely in that part of the intelligentsia. They lavished money on it, squandered resources to keep it content, loyal and trustworthy.

Not a single district capital remained without a theatre or an opera house. Ensembles obtained state sponsorship. The buying prices of pictures rocketed sky-high. The party headquarters, residences and monuments, the celebrations and the parades brought millions of leva to artists, painters and musicians.

The Union of Writers grew to 400 members. Pictures worth a record seven million leva were brought by state institutions. The budget outlays for culture in national and hard currency almost doubled in the course of several years. The number of business trips abroad tangibly increased to 'promote and popularize' Bulgarian culture. There was probably not a single country in Europe which subsidized its cultural development so generously.

Zhivkova was the subject of feverish name-dropping. People immediately capitalized on any chance contact with her. She was misquoted, directions were put into her mouth, her name was used to threaten and manipulate. In this way, 'a comrade with a high-school education' almost got a salary of 540 leva by a special decision of the Council of Ministers. Of course, she herself stopped much of the speculation and the blackmail attempts but still, too many people poisoned the atmosphere around her, made intrigues and demoralized society.

After Arbanassi we continued our work in Sofia at one of the UBO's weekend houses at 1, Angelov Vruh Street. The house had been the property of the Military Intelligence Service (RO–2), which had given it to the chief of the Abwehr station in Bulgaria, Dr Delius. Now instead of secret intelligence and counterintelligence operations, we framed sweeping cultural plans there.

The work was gruelling. All the time Lyudmila Zhivkova insisted that the report centre on the 'aesthetic education' phenomenon, a magic point in her view. I insisted on sections which would outline more clearly the link between culture, politics, economics and social environment. Still, the efforts of the working group achieved something. After long discussions we included in the report the intellectual dimensions of labour, discipline, and technoscientific progress.

After one of the working sessions, we stayed for dinner. We discussed why the cadres conformed, why they were not struggling and were afraid. I said, 'Small wonder they are afraid. If they make a mistake, their bread and butter may be put out of reach.' I do not know what she made out of it but she calmly replied, 'I am not afraid of that, either, because I can live on fruit alone.' It was then that I felt the gulf that divided our two worlds. She had almost repeated the words of the famous queen, 'If they have no bread, let them eat cake!' Zhivkova was not a blue-blooded aristocrat. She, however, had grown up and lived behind the walls of omnipotence where life and its problems seemed to have far different dimensions.

I saw for myself that she was not inclined to get angry at people who contradicted her. When we were working on the report for the Third Congress of Culture, we told her among other things that people found the film *Rome Revisited* written by Iliya Velchev quite incomprehensible. She said that she had not seen it but that people were probably not yet fit to understand such a film. Lyuben Nikolov (now a professor) spontaneously retorted, 'Or maybe, on the contrary, we aren't fit to understand them.' Lyudmila Zhivkova did not get angry and just said, 'I don't know, I haven't seen it.'

We were almost through with our work. Lyudmila Zhivkova was pleased. One evening, when everybody was there, she offered me work as her aide at the Committee for Culture.

At that time this was a high honour. I hesitated but refused. I told her that I was a lawyer, that my interests lay elsewhere and that I felt an outsider to the problems of culture and the arts. I was rather more interested in the problems of real politics, the economy and management. She was surprised by my flat refusal and said nothing. But I think she appreciated the candour of my answer and was not angry with me. That was how we parted.

In a couple of days' time, the draft report went to the Central Committee. There its original idea was modified. A progress report section was added and several concessions were made to the 'aesthetic beginnings', to consciousness and self-consciousness, to perfection and self-perfection, to discipline and self-discipline and so on. I tried to get in touch and managed to tell Todor Zhivkov that the report was spoiled. He answered quite rudely via one of his aides, ordering me 'to keep my nose out of it'. 'She knows her job,' Zhivkov had said. 'The comrades read it and liked it,' the aide said.

That was my first encounter with Zhivkov's tactics to endorse his daughter. He wanted everybody to see her as infallible and inimitable. In private, Zhivkov criticisized himself, but his daughter's plans and ambitions had to be immune to any criticism.

He wouldn't let even the slightest doubt be thrown on her actions. In the long run, it cost him dearly.

In the couple of days that followed I barely saw Zhivkova except at occasional public meetings and sessions.

In the autumn of 1979 I was called up for a 45-day stint in the reserve. I was surprised when they told me to present myself at Lyudmila Zhivkova's office at the party's Central Committee. She was already a Politburo member. She had been promoted together with Peter Mladenov, Todor Bozhinov, Ognian Doynov and Andrei Loukanov, all of them promising young people who were supposed to rejuvenate the Politburo personnel. These promotions were also intended to consolidate her own position. Lyudmila Zhivkova believed, for instance, that Andrei Loukanov would make the best prime minister. A couple of days after her father's ousting Loukanov did get this job – again, one of history's little ironies.

Alexander Lilov nominated her as a member of the Politburo. At that time he was in charge of the Secretariat and the Politburo in Todor Zhivkov's absence.

While Zhivkov was away on a visit to Italy, the Politburo met behind his back. With Alexander Lilov in the chair it took a difficult decision to name her as a Politburo member. Later on, at the 18 July 1979 plenum on the educational reform she was elected as a full member of the Politburo. Several months later I was urgently called to her office.

I went to her office on the second floor of the Central Committee in my captain's uniform. I entered and snapped a facetious soldier-like report: 'Captain Tchakarov, reporting as ordered.' She could not recognize me and was flabbergasted. It was only when I took my cap off that Zhivkova realized who was standing before her. She asked me why I was wearing that uniform. I explained in the same facetious manner that I was now far removed from the aesthetic beginnings and that I was being trained how to kill people. She took me literally. She stood up and began talking about how people should live in harmony, that violence destroyed man and the cosmic order, that war killed the creative beginnings in man and so on. After that she assigned me several tasks concerning the structure of the Ministry of National Education. Somebody had told her that I had worked on these matters at the Council on Administration with the State Council.

Several days later, she once again asked me to become her aide. I asked for time to think about it. Two or three days later I told her that I accepted. I remember she made a silly mistake then. I told her in so many words that I was perfectly well aware of what I was supposed to do, that I would work honestly and would seek to provide in good faith the link respectively between her, her office, and the incoming information on the situation in the intellectual sphere. She gave me an appraising look, pursed her lips contemptuously and said that she was in contact with other forces and that it was only they that could help the harmonious development of things.

Several days later she left for the seaside while I remained in Sofia. After she returned we left for Sweden on the first trip abroad on which I accompanied her. There she and the king of Sweden inaugurated the Thracian Treasure Exhibition. We visited sights which somebody had included in our programme. Outside Stockholm there was a camp for children aged from 10 to 15. We were told that it was there that they studied, worked, played music, learned how to cook and how to attend to patients in hospitals. I watched and racked my brains as to what was so interesting about this training. The children could hardly play their instruments and they demonstrated some kind of dance which was all too primitive. One of the Swedish policemen escorting us laughed and pointed to his head. He explained to me that that was a camp for mentally retarded children. But somebody had told Lyudmila Zhivkova that this was a prototype school conducting the education of her dreams – aesthetic education as a method of cultivating a versatile person.

That was when we clashed for the first time. She ordered gifts to be bought and I relayed this to the protocol people. The gifts were valued at 100 leva: ornamental boxes and handkerchiefs. She arrived and asked me about the gifts. I showed her the purchases, and she gave me a fierce look: 'Is that all?'

'Yes,' I replied, 'we are limited to that amount by the regulations. A larger spending requires a decision of the Secretariat and an order from the minister of finance.'

'You can go,' she told me abruptly.

She called the protocol people and gave them new orders.

That was the last time she assigned me and allowed me to decide financial matters concerning trips abroad and in the country.

Later on I found out that, as a rule, the gifts she took abroad often exceeded the spending limits laid down in the finance regulations. She, however, never signed bills. Instruments of payment were signed by Emil Alexandrov who was in charge of the international activity of the Committee for Culture. After her death he, too, found himself in the dock and served time in prison for 'unwarranted expenditures'.

There is a point I would like to make here. The only money matter she took lightly were the gifts for guests and delegations. She was pedantic in her own accounts. For example, on the island of Gotland she needed 5 dollars to buy a small ring for her daughter. She did not have money with her. I gave her 5 dollars and forgot about it at once. A month later she sent the money by one of the security guards. When abroad she went in for buying books which she gave to the National Library, to the universities and the research institutes. She spared little time for herself and never went shopping for clothes or jewellery, although in her younger years she had had a passion for jewellery.

After returning from Sweden our joint work went into a difficult period. I was torn apart in a reality full of contradictions, tensions and absurdities. Whatever report or reference paper I drafted, she would always add her sweeping ideas and thoughts.

It was a harrowing time for me. I had the feeling that something was beyond my understanding.

Another thing that weighed heavily on my mind was the little interest she showed in the economy, in party affairs and social policy. Working with her was nerve-wracking, with unexpected shifts of mood and conflicting directives. It had nothing to do with reality. She had made a fetish of cultural phenomena and would not seek a link between them and the other social spheres. She refused to realize that economy and politics inevitably influenced intellectual life. It began to dawn on me that I was helpless. My colleagues at the office and the security guards had realized that much earlier.

Once we visited Bourgas. The occasion was a conference on the development of the Strandja-Sakar region (23 April 1981). I diligently prepared background information on that backward place concerning its economy, settlement infrastructure and regional problems. The mayors of the three districts of Bourgas, Yambol and Haskovo attended the conference. They voiced concern over, among other things, the inadequate health service, water and food supplies and delivery and the persistently low birth rates. The cited facts created a painful impression. Then came the turn of Lyudmila Zhivkova to take the floor. She began with a trivial greeting and then spoke in the vein of her notions, of the role of culture and the harmonious development of the personality.

I saw the people exchanging glances. I fidgeted in my chair because I had the feeling that I, too, was the target of their derision and perplexity. I could see how remote we were from them, from their troubles and aspirations.

The sign of mysticism and the occult sciences hung over Lyudmila Zhivkova's life. How did she take up this idea which later became her destiny?

For years Lyudmila Zhivkova had led a life like all boys and girls of her age: she had gone out with friends, to parties and so on.

In the early 1970s she surrounded herself with a wide circle of friends, artists and intellectuals whom she gathered every Friday in her home at 18 Toulbukhin Boulevard. Some of the people who attended those parties later took positions of responsibility in culture, the state and the party.

Here is how one of the party goers, the future first deputy chairman of the Committee for Culture and subsequent president of the Union of Bulgarian Writers, Lyubomir Levchev, described those get-togethers: 'Along with the doyen Dechko Ouzounov, and cultural figures such as Georgi Djagarov, there one could also meet Nicolai Ghiaurov, Velichko Minekov, Vera Gancheva, Alexander Fol, Svetlin Roussev and Todor Ribarov. Perhaps at first some of them accepted these Friday invitations as a nice gesture, but today it is clear that Lyudmila Zhivkova worked very hard in those hours. She learnt about the ideas which excited the artists, about their quests and concerns. Different views clashed and this gave her a chance to evaluate them. Many of the artists, especially the younger ones, got to know each other better precisely because of those Fridays. They became close friends and later on their friendship grew into a close working relationship on the cultural front led by Lyudmila Zhivkova.'

Needless to say, in this eulogistic attempt at a biographical sketch entitled *Lyudmila Zhivkova, or the Flame on the Top*, published in 1982, one year after her death, Lyubomir Levchev says nothing about the end of these get-togethers, called pretentiously 'Friday Salons'. A high-ranking State Security officer found a way to let Todor Zhivkov know that anti-Soviet and revisionist ideas were aired at those parties. The 'Friday Salons' were held no longer.

The guests, however, caught the daughter's eye and were rapidly advanced. As a matter of fact she also needed them to secure her rear and to help her, just like her father, to make a breathtaking ascent. In this respect, her innate ambition knew no bounds.

At first she was promoted to the modest position of deputy chairman and later on she became chairman of the Committee for Culture. Then came the party and state posts. Starting as a rank and file research associate in history at the Institute for Balkan Studies, she reached the top almost at lightning speed.

Lyudmila Zhivkova realized that her private life was a failure. She saw that everything around her was motivated by her go-getting attitude.

After a serious car accident she went through a long course of medical procedures and self-cure. That was precisely how

Zhivkova came to learn about the Indian and Tibetan systems of treatment and hypnosis.

Slowly but surely an aversion to social life came over her. She withdrew into herself and decided to prove to the world that the body and matter should be transcended, that only the spirit and the ideas were eternal. That is how around 1975 she became strongly attracted to asceticism to the point of self-torture.

Her closest circle consisted of Bogomil Rainov, Svetlin Roussev and some other established party functionaries. They played a special role in her life. They bombarded her with books on the occult sciences and the transcendental states of the spirit. Bogomil Rainov had a particularly strong influence on her. He, however, refrained from meeting her openly. She visited him at his house where they held long conversations.

After her meetings with Rainov she used to receive books by the Indian mahatmas and the great gurus. She used to speak of the Mahatma Moria, of Elena Blavatska and Nikolai Roerich as her first teachers.

In 1977 Lyudmila Zhivkova made the long journey to India and Tibet. She met the famous Sai-Baba. She used to tell us how she went alone in the mountains to live in a cave like a hermit for a couple of days. She told me that it was there that she had learned meditation, the art of levitation, how to stop her breathing and to contact extraterrestrial powers; in other words she had been 'initiated'.

The Banner of Peace Movement was inspired by Svetoslav Roerich who conveyed to her the ideas of Russian artists Nikolai and Yelena Roerich. Only few could fathom what stood behind that movement and what its purposes were. In a rare moment of candour she implied that she actually wanted to lay the foundations for a world-wide spiritual fraternity of artists with markedly versatile accomplishments. They had to be kept on record in Sofia from a very early age. After that their growing up was to be monitored before they were eventually initiated into the great mystery of harmony. A depository was established in Sofia to keep the works of the participating children, their names and addresses were recorded and they were contacted for every following assembly in Bulgaria.

Zhivkova ordered a combination of bells, a globe and a cross (seen from above) for the Banner of Peace Movement and at every meeting she used the key words: 'miners of new ores', 'fire', 'light', 'cup', 'spiral'. At that stage, her thoughts were a mixture of the ideology of the 'White Fraternity' of the Bulgarian mystic Dunov (she thought he had been initiated but at a lower level), of Indian 'agni yoga' and the teachings of Yelena Blavatskaya (a Russian *émigrée* theosophist). Her speeches bewildered the audiences. A typical example was her speech at the inauguration of the Banner of Peace Monument (25 August 1979).

Lyudmila Zhivkova's last years passed under the sign of meetings with 'initiated' ones from India, Japan and Sri Lanka. Mysteriousness and thinly veiled irrationality began to engulf her personality.

The sad thing about all this was that many members of the establishment began to imitate her. They were instantly converted to vegetarianism in front of her while, of course, in private they would eat themselves sick. They and their families approached her on delicate issues, naively seeking her interpretation of their dreams.

It was disgusting to watch those people manipulate and take unfair advantage of a person who, in her heart of hearts, was so tragic. To them, however, hypocrisy and speculative interests were part of the mechanism which would secure them a fast promotion to the top or at least keep them there.

Lyudmila Zhivkova had no private life. She remained a vegetarian until the end of her life. Her meals usually consisted only of tea with milk, a morsel of black bread and dried fruits and fruit juices.

But the hard work as chairman of the Committee for Culture and Politburo member made her a nervous and mental wreck. Increasingly often she suffered from splitting headaches and nervous breakdowns. She never went to see a doctor, though. She used to say, 'If the spirit is sound, the body will follow suit.'

Some of the physicians failed to do their duty and covered up her true condition. In some cases, when she tried to get their help, they would wriggle out under different pretexts, fearing the responsibility, a possible mistake or her anger. They simply left her to the mercy of her fate, which was far from merciful.

In this way, day in day out, Zhivkova was overworking herself to death. Gruelling trips, meetings, talks and speeches combined with a harsh regime of self-exhaustion slowly undermined her frail constitution.

Her condition worsened. The symptoms of overwork were increasingly evident. Several times I suggested to her UBO security guards, remarkably intelligent and tactful, that we talk to her father and tell him everything. They listened to me but did not go along. They argued, 'They will come to terms like father and daughter and kick us out the next day.' I thought about it and realized that they were right. We were not physicians and we were not responsible for her condition. All the more so given that she and her father were very touchy. They would definitely not have been amused if their aides and security guards meddled in their affairs.

So many well-meaning people tried to get close to them and to help them in good faith with reliable information. Alas, they were usually turned out, accused of making intrigues.

I still managed to find a chance to tell Todor Zhivkov about Lyudmila's work. I had thought of what I was going to say when the right opportunity presented itself. At a meeting in Boyana, he noticed me and asked, 'How are you getting along, boy?'

I answered, 'I'm OK.'

When asked 'What are you working on?' I outlined our plans. I deliberately added, however, that the ideological premises of our cultural policy were unclear, that I had even heard people say that 'Bulgaria repeats the story of Stalin and Alliluyeva.' Todor Zhivkov immediately got my point. He could accept such an assessment. I did not tell him about the breakdowns, the yogas and so on; something which nobody would venture to tell him and go unpunished. I also told him that she was a young minister, that she had little experience and that was why people hurried to get from her more than they gave.

In the following days he had some strongly worded exchanges with her: 'What are all those scribblings about horsemen, fires and spirals, and so on?' He ordered all her materials and speeches to be checked at his office and at the Secretarial Department of the Central Committee.

But everything was in vain. They also gave in, pleading the 'modern critical apparatus' she used, and he resigned himself to it.

Maybe this is the fate of any long-serving ruler. He controls all the channels of information but, it appears, he does not know the most important things; even things concerning the life of his children. Nobody wanted to disturb him and bring him bad news.

Even the president of the Medical Academy, Atanas Maleev, who had every official and personal reason to do so (as brother of Todor Zhivkov's wife Mara Maleeva) would not do it. A person had to see and feel all this with his skin and senses in order to believe it. When I told some friends of mine that Zhivkov had been manipulated about obvious things, they would not believe me. 'Consider the tragic death of his child, and you'll realize the guilt of all those people at all levels who lied, withheld or hushed up the truth about what was happening or what was going to happen in Bulgaria.'

At the end of 1980 her condition deteriorated. Lyudmila Zhivkova kept starving herself. She began to seek and surround herself with only those people involved in occult affairs.

In my capacity as her aide I diligently compiled background information reports on which a lot of people worked hard. She needed them for her trips around the country. People were looking forward to their meetings with her. We discussed the socioeconomic targets with the top people in the State Committee for Planning and with the district leaderships. We singled out the most important problems and analyzed them carefully. Finally they were submitted at Villa 32 of the Boyana Residence (where she actually lived) several days before the respective meetings.

I found out, however, that she did not do anything with the prepared material. Once I asked her insistently about it before a visit to Pleven in late December 1980. She replied, 'I won't read them because they cripple me.'

The obsession with theosophy over her last years, however, was not the only striking thing about Lyudmila Zhivkova. I think she had inherited her father's strongly critical attitude towards reality in Bulgaria and in the world of socialism. Much of what I heard from her later on provided a clue to Zhivkov's own actions.

She showed no interest in the fate of socialism, in the life of the communist party. To her that was not worth talking about and she avoided such subjects. Lyudmila Zhivkova lived outside the intricate world of politics and social relations. I sometimes had the feeling that she did not hold any respect for her father's past and revolutionary merits which were extolled at the time.

Once when we talked I asked her, 'Do you seriously think that you can rule Bulgaria with Vanga? Isn't there a party in this country? You don't seem to be taking any interest in it at all.'

She replied, 'You are a vulgar Marxist and I don't know who taught you all that. What party? The party is a funeral procession of people who shuffle behind the hearse of a defunct political doctrine.'

She said that in 1980.

She even called the communists 'the party people' with a note of disparagement in her voice. She categorically objected to any mention of the leading role of the party or the role of the masses in her speeches and articles.

I wonder how that woman, unlike her father, was not at all interested in the authorities of the Ministry of the Interior which played a significant role in the life of the country. Department Six of the Ministry of the Interior even discussed theatre productions, reviewed exhibitions and gathered information about the intelligentsia. The so-called 'files' were nothing but a collection of memorandums, letters and other compromising material by which the intellectuals denounced each other. Many people were eager to become informers and trusted men and hastened to bring to the attention of the security services any compromising fact about a rival colleague.

That particular wave in the time of Lyudmila Zhivkova had no political outlet to the top. She herself plugged the channels of such information, ignoring the officers and the information coming from that department.

In 1978 she fired in a matter of hours the chief of Division One of the State Security Department Six, Colonel Naiden Petrov. The reason was 'compromising' material he had gathered on the first deputy chairman of the Committee for Culture, Alexander Fol, exposing his 'former' bourgeois background. He had found out that Fol's father had had connections with Tsar Boris III and had discovered photos showing Alexander Fol himself in the company of young Simeon and in the uniform of the Legion.

Colonel Petrov's dismissal was formulated in the following terms: 'The chief of Division One of Department Six is hereby relieved of his duties for raising obstacles to the implementation of the April policy line among the intelligentsia.'

In that case, it was not just a matter of protecting and patronizing the people with whom she worked and who were her close friends. Lyudmila Zhivkova would always do that and sometimes she was even very partial. In these cases she simply demonstrated her disgust at the methods of the security services.

While she was in charge, Zhivkova did not permit State Security to meddle in the affairs of artists and intellectuals. The State Security officers grumbled and intrigued against her, but they were helpless. Bulgarian intellectuals could travel abroad without restriction, they attended major cultural forums in the West, the doors were wide open to information.

Lyudmila Zhivkova knew about many of the political intrigues made against her by dogmatists and some State Security people; by the 'go-getters'. She was very careful to keep out of her entourage people connected or suspected of involvement with the special services of Soviet agents. She even suspected that they were bugging her and informing on her, but she was not afraid and used to say, 'The sword is tempered in battle, the spirit in struggle.'

In her plans for the future she staked everything on Alexander Fol, Svetlin Roussev and Bogomil Rainov. At the Twelfth Party Congress I had the opportunity to hear her exchange strong words with Todor Zhivkov. She shouted furiously that Svetlin Roussev be elected Politburo member. Her father, however, replied, 'Such things don't happen the way you think. You are rushing things.'

At that time Todor Zhivkov was preparing the grounds for Lyudmila Zhivkova's own election to some of the country's top jobs before the Thirteenth Party Congress. All personnel changes were geared to her future promotion and consolidation.

Lyudmila Zhivkova used to announce that she wanted to withdraw from the Politburo and to start work in science instead. In such cases her father would seek 'help' from the Politburo members and they would go to her and implore her not to do this. She 'reluctantly' agreed. Like her father, she was driven by a powerful ambition to get to the top and stay there.

Todor Zhivkov loved to hear somebody talk about his daughter as the Bulgarian Indira Gandhi. Sometimes he even showed unaccountable weakness and infatuation with respect to her. He would go so far as to be delighted to listen to how much more 'ignorant' and 'unqualified' he was compared to Lyudmila. He loved to be reminded that it was time that he go and that there was already someone who could replace him.

'Who will replace me?' he used to ask artfully.

'Why, Lyudmila is by no means inferior to you,' a young artist (I will not mention his name) had the audacity to suggest.

'Is that so? And what do the people say?' insisted Todor Zhivkov.

What followed was a flood of arguments, praise and dithyrambs.

They were added to by the members of Todor Zhivkov's hunting team, the leaders of the cultural unions, by numerous 'nightingales' of every stripe and rank, who sighed for her in rhymes, sought historical analogues for her and whispered them deftly and convincingly. In this way the cult of Lyudmila Zhivkova gradually developed and kept up an atmosphere of semi-Asiatic deification which was far removed from the 'laws of beauty' she loved so much.

Much has been written about the cult which has developed in the countries of Eastern Europe and Asia. Its political, economic, cultural and psychological aspects have been explored. But apart from these, there was always yet another side. It also has its 'systemic' character. The cult was not created by a single person. She was only a point of reference. Thousands of performers have contributed to the emergence and growth of that courtly atmosphere which for decades hung over Eastern Europe. Will this cult become tragic, or will it assume a comic image? This depends on the quality of the deified. In Bulgaria, at the time of Lyudmila Zhivkova, this cult was very often a political caricature. As is known, people idolize ideals and when there are not enough ideals, they idealize idols. Part of the intelligentsia had great fun playing that game. But whenever there was a chance to get hold of some sign of favour, they rushed to seize it.

Hundreds of people wrote to her, tried to get in touch, made a parade of their sham and real accomplishments. The correspondence in her office increased incredibly. She received two or three times more mail than any other Politburo member. Of course, ordinary people also wrote to her, seeking help, medicines and treatment abroad, complaining of abuses and injustice.

That was a hard time for all her office aides. We usually worked 12 to 14 hour days. She monitored the correspondence and herself gave directions, she remembered what she had said and wanted only productive interference. But she soon tired. 'There is no end to it!' she used to sigh when I reported about the numerous applications for weekend houses, specializations abroad, for roles and exhibitions, and so on.

If we disregard these personal aspects in her style, Lyudmila Zhivkova's cultural policy was a really new political thinking in action. As early as the late 1970s she boldly called for the self-centered ideological and class interests to be overcome and put behind universal human purposes and interests. Her speeches at all international forums were free of the apologetic and propaganda clichés that were so typical of ideological life in Eastern Europe at that time. She was not afraid to share her view of the Soviet Union, either. She made no secret of her antipathy to Moscow. 'We embarked on a fatally wrong historical road by becoming allied with the most uncivilized country in the world,' Zhivkova told me once. She was deeply convinced that 'Hitler was the product of Stalin and of his system.' We had a long dispute over this. Then, again, I was convinced that she hated violence in all its forms. It was for this reason that she had no sympathy with the Soviet Union where, as she saw it, 'violence has always triumphed'.

The international meeting of cultural figures and politicians in Bulgaria in 1980 became, as the participants themselves put it, a second Madrid. The reference was to the formal CSCE meeting held in the Spanish capital at the same time. According to some of the participants, the meeting we had organized was a much greater success because people were absolutely free to speak their minds. At the conference she kept repeating the thesis that the planet was our common home, that planetary thought should triumph.

Many important political figures in the world showed interest in her political performance. US President Jimmy Carter met her by chance. He was in New York and decided to see the Thracian treasure which was then being displayed for the first time. The now former emperor of Japan also visited this exhibition. She met Indira Gandhi, Mexico's president, kings and other VIPs of Europe and the world. These meetings and her cultural policy gave our country a more favourable image, different from that which dominated.

But her father could not understand all this. He did not have enough flair to realize that the atmosphere which Lyudmila Zhivkova created could give our country a real international political chance. Wary of the political future and bowing to the apparatchiks' open disapproval of her 'quirks and Indian nonsense', he rejected her positive steps for the relaxation of the atmosphere inside and outside the country.

She vehemently stood up for the right of this country to walk on the road to Western Europe. For example, during the meetings, visits and contacts of Bulgarian cultural figures with their Western colleagues, this frail woman protected them from encroachments, police sanctions and intrigues from any source. But few people were grateful and many more were the unreliable ones who secretly undermined her authority. Her idea was to seek a new balance in Bulgaria's international relations. Some people may now find this understandable and easy, but those were the 1970s; the war in Afghanistan was forthcoming, the crisis in Poland was coming to a head.

Lyudmila Zhivkova, however, had no clear idea of the political and economic organization which society needed to this end. That was part of her tragedy. She had little interest in political realities, or at least created such an impression.

In the meantime, she had found out that there was something wrong with the Cultural and Historical Heritage Fund. She was informed that some people there had started to embezzle the funds allocated for that patriotic activity. With her consent the people in charge of that undertaking and especially Zhivko Popov's group were subjected to a top secret investigation. At that time I did not know that an investigation had been launched and I wondered why Lyudmila avoided meeting Zhivko Popov and his family. When I told her of the people who wished to see her she warned me, 'I am not here to Zhivko Popov and his family. No appointment is to be arranged.'

On various occasions she started saying, 'Every cause needs clean-handed people,' or, 'I want strict accountability. Someday the people will hold us responsible for every leva we have spent.'

But this accumulation of so much negative information seemed to transform her character. She lost her good mood. She kept silent for a long time, listened distractedly and spoke ambiguously.

There was nothing left of the years when she used to speak with fervour and enthusiasm about her plans. They were grandiose indeed. She wanted to restore the Bulgarian churches, monasteries and chapels. She was contemplating a programme for training of Bulgarian ecclesiastics in world theological academies and centres. So as to speed things up and to make up for the low-standard qualifications of the country's personnel, she assigned me to draft a programme under which world-famous experts and scientists would be invited to work in Bulgaria, to found schools and to help directly in personnel training.

The first area of this programme was health care. As an integral part of her plans, she intended to organize in Bulgaria the publication of the wealth of the world's philosophical and political thought without distinction of ideology and prejudices. She knew what kind of help we could expect from each West European country in terms of information, experts, curricula and financial aid for cultural programmes. She had particularly ambitious ideas to win over as friends of Bulgaria some rich and influential people from the world's major financial and cultural centres who would invest in culture and education. She worked with them individually, continued a personal correspondence with them and made sure that they be accorded special attention. Those who are still our friends were won over at that time by Lyudmila Zhivkova. But we underestimated her ambition to win friends for Bulgaria in each European capital, to 'invest' in people and to gain ground.

In this way, far before the advent of restructuring was announced, Lyudmila Zhivkova was campaigning for a world without frontiers, dogmas and prejudices – not in words but in deeds.

She paid an incredibly high price for it. Just remember the hatred and the rumours that rained down on her, how everything was distorted and belittled, how she was mocked and denigrated.

But let us go back to the atmosphere of those days.

Her fatigue gradually began to catch up with her. The glimmer in her eyes visibly faded. Before leaving for Austria on 12 June 1981 she called me and ordered her schedule for the visit to be limited to Vienna, and to seeing its sights. This was unusual because she was normally tireless on such trips. Obviously, she was near the end of her tether.

At the end of June a scandal broke out at the Committee for Culture between her office aides. Lyudmila Zhivkova quarrelled with her long-serving personal secretary Katya Chalukova and fired her. The secretary had told her about the intrigues made against her by the deputy-chairmen of the Committee. Chalukova asked to see Todor Zhivkov and threatened that she would make disclosures. She was not received by Todor Zhivkov but her conduct was a great blow to Lyudmila Zhivkova. I was surprised that she could be so strongly affected by this. She called me time and again and asked me what to do. I was even more surprised by the fact that there was not a trace of the romantic and confused Lyudmila. She was very rational and cool and asked what people said about her in reality. Obviously, the shock had made her face up to the truth, it had made her businesslike and energetic. I remember what she said at one of our meetings of the board of directors of the Committee for Culture in 1979: 'All complaisance is deadly. One should better make mistakes, but act.' And now she was trying to act.

I took this first opportunity to tell her how all her actions and steps to organize 'societies' around her were known, that many of the 'initiated' brazenly lied to her and capitalized behind her back. She agreed. She had learnt that her deputies at the Committee had secretly opened her mail, that they had been intriguing against her and had been 'selling' her. It was obviously the right time for openness and I told her that a courtly atmosphere had been created, that people were tired and did not understand her.

'Yes, I kill myself with work for these people and they reward me by spreading rumours that I sleep with my driver,' she said bitterly.

Then she pondered and said, 'I have actually built everything on sand.'

There was no trace of her mystical wrapping. I was astonished at how accurately she could assess things.

'They all betrayed me. Actually I have only a few people on whom I can rely. At the Politburo one or two are with me, among the intellectuals only a handful of people really understand me. All the rest swarm round me because they are self-seekers and go-getters. I gave them everything, posts, honours; and yet they are ready to betray me any time.'

She spoke long and bitterly about herself and the country. That was the first time that I heard her reason in so down-to-earth and realistic a way.

'Being Zhivkova is my biggest handicap. I can do nothing on my own. If I do something good, it is not acknowledged but they say I can do it because I am Zhivkova. If I do something bad, scold or criticize someone, it is again because I am Zhivkova. If someday you write something about me, please include this,' she added.

The dread of the scandal with her secretary lingered, however. Everyday she asked me what to do. She was afraid of disclosures, but she did not say what she was fearing. She only mentioned her correspondence with some personalities and people in the entourage of the Bulgarian tsar in exile, Simeon II, and with prominent figures in India, Switzerland and Italy. But that was all.

Several days after the scandal she left for Borovets with her father. He had finally realized that his daughter really needed medical treatment and some rest.

I heard her for the last time on the phone from Borovets where she had put up at Tsarska Bistritsa. She asked me absent-mindedly about some bibliographic reference and I wished her a complete rest to which she laughed in a strange way.

Lyudmila Zhivkova died on 21 July 1981.

To say that it was a shock to me would be an understatement. Apart from everything else she was so young; she didn't even live to be 40. It was only human that I should feel bereaved. I was shocked by the nationwide reaction. People who until yesterday derided her now grieved sincerely. Tens of thousands came to pay their last respects, thousands wept without hypocrisy. It seemed that the Slav compassion had been awakened in them and many realized that an extraordinary person had passed away; someone unusual in her thoughts, character, actions and plans. I heard somebody in the crowd say, 'The grave remains the best stronghold against the blows of fate.' Then it sounded somewhat pretentious but now I understand the truth of these words.

I asked myself, 'How is it possible? How did it all happen?'

I began fitting together the jigsaw puzzle of her last days and hours.

In Tsarska Bistritsa she had been severely depressed. She wanted to see her husband but he was busy. 'Is my father really aware of how I feel?' Zhivkova asked the nurse Ani Mladenova. She answered in the negative. Zhivkova told her, 'It's much better that way.'

On Sunday 19 July, she telephoned her aide Kiril Avramov and asked him to prepare the slides on Vladimir Dimitrov. She told him that she would fetch them on Monday. He waited for her on Monday but instead of coming she sent the security guards to receive the slides.

The following day she had lunch with her father and told nobody of her intention to go to Sofia. After lunch everyone retired to their suites. She locked herself in. Suddenly she emerged and said, 'We are leaving for Sofia.'

The guards replied that they should at least tell her father.

'No! Under no circumstances,' she ordered.

Early in the afternoon they arrived in Boyana, Home No.32. There she started burning documents in the fireplace. It turned out later that she had also destroyed some documents before going to Borovets.

At about four in the afternoon she asked for some fruit juice. There wasn't any because she was not expected to come. They asked whether they should go and buy some.

'No, don't bother. It doesn't matter anymore,' Lyudmila replied.

An hour later she told the housekeeper Violeta that she was free to go. She told her, 'You can go home, your daughter is studying for entrance examinations.'

Between five and eight in the evening she took three consecutive showers. On the third time the house maid Liliyana told her, 'Comrade Zhivkova, please don't. You will be travelling and you might catch a cold.'

'Mind your own business and don't meddle in my affairs,' she snapped at her.

At around eight in the evening, the woman, worried, knocked on the door but there was no reply. She entered the bathroom and her scream drew the attention of the security guards and the driver. They found Lyudmila in the bath. They took her out of the water and tried to resuscitate her by artificial respiration. She gave a faint groan but did not come to. They telephoned the government hospital but the ambulance took 55 minutes to arrive. They had had a puncture, the doctors explained. They started some sort of manipulations to justify their presence. But everything was already over.

They telephoned her father who arrived at around eleven at night from Borovets. He wanted to see what kind of medicines she had been taking and insisted that he entered her room, but the doctors did not allow him. 'She is in a critical condition. Please don't.' He realized the truth and left for Bankya. Until his ousting on 10 November 1989 Zhivkov never set foot in that house.

On her desk they found a diary with some of its pages torn out and destroyed. One of the surviving pages contained notes on a dream and an attempt at its interpretation. The notes were intended for a well-known party functionary of that time.

The death of Lyudmila Zhivkova brought to a close a chapter of the country's political history. Everything which for a decade had been built with a view to her promotion now collapsed.

People and institutions suddenly became useless. I remember the reaction of a well-known Bulgarian historian after her death was announced: 'Now everything in the hierarchy will crumble to pieces, there will be an instant shift of layers.' He was proved right.

Alexander Lilov was the first one to feel the difference. He received a large advance. Todor Zhivkov began to shower praise on him, he created for him the reputation of a major politician, theoretician and modern architect of socialist Bulgaria. He had never praised anyone like that, least of all the number two in the party and the state. The new situation, however, suddenly gave the young politician a rather dangerous lead. The person who was to balance this comet's rise was no longer there. In a matter of days, Lilov found himself in isolation. His colleagues, the Politburo members, hastened to search out his faults, blunders and indiscretions. After a difficult period of isolation for Lilov, in 1983 he was removed from the Politburo on the absurd grounds of inexperience after almost 12 years as secretary of the Central Committee and Politburo member. They allowed him to keep his salary and car. Here, once again, Zhivkov observed his rule: a gesture of compensation to an ousted political rival.

Another almost illegal structure collapsed: the Cultural and Historical Heritage Fund. This fund was set up to finance the purchases of paintings and collections of art works abroad and in Bulgaria and to procure historical archives which were of interest to Bulgaria.

The standard procedure was that when the news about the sale arrived, the painting was considered from the point of view of its artistic merits and approximate price.

This very often happened in face-to-face meetings. There were no papers. Everything was shrouded in secrecy. It was easy to achieve because Zhivko Popov was one of Mircho Spassov's trusted men. Alexander Fol was responsible for the scientific valuation of the works of art or of the acquired historical memorabilia.

The funds were appropriated by the signatures of three government departments: the Committee for Culture, the Ministry of the Interior and the Ministry of Foreign Affairs. That fund was actually the mysterious source of rumoured riches and enrichment.

A number of embezzlements were detected. Zhivko Popov was sentenced to a 20-year prison sentence. Nevertheless, many of the 'squander-maniacs' got away with it.

The One Thousand and Three Hundred Years Bulgaria Commission was also disbanded. Its head, ranking as deputy chairman of the Committee for Culture, was Todor Ribarov, a fellow student and trusted friend of Lyudmila Zhivkova. She herself had spared no effort and energy on the monumental campaign to 'celebrate' the 1300th anniversary of a Bulgarian state, which was to take place in the autumn of 1981. But she did not live to see it.

Todor Zhivkov ordered a covert investigation of us, the people working in her office. Several years later I found out that our property status and way of life had been investigated.

Scores of people from Lyudmila Zhivkova's entourage disappeared from the limelight. Her deputies at the Committee for Culture were replaced.

Others, scientists and artists, who had received her attention, were now subjected to 'creative' reviews. They quickly lost their ground in the officialdom of the country's cultural life. Panegyric books about her were published, her ideas were glorified; but practically everything created by her was being demolished. The conservative forces which had dwindled in her time, now took the offensive.

Only two structures survived: The Banner of Peace Assembly and the newly established Lyudmila Zhivkova Foundation. The former was headed by her brother, Vladimir Zhivkov. The initiative for the establishment of the foundation came from Italy. The person who organized and held the first founding meeting was Roberto Galo, later on rumour linked him with the secret Italian Masonic Lodge P-2 and with its head, Licho Gelli.

A lot of time has passed since those years. There was something inspiring and yet grotesque about them.

What was grotesque was the means and the ways by which Zhivkova wanted Bulgaria to become 'a cultural centre of the world' and 'to make the world speak of Bulgaria by 1990'. Those attempts to push development ahead through 'initiated' ones involved people who, having received unlimited earthly wealth in this world, wanted to take it with them to the afterlife. That is why they discovered 'reincarnation' in themselves. Lyudmila Zhivkova was a reincarnation of Alexander the Great, others had discovered in themselves Catherine the Great and Napoleon. In spiritualist seances those people wanted to find in themselves the next, higher 'Karmic circles', until they could merge with the absolute spirit and harmony – with God.

What was modern and meaningful were the objectives and ideals which Lyudmila Zhivkova set to the cultural policy of Bulgaria in those years. They helped this country obtain a new image in the eyes of Europe and the world. Many good things were said about Bulgaria, we won confidence during those years of cold winds in Eastern Europe. Bulgaria in the Balkans turned out to be an oasis which promoted non-conformism and cultural identification with the real processes in the world. I think that it was precisely during those years that our intelligentsia charged itself with civic courage on a large scale, when many artists and scientists shaped their own stand and view of the world they wanted to build. In essence, the period since 1981 saw an escalation of the protest of the intelligentsia which already had a criterion for progress because it had witnessed the good times.

Apart from courage and innovation, Lyudmila Zhivkova allowed the allocation of much money for Bulgarian culture. Now that the intellectual sphere also confronts 'market socialism', now that things will be measured in terms of the consumer and his purse, I think that the disproportionately developed sphere of Bulgarian culture will face hard times ahead. With its dense network of institutions and personnel, clashes and disappointment, purely human dramas will be inevitable.

Let us leave future researchers to sift out all the contradictions, the good things and the bad things in Lyudmila Zhivkova's life. Time itself will determine of which there were more because, as the American writer C. Darrow wrote, 'History often repeats itself and this is one of its faults.' I still think that even today the intelligentsia can tell the story of Lyudmila Zhivkova properly, without affectation and fear of being accused of nostalgia for totalitarian thinking and the stagnation phenomenon. At any rate, Lyudmila Zhivkova proved that with her life.

5. The End

There is something common to all totalitarian systems. Consider Hitler's last days; the Allies' bombs were falling over the Reich Chancellery's bunkers, Berlin was under siege, yet he and his political and military staff kept planning strikes and moves till literally the last hours. The mechanisms of the totalitarian machine function towards one and the same end, disastrously, but flawlessly. Information continues to be manipulated and people remain as obedient and servile as ever. Once finely tuned, the machine runs on its own momentum, and only a counterstrike can make it stop.

The same was true of Todor Zhivkov's last years of rule. No bombs fell, of course, but social tension rose to pre-war heights. The Politburo had its sessions, the Council of Ministers adopted decisions one after the other. The people applauded at meetings and the ever-festive parades streamed in streets and across squares. Everyone seemed to turn a blind eye to the changes, which had arrived.

It all began some time around 1984.

What was happening in the country's economy?

The wrong investment policy of the last 10–15 years began to disintegrate by 1984.

The first echelon industries felt this first: the ferrous and non-ferrous metallurgy, as well as the petrochemical industries had used up all the raw materials necessary for their development. The privileged Soviet supplies began to dry up. After 1984 the Soviet deliveries became less lavish and more tied in with adequate barters.

In 1986, as deputy chief of the Central Committee's Economic and Technical and Scientific Policy Department, I headed a working delegation to the Soviet Union. We were received by Nikolai Slyunkov, a Politburo member and secretary of the Central Committee of the Soviet Union Communist Party. In the course of two and a half hours, he explained to us the Soviet decision to eliminate a relationship which his country had started to view as an unjust, colonial structure of trading.

When I returned, I asked for an urgent appointment with Todor Zhivkov since he himself was leaving for the Soviet Union the next day. I reported the graveness of the issue and proposed that we immediately seek both political and economic ways to come out of the difficult situation which we were facing after the radical change of policy of our major trade partner. Prior to his departure, he appealed as usual, to the ambassador Georgi Pankov to do all he could to retain the level of Soviet supplies – an impossible task to fulfil under the conditions of Gorbachev's new political leadership. The decades-old political, administrative and economic guarantees had become a thing of the past.

Still, the unsound economic structure continued to function. Electronics, machine-building – the prestigous sectors – skimmed the cream off the national resources. Our participation in the international division of labour was becoming ineffective.

Our entire technological development depended on imports from the West. Our electronics had swallowed in a single five-year period around 800 million dollars, but its output was only 15 million. The difference was pumped out of such traditional sectors as agriculture, food and light industries. But these were also hit by stagnation, as they were left with no means for simple reproduction.

The accumulated petrodollars proved treacherous. With them we had built industries which annually required a portion of imports worth around 4 billion dollars while exports earned only 2 billion. From 1985 onwards, Bulgaria began to sink annually at a rate of 1.5 to 2 billion dollars. No less than three quarters of the imports were used inefficiently to sustain industries which ran for their own sake and had no market. By the end of 1988 the country's foreign debt ran at over 8 billion dollars, a fact which was diligently concealed from the nation as much as from Todor Zhivkov.

How was this done?

For years on end, at the end of the third quarter, the government would order a moratorium on imports and figure its costs for the nine months of the year. Imports in the final quarter were charged to the *following* year's costs. This perpetually hid the country's catastrophic deficit from Todor Zhivkov himself who, as late as 1989, still talked of a 6 billion dollar foreign debt.

But he was obviously loath to learn the truth. The periodical national bank reports and a series of alarming memos, which I prepared with the help of the then president of the Bulgarian National Bank, Vassil Kolarov, were intended to reveal the real situation. As always after such meetings, Todor Zhivkov was surrounded by politicians who calmed him down by drawing a brighter picture of reality. As a result of this he began to eye us angrily, calling us 'panicmongers' and 'pessimists'.

The country was sinking slowly and inexorably. A large part of the debt was literally eaten up by the population because we imported mainly consumer goods – foods and durables.

On several occasions I proposed to raise prices in order to protect the impoverished commodity stock from the money which was being funnelled into unprofitable industries, and to compensate only the low income population. He, however, did not find the courage to do this. Sometimes he used to say, 'Don't worry! We'll start drawing from Uncle Todor's money.' He was hinting about the part of the national reserve deposited in Swiss banks. And in 1968 he did allow the withdrawal of around 150 million dollars which were auctioned off among the commodity producers, so that an additional output worth one billion leva was created. But against the background of a depleted market and obsolescent industries, this was in no way reassuring.

Anyhow, by late 1988, all disproportions and deformities in the Bulgarian economy came to the surface: a market disbalance, an economy which depended on hard currency and resources, a manpower shortage, and a host of ecological problems. Social and political tension intensified. The people wanted to live well; what was more, a large part of them remembered the good and calm years of the past. Consumption rose considerably and people became more choosy. Their models were the Western goods. This comparison became the strongest weapon against peoples' rule. Each product coming from the West carried with it a propaganda charge which disintegrated the pro-socialist public mood in Eastern Europe. People would say, 'Look at the two Germanys – one makes the Mercedes, the other makes the Trabant.'

Still, despite the heavy food imports and the foreign exchange structural problems, the unceasing changes in the administrative apparatus of the state and the economy continued.

All public energy was channelled into useless 'mergers' and 'openings' of new ministries and enterprises. When the economy was stable this used to be seen as a novelty. But the 1987 reform had changed the situation. It had heavily affected the central planning organs and the state's financial system. The decisions were made in full secrecy in Euxinograd.

Actually nothing had changed, because the old structures and systems under the umbrella of a superministry had remained. As a result of this, bureaucracy increased and the country became even more uncontrollable. The information channels were clogged. All processes were getting out of hand. Priorities became mixed up, as were responsibilities. The economy was engulfed by chaos and ruin. The economic cadre lost their bearings. Mass dissatisfaction could be felt everywhere.

Along with the crises in the economy deep social changes started taking place in the country.

Slowly but surely, as a result of the higher education and all-round cultural development, a new generation of a broader culture and stronger civil conscience appeared.

The communist party itself was joined by people of pronounced intellectual capacities. Those were people of a new political thinking, albeit timidly expressed and somewhat restricted. The economy, culture, education, foreign policy, administration and science saw the growth of a new élite who in style, interests and motives wanted fully to participate in government and decision-making. Covertly at first, they gradually began to demand their rights even more openly.

The first telltale sign that the layers of power had shifted was the closing down of different departments at the Central Committee of the Bulgarian Communist Party, which had until then worked with confidence and unrestricted control in all public spheres. Power was concentrated in the hands of the Politburo and the Secretariat, but subsequently some 'disobedient' cadres began to bid for the power of the high-ranking party leaders themselves. In such cases, Zhivkov remained as a last reserve for the party apparatus, something which I think wasted him most quickly. Every conflict of the day was passed on to him for solution.

The radical changes in the power structure matured and they were aimed directly at the party monopoly. Zhivkov understood this, undertook tactical steps and was ready for any kind of changes with the exception of one, to be deprived of his personal role over the party and the state. Increasingly he started to behave in public as a bad actor.

It is early to draw conclusions: it is much better to follow through his actions more closely during the time at which they took place with the help of my office diary. They cover above all Zhivkov's personal evaluations, notes and the tasks which he assigned to us privately during our meetings with him or in the presence of the others.

> The all-union conference of the Soviet Union Communist Party is being held. Our stand is supportive because it reflects the new attempts of the socialist countries, ourselves included, to separate the party from the administrative government. From a historical and theoretical point of view, the road is clear for the construction of a civil society, self-government and control over technical and scientific progress.
>
> But at present our economy has many 'enemies'.
>
> In agriculture such enemies are the agro-industrial complexes, the National Agro-Industrial Union, the Ministry of Agriculture, the Ministry of the Economy and Planning and the Council of Ministers. All of them work as bureaucratic tiers of government. The situation in industry is similar.
>
> As to Boris Yeltsin's political views, they are in essence petty-bourgeois and adventuristic for a country such as the Soviet Union [4 July 1988].

> At the forthcoming Business Forum in Varna we must clarify our stand towards the world.
>
> We still talk on the new historical essence of socialism. We have to take into account the changing realities. The new political thinking is a synthesis of the experience of all socialist countries, not only for the preservation of humanity, but also for its restructuring.
>
> Our economic organizations have all the necessary rights and we are prepared to continue with all sorts of contacts and ties [morning coffee meeting, 19 September 1988].

On 20 September he had a meeting with Giulio Andreotti at the Pravets Residence. The meeting passed in a friendly atmosphere. The Italian side demonstrated the desire to work with Bulgaria.

On 21 September, at breakfast time, I made use of the opportunity to put forward the question of the unlimited lease of land with the right to inheritance. We had to break free of the land-lease system which bred predatory attitudes towards the land and agricultural production. I quoted from foreign sources that for instance, in the USA, 24 per cent of the land was cultivated by leaseholders. I also expounded on the legal essence of leases. Zhivkov agreed and accepted my argument, and told me to incorporate them in the materials for the forthcoming plenum on agriculture.

But the land-lease idea ended unsuccessfully after one philosopher told him that that was a feudal category. Zhivkov began to hesitate and in the papers I prepared, the word 'lease' was left as a good wish.

Zhivkov spoke about his meeting with Kaison Fomvihan of Laos. I wrote down the following: 'Who the hell is fooling them, too, that they are building socialism? They neither have market relations, not a material base, yet they are haughty enough to lecture us and won't heed what we have to say. The black devil is really fooling them [22 September 1988].'

The following quotes illustrate some of Zhivkov's evaluations of certain events which occurred towards the end of 1988.

> The article in the magazine *Ogonyok*, according to which I have told Soviet State Security Minister Ignatiev of my negative attitude to Khrushchev, is a complete fabrication. Even though during my last visit to the Soviet Union we failed to reach agreement; he cursed and threatened at the top of his voice. After my meeting with him I confided to Stanko Todorov, who was accompanying me, that Khrushchev could no longer control himself [1 October 1988 concerning Bulgaria's relations with the Soviet Union].

> My deep conviction, which I expressed before Richard von Weizsecker is that the United States and the Western Allies will oppose Germany's union because that will create an European colossus whose future actions towards the Allies themselves cannot be predicted [21 November 1988].

> In our plan for next year there are elements of autarchy: the foreign economic ties of the country are not attuned to the new world realities. Not should we make concessions in terms of import of technology. Today only a complete dud could not be able to solve these problems because we have created all conditions for direct contacts with Western partners.
>
> Major burdens are the heavy engineering works in Radomir and Rousse, and so are the specialized industries which have prospects [6 December 1988].

> How should future changes be carried out in our country?

> The government of the state has to change its nature. It must be present, but not as an administrative umbrella. We should create a new hierarchy of power, but on an economic, not administrative basis. We must create the conditions of competition, both internal and external. Capitalism preserved itself because of competition. We must defend our firms, but we should not guarantee unconditionally their survival [8 December 1988].

> The cadres which are now at our disposal are 80 per cent useless to us under the new conditions. That also holds true of all of us who are present here. We too cannot work and rule properly any more [15 December 1988].

On 16 January 1989, in conversation about the detention of a group of human rights activists in Plovdiv: Zhivkov said, 'Today they are few but we must not delude ourselves that these will remain isolated acts. We will not remain an island of peace in the contemporary world.'

In connection with his postponed visit to the Soviet Union and his meeting with Mikhail Gorbachev (due to the busy schedule of the Supreme Council of the USSR), on 26 January 1989, I told Zhivkov the elements of isolation between our two countries were growing. I pointed out that the Western press gave increasing attention to the deterioration of his personal relations with Gorbachev. If this situation was not overcome, the negative attitudes would increase. He asked me what I thought the reasons were for that state of relations. I replied that Gorbachev would not want to work with him because he was a representative of another epoch and he wanted to differentiate himself from that particular political style. All the more so as there were signs of economic deterioration, and the people were expecting with alarm and nearly *en masse*, major personnel changes.

I ended the conversation with the feeling that Todor Zhivkov was hopefully awaiting Gorbachev's fall and the 'normalization' of Soviet perestroika. He said: 'Restructuring and democracy are pure demagogy if they lack a firm economic base. Who will be the winner of that game? The common people will suffer the most. We must pursue democracy without setting unfeasible objectives.'

On 30 January 1989 I made a progress report on hunger-strike poet P. Manolov to which I called for a reaction. His papers, which were of no value whatsoever, had been taken from him and, by such actions, we were only becoming the world's laughing stock. Zhivkov ordered the case closed. Later on General Radoulov arranged the return of the papers and with that came the end of the hunger strike.

Several days later I asked Zhivkov's permission to attend the seminar at the Union of Bulgarian Writers with the chief of the inquiry, General Kotsaliev, about the poet whose papers had not all been returned. I verbally reported to Zhivkov on how the meeting had passed.

Several days later, I had the opportunity to confide to him that a troubling tendency was taking shape which showed that instead of the party, State Security dealt with the political manifestations of intellectuals. I said the following in the presence of all: 'We have become a party of idlers. We work only with those who applaud us, and State Security deal with the complaining ones, when it is our job to do so. Why are we hiding, why don't we bring it out on television and in the newspapers?' Zhivkov apparently agreed with me but said that they should not be left just like that.

Two things, I think, led to the increased tension in the relations between the party and the intelligentsia.

One of them was Todor Zhivkov's confidence after so many years of uncontested rule. For many a year it was precisely State Security that suffocated the intelligentsia's protestations in embryo. Zhivkov's inertia in this respect was strong. He still believed that the repressive organs were the magical cure. He knew that the world had changed but he did not feel this change personally and he was not prepared for it.

On the other hand the security organs themselves were dominated by leaders of the old school, who also gained acknowledgement by trying to outdo the political organs with their effective interference in events. They persistently scared Zhivkov with conspiracies and 'counterrevolutionary plots'. A number of actions aimed against the different representatives of the intelligentsia were the fruit of these extremists in the security service, who acted on their initiative.

Politburo member Yordan Yotov and I managed to persuade Zhivkov to have the *Rabotnichesko Delo* daily set aside one page for coverage of the work of the Glasnost and Democracy Club. But while we were talking him into it a group of activists from the club gave a barrage of interviews on Radio Free Europe and the plan fell through.

I tried to create a bridge between him and part of the dissenting intelligentsia and was not the only person doing so. I kept on assuring him that many of the dissidents were honest people, while others who strived for careers wanted to be front-rankers again, so he should not view their conduct as aimed against the state. But the Sixth Department of the Ministry of the Interior probably had reliable informers in the newly founded Club for Glasnost and Restructuring, because Zhivkov knew about their private conversations and considered me naive. I heard several top-level officers from that department say that I was misleading Todor Zhivkov. All this was intensified by the fact that the Central Committee's departments chose to stay on the sidelines. They were not informed and rested idle. The Ministry of the Interior thus became the most prominent 'defence line'. The ideological cadres prefered to remain out of this. Todor Zhivkov remained an opponent to the use of brutality against the intelligentsia, but the two elements of government, – party and state – continued to work separately, as in the old days. He could not work out a more modern, politically grounded line of action corresponding to the changing realities. He was confused, but he would never resort to extremist measures. Some extremists at the security organs began to talk of 'sharp and out-of-court actions' with respect to the active public figures (provocations, beatings and blackmail). I reported this to Zhivkov and he simply jumped up and brusquely said,: 'Under no circumstances! Who was the person who could think of doing such a thing?' And he created at the Central Committee a headquarters where the minister of the interior had to report anything he undertook.

History shows that in a political system such as ours, the balance between the party and the repressive apparatus is very delicate. The equilibrium here depends to great extent on chance. The repressive apparatus is such that it persistently seeks to expand its scope of action independently of the people who work for it. This is a product of the system. The minister of the interior (later a Politburo member and secretary of the Central Committee), Dimitar Stoyanov, was to me an honest, modest and uncorrupted man. But under the burden of the system he was the first and natural conductor of its interests in the apparatus and in the political leadership of the country. The language of the organizational workers at the Central Committee began to become enriched by such notions as 'operative situation' and 'to be placed under surveillance'.

In this situation the best way to neutralize negative feelings was to talk with Zhivkov. Among the scenarios proposed was the following one: 'Comrade Zhivkov, why are you angry with the dissidents? What do they want, after all? They want changes in the system. You personally said that it was unsound, and you keep talking of its deformities. They are saying the same thing. Why do you have to be angry with them? Let us stop attacking them and work together with them.' Such considerations calmed him down, because they separated him from the system. It could be criticized and spat upon, but not him, because he had the feeling that he was the pillar and support of the system. That is how we all react – we have an excuse for ourselves, but not for others.

The other way to argue with him on these matters without being accused of petty-mindedness and panicking was to acknowledge someone of the intelligentsia who was honest and well-known to ordinary people but who also took a critical stand towards the style of government. It is a fact that Zhivkov personally knew almost all of the most prominent representatives of the intelligentisia, knew their work and even their private affairs. When some of them lined up in the ranks of the discontented he was shocked by their impudence. They had worked for 15–20 years as leaders and had created nothing as scientists or citizens. Some of these late allies of democracy were high-salaried 'dissidents'. Some had previously played up to him humiliatingly, while about others he had compromising evidence. By that time, the bulk of them were pensioners with generous retirement benefits, yet they were the ones to 'dare and teach us democracy'. This enraged Zhivkov and he declared that he would not have been surprised and would not have had ill feelings if the workers had been the ones to revolt. He said they had a right to. He even said that the workers at Kremikovtsi should be the first in the list of the dissatisfied. But when it concerned people who had all their lives been fed from 'the social cauldron' and had not produced a single passable book, film or scientific contribution, he could not reconcile himself to that. His evaluations became extreme. Blinded by such conduct he forgot that there were many honest people among the dissatisfied. When I reminded him of them, he became pensive.

On several instances I told him that among their leaders there was one Zhelyu Zhelev, persecuted by Todor Pavlov himself – a person for whom Zhivkov had no respect. I never heard him say a bad word for Zhelyu Zhelev or even hint that he dismissed Zhelev as a personality.

In fact, Zhelev was the only person Zhivkov seemed to accept as a worthy political opponent, and even hold in respect – as far as Zhivkov could accept any political opposition, of course. I often heard him compliment the late writer Georgi Markov and the writer Hristo Ganev. He had respect for open and honest adversaries and he gladly welcomed any gesture of theirs, suggesting friendliness.

But let us return to the chronology of events:

On 13 February 1989, in the morning, we discussed the situation in Poland and Hungary. Zhivkov noted: 'Why is the Economic Community making concessions to Hungary? If we, too, make a compromise, will they accept us in the same manner? Probably, but this would spell an end to socialism. We are not prepared for pluralism, there is no social base for other parties in our country. When such a base is created, we'll see what happens, but now we have to rebuff the informal alliances and structures.'

The week from 7 to 14 March 1989 was very tense for Todor Zhivkov because of the Artistic Union Congress. The situation was tense everywhere. Especially tense was the congress of the Writers' Union and that of the film workers about which Todor Zhivkov was informed several times a day. Sharp statements were made aimed at the 'April line', at the situation in the country and at the persecution of the intelligentsia.

These congresses represented the political culmination of public opinion which displayed the actual correlation of forces in the country. It had become clear that we were entering a situation of intense political struggle. Todor Zhivkov was trying to contain the disintegration and chaos, but he failed to curb the events. What was more, his most active critics were precisely the communists in the artistic unions – an indication that the party members had completely separated themselves from the nomenclature leadership.

Todor Zhivkov summoned the writers who were members of the party's Central Committee and spoke about their conduct at the forthcoming congresses. Several of them including Bogomil Rainov, Pantelei Zarev and Georgi Djagarov, were personally asked by him to defend the party line. But their voices remained unheard. What is more, Djagarov, who at that meeting toadied before Zhivkov, at the congress itself not only did not make a statement but carelessly flirted with the dissidents. It was funny and sad to watch his efforts to appeal at all costs to the opposition at the congress. He constantly switched partners in that indecent political dance. But he was cold-shouldered by practically everyone. Even Zhivkov felt that Djagarov was playing at the meeting, but he could not believe that one of the most servile members of his entourage would so readily betray him.

I was present at all four congresses. The last one, that of the Union of Film Makers, ended early in the morning on 16 March 1989. Tired, I went to the morning meeting at the office with a brief report.

> Comrade Zhivkov, I was at the four congresses and I listened to over 200 statements. I spoke with scores of artists. What are my impressions and conclusions?
>
> Something completely new is happening in Bulgaria. We are facing a mature, young, intelligent and flexible opposition. It displayed more brightness everywhere – in the statements, in the analyses, in the proposals. Those were born orators who gave the tone and took the congresses over. Opposing them was a defeated and confused ideological apparatus with a handful of officially approved artists. Such is the truth and if we do not make correct assessments and conclusions, the party will continue to be isolated by the intelligentsia.

Todor Zhivkov stood quite impressed by the firm and open description of the events. Up to then he had talked of disbanding the local party organizations, of the setting up of 'workers' posts' among the dissidents and other outdated and futile means. But the fact was that nobody proposed to him anything better. Everyone lay low, nobody wanted to come out and speak honestly of the new situation. They waited for him to decide what was to be done. But he also did not know how to react. He vacillated between his primitive sense of discipline and obedience on the one hand, and the hope that it was all just a passing thing on the other.

Around lunchtime he suddenly had an idea how to avoid an eventual clash with the disobedient cultural figures. On hearing this I called his secretary and arranged an appointment. Todor Zhivkov received me at once. I offered him a compromise. I told him that to confront the intelligentsia would be the greatest political mistake of our lives; we would prove to be hypocrites and demagogues who proclaim democracy but seek conflict and adopt unpopular measures. I reminded him of our decision that from now on all kinds of informal societies could exist, that there would be discussions and freedom of expression, a new thinking which we would support. The congresses were an illustration of this. What was more, they confirmed that the party's decision to work with the intelligentsia were in principle correct, and that now we were simply implementing them. Therefore what happened at the congresses was also partly to our credit – an expression of the new policy rather than a hostile act against any particular person. I suggested that the Politburo needed only to give a high assessment of the congresses and to do so publicly. People were expecting a crackdown but instead of this, the party would extend its hand in search of conciliation.

Zhivkov immediately approved and asked me to draft the Politburo resolution. I wrote it enthusiastically, but the draft was subsequently corrected because it was considered too conciliatory and unjustifiably optimistic. Some negative assessments were also incorporated. The published version was lame and vague.

A curious episode took place during these days, which I think sheds more light on Zhivkov's character.

Returning home one evening, off Orlov Most, near Svetoslav Terter Street, I heard gunshots and cries that someone had been wounded. When I got home, I telephoned the investigation department and was told that a person had been wounded after resisting arrest for writing wall slogans. Plainclothes men had been posted on the block, where similar slogans had previously appeared. The wounded man was Simon Varsano, a photographer for the Pirogov Institute of Emergency Medical Aid.

After the morning meeting I asked permission to stay behind and reported the incident to Todor Zhivkov. He was amazed and asked if the man had been killed. I told him that he had not, but that his life was in danger, due to loss of blood. Zhivkov immediately ordered me to do what I could to help and to follow the case closely; he was ready to send the governmental doctors' team to assist if necessary. It was not easy for him to forget what had happened. That is why I am convinced that he had never been emotionally prepared for rough physical actions and violence. That which did occur was the fault of the functioning of the system which had its supporters at all levels of government.

On 25 April 1989 we discussed the plenum of the Central Committee of the Soviet Union Communist Party which relieved 110 members and candidate-members of the Central Committee and sent them into retirement. I carefully asked whether the same might occur in Bulgaria as many members of the Central Committee had lost their worth or had been compromised, and whether we had to wait until the congress for their release. Zhivkov replied briefly: 'Bulgaria is not the Soviet Union; our problems are not the same, and they cannot be solved in similar ways.'

On 5 May 1989 the agricultural plenum took place at Boyana Residence. Colonel General Slavcho Trunski sharply criticized the agrarian policy and its results. He was right and spoke objectively. During the break I went to give Todor Zhivkov a letter to sign and, as we walked from the meeting to the aides' office, he asked, 'How do you think the plenum is going?' I replied, 'Fine, calmly,' but I knew that what he wanted to hear was my opinion on Slavcho Trunski's speech.

Suddenly he said angrily: 'The revolutionary cadres will either change or will have to go. Society cannot stand them any longer. To hear Slavcho Trunski! He is of the offended ones, having spent his life waiting to be elected to the Politburo. . . .' He was girding up to reply, but the aides managed to dissuade him.

On 8 May events began to unreel vehemently and chaotically

A group of activists had been detained at the Club for Glasnost and Restructuring. The date of the meeting had been learnt by the security agencies several days earlier and the minister of the interior requested in writing instructions from Todor Zhivkov. Zhivkov hesitated for a couple of days. In the meantime one of his bodyguards told me that one police chief had telephoned Boyana Residence, where Zhivkov lived, and asked permission to make arrests and confiscate papers. (These were actually the club's political documents which contained nothing secret.)

Todor Zhivkov agreed and the group of intellectuals were detained. The effect was nil. They were taken to the investigating department to be interviewed. No arrest warrants were shown and a confusing situation ensued, in which they were not prisoners, but neither were they free to leave.

Those detained started behaving haughtily. The investigators were taken aback. Their position was ridiculous and sad at the same time.

Meanwhile the arrests were reported by all major foreign radio stations. Another group of intellectuals immediately organized a protest and several hours later the detainees were released.

Those actions displayed the complete pointlessness and helplessness of the repressive system. It applied by force of habit Article 273 of the penal code. Neither field workers of the Sixth Department of the Ministry of Interior nor the investigators themselves truly believed in what they were doing. I know many of them who even then had the courage to voice openly their protest over the fact that they were expected to 'catch smoke with a fishing net'. Nobody at the Central Committee had been notified, not even its sector responsible for the Ministry of the Interior. The political decision-makers were angry that the ministry had acted on its own. And the officers at the ministry were angry that the party had shifted the dirty work onto them.

That was how tension increased not only between the rulers and the intelligentsia but also within that part of the intelligentsia which was in power. In just a couple of days Zhivkov had succeeded in losing his entire prestige before the intelligentsia – a prestige he had created despite the lack of intellectual contributions, with a sustained handing out of appartments, villas, cars, commissions, jubilees and festivities.

Was Todor Zhivkov the manipulator or the manipulated?

I recall one instance which is indicative of the fact that during the last years at the top, his political reflex began to fail him.

He received the editor-in-chief of the newspaper. *Literaturen Front*, Lilyana Stefanova. She told him certain things and turned him against a large group of writers. Among other things she mentioned that the well-known dissident writer Radoi Ralin received a 450 leva monthly salary as the newspaper's observer but had not published one line in the past five years or so to justify his salary. She thought that he had to be fired and pensioned. After his conversation with her, Zhivkov summoned me and as a lawyer he assigned me to check out the story and see what grounds there were to sack Radoi Ralin. I called Ivan Popov, one of the political aides at the Economy Department, who was the best expert in labour law. I asked him to go to the newspaper's office and to check things out. I phoned Lilyana Stefanova to notify her that I was sending an expert to be given by the personnel department all the relevant documents for verification and to obtain its legal stand. She agreed. Popov went to the personnel department and asked for Radoi Ralin's file. They told him that they had not been notified and phoned the editor-in-chief, Stefanova. Popov heard her shout angrily down the phone: 'Why wasn't I told anything about the case?' and, at one point, say indignantly: 'What do these Central Committee guys want?' Perplexed, Popov phoned me at once and asked me what to do. I told him to return right away.

This was a real manipulation with the consent and in the name of Todor Zhivkov. Lilyana Stefanova wanted to fire Radoi Ralin through the agency of Todor Zhivkov.

I went to him and told him what she had done. On the following day the whole country would be aware that it was not Lilyana Stefanova but Todor Zhivkov who had dismissed Radoi Ralin. I also told him that the editor-in-chief had all the power, if there were grounds for dismissal, to pension off Radoi Ralin even without the help of Todor Zhivkov. He agreed and, referring to her, said, 'Don't waste your time with that shit. Tell her to face up to her own responsibilities.'

This wasn't an isolated case. Everyone who had to clear their unpopular decisions shifted the responsibility on to Todor Zhivkov and, very often, they later claimed that he had ordered the witch hunts and crackdowns. All confrontations with the intelligentsia were referred to him and were decided at the Politburo, while the people in charge of the state cultural policy steered clear. They controlled the money and the administrative authority. They could have done a lot to solve the problems where they arose. Instead, they preferred to go to Todor Zhivkov and ingratiate themselves with him, to slander and to say how outraged they were, while otherwise they passed themselves off as his victims who were made to crackdown on the intelligentsia against their will.

Particular instances included the Rousse Environmental Protection Club, the punishment of four Sofia University professors and the Club for Glasnost and Restructuring; these cases grew into all but national political issues in a matter of hours. The government culture chiefs merely organized floral tributes, anniversary celebrations, and exhibitions. They couldn't bring themselves to defuse a single conflict, although they had the money and the power to enforce a civilized style based on the law and on peaceful dialogue. Instead, everything was left to the discretion of Todor Zhivkov who, without them, could only resort to the arm of repression and the associated political apparatus with their familiar methods.

At one morning meeting I told Todor Zhivkov that I disagreed with the use of repressive methods and I insisted that we abandon that style of work. I told him that resentment was running high in Bulgaria and that many people believed he had adopted a police style. I insisted on the start of a dialogue with the Club for Glasnost and Restructuring and on an end to action, which achieved nothing other than allow 'good-for-nothings', among others, to pose as national martyrs.

The persecution of some such people won them popularity at home and abroad. Even those whose talents had run dry turned to politics as a chance to stand out against the background of the national and East European revolutions. Our political ignorance enabled even inapt dissidents, well paid until recently, to assume an aura of victimization and martyrdom. Of course there were people who struggled not out of vanity or to make political capital for the future. Many of them were and still are genuine champions of democracy and they deserve credit.

Much more alarming developments unfolded by 20–22 May, 1989. Reports started coming in of tensions in north-eastern Bulgaria, as well as in Bourgas and Kurdjali. Some opposition activists there had turned to the Turkish population and campaigned for hunger strikes and disobedience. Todor Zhivkov became increasingly worried. 'They are playing with fire,' he told us wistfully.

By 26 May the situation in north-eastern Bulgaria deteriorated further. Todor Zhivkov started looking for ways out. He ordered the minister of the interior to expedite the issue of foreign travel passports so that the most active and authoritative representatives of that population could be expelled from the country at an early date.

In the early morning of Sunday 28 May, his secretary called us for an emergency meeting at his Central Committee office at half past nine. There was obviously an emergency; he rarely summoned us on a Sunday.

He arrived looking very anxious. He had received information about the situation in north-eastern Bulgaria and more specifically in the area of Shumen where civilians had clashed with the security forces. The reports of casualties had upset him. He asked us what to do. We were all silent. I put forward a question: 'At the national conference, just a couple of days ago, Comrade Dimitar Stoyanov said that the regenerative process is making progress and that with the exception of some extremists, it is well received by that population. What were these evaluations based on, when just in a matter of days riots broke out?'

He cut me short, 'It is easy to be wise after the event . . .'

I did not give up and continued: 'Does this mean that we can mislead each other on a large scale and be so totally unaware of what's going on in the country that we can't sense that riots and revolts are imminent?' He did not reply.

After a short discussion we approved the idea that Todor Zhivkov should address the nation on television. I objected, saying that the address was a good idea but someone else should deliver it, the minister of foreign affairs, Peter Mladenov; the chairman of the Council of Ministers, Georgi Atanassov; or the chairman of the National Assembly, Stanko Todorov. I argued that an address by the head of state was a great risk. The situation was unfavourable in the Warsaw Treaty countries too, and we had better leave ourselves some backtracking room. He thought about this, but then said that the 'patriotic upsurge' still mattered more.

The address was drafted by the evening and on the next day, Monday 29 May, he came out and with some emphasis called Peter Mladenov to coordinate the text of the declaration with him, too. While we were waiting, I once again suggested to him that the Politburo consider whether the head of state should commit himself or whether we should leave it to a lower-ranking official. I said I was convinced that if it came to a confrontation and the many-times-stronger Turkish army invaded, the Soviet Union would refrain from the use of force at this point. It would limit its reaction to a declaration and a protest at the United Nations.

He hesitated for a moment, but finally opted for the idea that patriotic upsurge was needed and that it would work only if none other than Todor Zhivkov himself addressed the nation.

In a short while the meeting began. The Politburo approved the text and assigned Todor Zhivkov to deliver a televised address to the Bulgarian nation.

That was the beginning of the largest exodus since World War II in which over 300,000 people decided to leave Bulgaria in a short span of time. The exodus completely disrupted the political and economic life of the country. It also precipitated Todor Zhivkov's downfall. The cause of these events can be traced back to several years earlier.

Few people know the way the ethnic question has developed over the last few years. It unfolded as an undercurrent which sometimes surfaced as a surprise conflict after which it soon subsided. The events in the summer of 1989 were actually prepared in 1984. Judging by insiders' accounts, the so-called 'regenerative process' caught many people by surprise. Only a handful were in the know. Generally, Todor Zhivkov was a very secretive person. That was a great advantage in the conditions of that type of rule. He never boasted and his questions were confined to the matters he really wanted to know and he put them to the right person. He asked questions as if absent-mindedly, without an apparent coherence or logic, and only later would his long-term aims and secret intentions come to light.

The regenerative process in Bulgaria has a long history. It had been the subject of partisan strife and passions; national nihilism or national chauvinism have always taken the upper hand. It is an intricate affair in terms of politics, history and religion, combined with espionage and diplomatic intrigues.

In recent times this process began in the 1960s in the Rhodopes region where the Muslim Bulgarians started rapidly to adopt more Turkish attributes. The phenomen became widespread in the Kurdjali region where it is concentrated. What happened in practice was that people with Bulgarian and Turkish names lived together in one family.

The regenerative process actually began in 1970 with the change of the names of the Islamized Bulgarians. The process started on the initiative of the leaders of several districts inhabited by this population: the districts of Kurdjali, Smolyan and Blagoevgrad. The political direction and supervision of the process was the responsibility of the propaganda department of the Central Committee of the Bulgarian Communist Party, whose secretary at that time was Stoyan Mihailov. Alexander Lilov was also involved in its direction in the 1970s.

In 1983–84 the process was extended to the regions compactly populated by people with Turkish ethnic identities. That was precisely how the regenerative process flared up and surfaced.

The people who insisted on taking the process to those regions were the then first secretary of the party's district committee in Kurdjali, Georgi Tanev and the Kurdjali Member of Parliament, Georgi Atanassov who was then secretary of the Central Committee of the Bulgarian Communist Party.

What was Todor Zhivkov's role at that point?

In the first days he was sceptical about the reports coming in from Kurdjali, he even warned against overdoing it. But the assurances that everything was fine and was going smoothly put him off his guard and he gave the go-ahead, and the operation was carried through. The whole population adopted Bulgarian names. Incidents took place in only two regions: Momchilgrad and the village of Benkovski.

The events in Kurdjali came as a surprise for the Politburo of the Central Committee of the Bulgarian Communist Party. They met to discuss the new political situation in the country. In a heated debate, they considered whether the movement should not be extended to north-eastern Bulgaria. Pencho Koubadinski suggested that the process spread only to those areas where there is no compact population with a Turkish ethnic identity. Todor Zhivkov's idea to cover all regions prevailed. A political direction was formed at headquarters at the Central Committee of the Bulgarian Communist Party. It was headed by Todor Zhivkov and included Milko Balev, Georgi Atanassov, Pencho Koubadinski, Dimitar Stoyanov, Peter Mladenov and Stoyan Mihailov.

Todor Zhivkov was seriously concerned about several parallel processes which I think outweighed other considerations in making the 1984 decisions. Those were the extremely negative demographic characteristics of the population: ageing and low birth rates. The migration had forced large numbers of the Bulgarian population to leave those regions and to converge in urban areas. They left behind deserted villages which were immediately occupied by the Turkish-speaking population. The villages in entire regions looked like eighteenth or nineteenth century settlements, with their imams, surviving Turkish lifestyles and rituals and pronounced religious fanaticism. Worse still, the population of those regions was firmly bound to the land and to stockbreeding. Labour had acquired a family character which made their organization and way of life extremely stable. No full statistics and census figures on that population were available, and that made the picture even more unclear and disturbing.

The other adverse factor was the growing self-consciousness of the intellectuals bred by that population. These were young people, admitted to the universities on a priority basis, and almost all of them had civil professions: teachers, doctors, agronomists. They drifted apart from the rest of the population and showed alarming signs of integration with Turkish culture. Everything that had been done until then for that population in terms of improving its living conditions, culture and education, merely intensified the process of its ethnic segregation.

From an international point of view, another adverse geopolitical factor was and still is our neighbouring proximity with multimillion-strong Turkey. Its rapid economic growth and its military capability, huge by the standards of the Balkans and Europe, should always be a weighty consideration in our relations, then and in the future. With its economic and human resources, Turkey will always be preferred as a partner by the large European countries.

Here is how Zhivkov himself set forth his stand on these issues only a month after the 29 May, 1989 declaration (when the exodus was at its height). Addressing graduates of the Academy of Social Sciences and Social Management, he said:

> Unfortunately a similar problem arose in this country with the so-called Bulgarian Muslims.
>
> What is the essence of the question? History has so decreed that after the liberation, the Bulgarian state and the Bulgarian people constituted two communities.
>
> One of them is the community of the Eastern Orthodox church. That was by far the larger part of the Bulgarian people. But there was another community, the Muslims. These two communities are a reality resulting from the Turkish yoke. Even in their early period, the Bulgarian national revival figures worried about Bulgaria's future. Even the capitalist governments and many of the then ruling regimes and people were aware of this problem. It was not by accident that they banned Turkish schools back in 1921. But what happened afterwards? Our party came and introduced schools, language teaching, and so on and so forth. Our party, too, introduced Macedonian cultural autonomy.
>
> That was our legacy after the April plenum of the party's Central Committee.
>
> The question is this: either we cope with this problem reasonably, calmly, without yielding to provocations and by studying the present-day international realities, or tomorrow we will be another Cyprus or something worse than Cyprus. Bulgaria is at stake. I am being perfectly serious and I say

> this in all responsibility. We know about their plans. We are perfectly well aware of the plans of those who are in charge there. When Kenan Evren arrived on a visit to Bulgaria, he raised a single matter – stopping the emigration. He was not interested in anything else. I tried to discuss many other issues, but he was indifferent and only went through the motions. The only question he raised was, 'Mr Zhivkov, we must eliminate the emigration issue and stop dealing with it. There are 100 humanitarian cases, let them be considered favourably.'
>
> When I went to Turkey to pay a return visit, that was two or three years later, those 100 people had increased to 3,500. . . .
>
> Why should one part of the Bulgarian nation which was put to fire and sword to convert to Islam, not be considered part of the Turkish nation? Why, on what grounds? Clearly, this is a fifth column. They have gathered along the border and in all mountain passes which are vital in case of war and, generally, for running a state. How did this happen? Who engineered it? Obviously we did not engineer it.
>
> Therefore, our nation and our intelligentsia realized the gravity of the issue; that it is socialist Bulgaria that is at stake. That is the problem of all problems.

That was the political and the intellectual motivation of Todor Zhivkov's 1984 decision on the regenerative process in Bulgaria.

At that time deep down I opposed Todor Zhivkov's actions. I thought they were pointless, that we could do without them. I sought and suggested other decisions, including an immediate and unconditional restoration of names. The events at the end of last year and the beginning of this one, however, have convinced me that Todor Zhivkov still had a reason to seek a radical solution to that intricate problem, even though the solution was all too late. History shows that no ethnic question in the Balkans has ever been solved in a peaceful and democratic way.

One should bear in mind that Bulgaria is the gateway to the Orient. Here the recipes of abstract democracy cannot be applied as a measure and a method to seek a way out. I do not know of a single American political figure who has been brought to trial for the crazy war in Vietnam which had all the ingredients of genocide: tens of thousands killed, hundreds of thousands wounded, whole parts of Asia contaminated. The United States national interests had been defended thousands of kilometres away from its borders. There are such examples in the contemporary history of all European democracies.

The coming years will be the judge of our times. My faith is pinned on the building of peaceful and stable structures in Bulgaria and in Turkey under the control and standards of Europe, which is interested to have stability throughout the continent. Failing this, Bulgaria will have to brace itself for a grave and unhappy future.

This, however, is my personal opinion which I do not press on anyone. Let us see what happened next in those troubled days.

On 29 May 1989 Todor Zhivkov arrived and asked us to emphasize certain points in the declaration which would strengthen our positions, to stress that Bulgaria observes the Vienna Concluding Document, that it is opening its borders and allows everybody to choose his own national identity. Let Turkey stop playing games and open its borders too.

In the evening he read the declaration on television, and it made a strong impression because Bulgaria had not witnessed such dramatic confrontations for a long time.

The following day Zhivkov looked contented. Obviously, the declaration had received great acclaim.

He insisted on the patriotic upsurge and became so carried away that he ordered the Secretariat and the Civil Committee to direct this upsurge against the national apostate intellectuals. (This was a big mistake. Several pitiful slogans were held up at rallies and nobody wanted to shout 'the traitors' and 'the national apostates'.)

Zhivkov proved surprisingly uninformed. I think that in a crisis there was always somebody who would report to him facts which suited his notions. That was probably the case then, too. Pleased with himself, he said, 'Well, we told them point blank to leave for Turkey and they got scared. They handed out the application forms, but only 15–20 people took them, the rest refused.' The vice-president of the Central Bank, Todor Chavdarov, had told me only a couple of hours earlier that in Silistra alone some 15,000 people had started to withdraw their money from the bank because they were leaving. I said, 'Comrade Zhivkov, this is not true. The information is quite different.' I told him what I had learned from the bank. He was unpleasantly surprised but said nothing.

I think the system just malfunctioned, or maybe in such cases some self-seekers simply disinformed him. That was further evidence that a system built on the principle that you could gain personal benefit from disinformation worked trouble-free despite the fact that everything around was crumbling and perishing. It was only logical that the pillar of this system himself should be its victim.

Tensions ran high in the days between 1 and 9 June. The Politburo commended Todor Zhivkov's declaration. He was convinced that it had halted the rioting, that the Turkish delegation at the Paris conference was in disarray, that the people were in a patriotic upsurge, while the dissidents were crushed and terrified. He gave orders that the emigrants be seen off with music, songs and mass celebrations organized by the local councils. In reply I ventured to tell him that 'no country loses its population except at war. Agriculture will collapse and the economy will sustain enormous losses.' I dreaded his reaction, but he said nothing.

He came back radiant from a Politburo meeting and announced that he had received their unanimous support, that 200,000 people might be allowed to leave the country. (That was the figure given earlier by Pencho Koubadinski. Another person cited a larger number of emigrants, saying 'If we want to solve our national question we have to drive out 200–300,000 people.)

After 10 November, that same person described this policy as 'criminal'. This staunch support came as a pleasant surprise for Todor Zhivkov.

Around 9 June, ever more alarming news started coming in about deserted villages, abandoned and roaming livestock, looting and endless lines of emigrants on the roads to the Turkish border.

On that day I jotted down an intriguing episode in my notepad: over the morning coffee, Dimitar Metodiev reported that the Spanish football club, Barcelona, was prepared to pay between five and ten million dollars for our footballer Stoichkov.

I mentioned that such an amount would be enough to import ladies' footware and underwear which were virtually unobtainable in Bulgaria at that time.

Todor Zhivkov took notice and I took the courage to insist that we shouldn't waste time, as our teams were not due to play in any major tournament where Stoichkov would be missed.

Zhivkov replied, 'All right, see to it, tell the comrades who are in charge to think about it and make a decision.'

I phoned the president of the football federation Andon Traikov who said that he would not make a decision without the minister of defence Debri Djourov (Stoichkov played for CSKA, the army football club).

An hour later, an urgent call came from the office of Dobri Djourov. He was put through and he reacted sharply to the idea. He accused us of misleading Todor Zhivkov and told us that Stoichkov was indispensable for Bulgarian football and that it would be a criminal act to sell him (actually two rounds later, the team dropped out even though the star played on). He said that Todor Zhivkov should not be misled and talked about ethics and adherence to party principles. I replied that the matter was not prejudged and that the directive was that the federation and the minister consider the situation and make a decision.

Djourov called Todor Zhivkov and then called me back and told me not to pester him with the Stoichkov case any more.

At lunch I told Zhivkov that the case was closed and added jokingly that the minister of defence was ready to send three heavy tanks and stage a coup and have us arrested. Zhivkov laughed contentedly but then grew serious and said as if to himself: 'He would never venture on something rash! Still, he too has started playing games, distancing himself, but it is too late! Look,' and he started counting on his fingers those who he thought had to go in the not too distant future, 'Milko Balev, Grisha Filipov, Dobri Djourov, Pencho Koubadinski and some others, I don't know, but I'm certain about those.'

This gave me food for thought. Zhivkov never tolerated people whom he could not trust, especially people holding key positions of power. But now it was a question of no less a person than the minister of defence himself. It was out of the question that he had put up with his fellow partisan merely for sentimental reasons. Zhivkov never forgave anyone the faintest disloyalty and reacted to the slightest suspicion. And yet Dobri Djourov had been the irreplaceable minister of defence for nearly 30 years. What held him on even though they were openly intolerant of each other? Dobri Djourov obviously resented many of Todor Zhivkov's actions, especially his despotism. He himself was modest as a soldier, impervious to corruption and there were no compromising facts in his life and career. That, too, made him dangerous. Anyway, the two of them had tolerated each other for nearly 30 years.

Between 14 and 20 June 1989 the situation in the country became increasingly aggravated. The emigration momentum reached enormous proportions. If that rate was maintained, 500,000 people would have left Bulgaria by the end of the year. Disastrous losses were imminent in the economy and especially in agriculture.

At that time Todor Zhivkov began to suggest new steps in the policy towards that population. He ordered a report, which should take into account the specific aspects of our culture and life.

> Why some people think that culture is a one-way process? It is evolved by different social groups. What's wrong with bagpipes and zourlas playing at weddings and parties? What's wrong with horo dances and belly dances?

But the situation called for other measures. It was too late to reverse the deep rooted ethnic processes by the methods of culture and psychology.

At that time the American president assured the Turkish prime minister Turgut Özal in several telephone conversations that Turkey had America's backing, while the Soviet Union would not commit itself to Bulgaria's ethnic policy and that was evident with every passing day. We were alone in our own political and military bloc.

It was becoming increasingly clear that the Bulgarian–Turkish conflict was being taken over by outside powers. They placed this conflict in the context of global politics and East-West relations. Our stake in these politics was infinitesimal. We could expect no dividends from the conflict because we were the most loyal and steadfast ally of the Soviet Union.

Admittedly, at that time Todor Zhivkov proved a courageous and astute leader who would not shrink back from difficulties and was not afraid to defend Bulgaria's positions and interests.

On 13 July he received the Turkish ambassador in Sofia, Ömer Lütem, at his request.

After the routine diplomatic civilities, Todor Zhivkov reminded him that during his meeting with Kenan Evren, the then president of Turkey, they had reached a common understanding to drop the emigration question from bilateral relations. They had expressed readiness to consider individual humanitarian cases. At that meeting Evren had raised the question about the solution of 100 cases but later on they had laid claim to 3,500 people. After that, those claims increased in number and the Turkish side had started talking about one, two or even more than three million Turks living in Bulgaria. In this connection, Zhivkov called on Turkey to open its borders and receive all those who wished to settle there.

Zhivkov reminded him that the Vienna Concluding Document opened up unlimited legal opportunities for the solution of these problems. 'These documents made the emigration agreements unnecessary. The terms 'minorities' and 'emigration' were already obsolete. Turkey was keeping up a campaign to predispose Bulgarian citizens to emigration. Now our borders were wide open. It did not matter to us how many Bulgarian citizens were going to leave. We were not worried if three out of nine million Bulgarian citizens left the country. Once Turkey had promised the world to accept three million Turks from Bulgaria, let it accept them, if these people wished to go, of course. We had no intention of making difficulties. We refrained from all actions directed against Turkey. We had turned down the request of both the Communist party and of the Kurdish organizations to establish their headquarters in Bulgaria. Why was Turkey forcing us to associate with the Kurds and the Turkish Communist Party?

Further on he said that we must revive business between the two countries. As to the emigrants, we would not have any special problems with them. The Ludogorie was a wonderful region with excellent land and many young people would want to settle there

After that Todor Zhivkov discussed the advantages of our geographical position. The shortest routes between Europe and the Middle East and south-west Asia lay across our two countries. Under the circumstances, other roundabout routes would have to be sought. Our Soviet friends would be only too glad if these routes to the Middle East and south-west Asia crossed their territory. The Turkish vehicles and citizens who crossed Bulgaria free of charge were over three million annually. They, too, could look for roundabout routes to Europe. It should be seen who stands to gain and who stands to lose, but even at that point it was clear that Turkey would lose more.

As to the bellicose calls for another Cyprus solution, one should not forget that Bulgaria was not Cyprus.

Todor Zhivkov also proposed a settlement of bilateral relations and warned that 'if someone in Turkey counts on the coming to power of a new government in Bulgaria which would revise this country's policy on the matter, he was greatly mistaken.' (He proved the one mistaken: Özal became president, and Todor Zhivkov found himself detained on remand. Will history set the record straight someday?)

He went on to say that Bulgarians were living in many areas around the world – 400,000 in Moldavia, 300,000 in the Ukraine – but Bulgaria did not lay claims to 'minorities' or to the emigration of that population. We had grounds to lay claims to Turkey on account of the 400,000 Bulgarians now living in that country. But Bulgaria had never raised this question, although she had the right to do so.

Todor Zhivkov said that we do not appraise Turkey by the number of her Phantom fighter planes or other military equipment (which could be reported to Evren and Özal) but by its potential and role in the Balkans. If we did something rash, we could exterminate each other in a matter of hours. Therefore, we had no other alternative but to seek peace and understanding between Bulgaria and Turkey.

That was the position from which Todor Zhivkov defended our national interests. Perhaps his policy would have been successful if this conflict had not turned into an arena for the two blocs to test themselves against each other. Each East European country was preoccupied with its own economic and political problems. The Eastern bloc had turned into a goat's skin on the map of the world which had long ceased to frighten anyone.

At the morning meeting (21 June 1989) I saw for the first time a tired, faint and depressed Todor Zhivkov. He kept silent and did not ask questions. From time to time he tried to concentrate and listen but managed to do so only for a short time. At the end of the meeting he said, 'The Soviet Union is in crisis. We, too, are on the brink of a crisis.'

On 3 July I noted down an event which was interesting from a psychological point of view. A colleague, Dimitar Metodiev, the only veteran aide of Todor Zhivkov still serving, reminded him that those National Theatre actors who were most deserving but were pensioned on very unfavourable terms, were an outstanding issue. Todor Zhivkov looked at him and said, 'All right, I have already arranged it, haven't I? How many times are we going to discuss the matter?'

Dimitar Metodiev insisted, 'Nothing has been done about it. Whom did you tell?'

Todor Zhivkov replied, 'More than a month ago I referred the case to Georgi Yordanov [deputy chairman of the Council of Ministers, in charge of the cultural sphere].'

Dimitar Metodiev was surprised, 'Why then when those people keep going to Yordanov does he tell them nothing?'

Todor Zhivkov laughed, first sniggering and then in roars, 'Dimitri [that was what he used to call him], you have been working with me for so long but you haven't learned a thing. Well, if they ask him more earnestly it will look as if he has solved the question and he'll take the credit. The old man [referring to himself] needs no credit and capital. He is leaving. Everybody is wondering what will happen when I'm gone. They are looking for options, they are playing up to somebody. Haven't you still made your own reckoning? Hurry up, everybody's scrambling to desert the sinking ship.' He laughed for a long time and I think he was really amused; although, there was sadness in that laughter.

In point of fact, he himself had realized what was going on. He had not lost a fraction of his skill to judge people. His sensitivity had edged. He felt that everybody was preparing to desert him. He could sense it in their glances and in the compliments they paid him, many of which sounded openly hypocritical and unconvincing.

A tour of the diplomatic corps to Smolyan was organized on 5 July 1989. It was interesting to watch the way the inner circles of the regional and local bosses at the dinner talked to Todor Zhivkov about the development of electronics and all other industries in that scenic mountain area. They didn't say a word about the development of tourism and stockbreeding! They all tried to touch the right cord in Todor Zhivkov's notions of Bulgarian economic priorities. It seemed we felt ashamed to talk about such 'simple' issues as agriculture, tourism, and craftsmanship, especially in places where they could flourish.

On 6 July, Todor Zhivkov left to attend a session of the Warsaw Political Consultative Committee.

Upon his return between 6 and 10 July he ordered the disbandment of all Central Committee structures which duplicated the Council of Ministers. He was enraged by the fact that he was waiting for the third consecutive year for the government to do something worthwhile rather than just holding back. For the first time he began talking in our presence frankly and with displeasure about Prime Minister Georgi Atanassov and the minister of the economy and planning, Stoyan Ovcharov. He accused them of incompetence and of trying to hide behind his back and do nothing. After that, he shared this view with the Politburo members, which implied that he had decided to go ahead with major cabinet changes. That provided everybody who expected to be affected by the changes in government with a natural rallying point.

During that period Todor Zhivkov's mind was ripe for radical decisions. Quite unexpectedly he agreed with my suggestion for Council of Ministers decisions which would lift the restrictions on, among other things, owning property, residence rights, private ownership and free enterprise. Maybe that had something to do with a report he had ordered on a number of laws which bred social tensions in the country and crippled the country's civil and economic life. The fact that Ceausescu's Romania was the only other country to have such laws, seemed a crucial argument to him. When this argument was advanced, he immediately agreed with the idea to abolish bureaucratic restrictions. He also seemed ready for a decisive review of ideology. In this connection, the following quote from one of the numerous speeches from the period (before the graduates at the Academy of Social Sciences and Management on 29 June 1988), I think, shows no fundamental difference between his views and the platforms of some of the present opposition parties.

> And yet, which is the main question, the question of questions, without which we cannot start any kind of restructuring on a sound foundation?
>
> The main promise of Marxism concerning the socialist society is that socialist society would emerge after capitalist society. Therefore, neither Marx nor Engels ever claimed that a socialist society could be built without the creation of all those objective and subjective conditions necessary for the development of capitalism itself, which would then be succeeded by socialist society. That is the main and most basic thing. That is where our entire Marxist–Leninist political economy has been mistaken because, contrary to Marx and Engel's expectations and predictions, socialism did not triumph in the most advanced countries. Socialism

> triumphed in the least developed capitalist states. After World War II it triumphed in underdeveloped countries, with the exception of the German Democratic Republic and Czechoslovakia. Before World War II, under capitalism, Czechoslovakia ranked third or fourth in the world. Now it ranks fourteenth or fifteenth, I'm not sure which.
>
> The crux of the matter is this. We can hold seminars to discuss the question, but if we don't agree unanimously that socialism is premature, we cannot carry out any restructuring, we cannot make scientific advances, we cannot make any progress. We cannot rally the millions of people behind the idea of restructuring.
>
> True, history did not throw out that premise. Nothing of the kind. It endorsed it and it grew up. We cannot imagine many things in the world after the victory of the Great October Socialist Revolution. They could not have happened without the victory and without the creation of the socialist community.
>
> The premise must grow up a sturdy child and will grow up a sturdy child. But the fact is that socialism triumphed prematurely. That was how history decreed. You might ask, why and how? I make no pretence to be a scientist. I am a public figure, a statesman and a communist. I lay no claim to scientific knowledge or erudition. My fate decided it that way.

It is a different question that Todor Zhivkov had no think tanks to launch on the practical dismantling of this system. Either fear of mistakes or incompetence had paralyzed all 'brain trusts' of the party and the state. He himself was partly to blame for this. If somebody came up with an original suggestion, he hastened to turn him down or to lecture him as an underachieving student. Much of the responsibility for that rests with the insinuations of some philosophers who flattered him as a theoretician and innovator of the communist movement and as the top reformer of socialism.

In such a way, in the face of urgent practical problems, Todor Zhivkov's materials, reports and speeches presented an endless stream of claims to innovation and theoretical contributions. They involved an underhand struggle between aides, scientists and experts who worked in the dark and suggested 'discoveries'.

In those days he began to complain of overstrain, something which he found hard to tolerate. He wanted to work the way he had worked all his life; 10 to 15 hours a day. For the first time events caught up with him. He was oppressed by the Turkish issue as well as by the situation in the Socialist countries.

I saw him standing up, lost in thought for the first time. As if trying to explain his reflections, he deliberately asked himself aloud, 'Is it possible that I acted rashly in 1984?'

He was severely tormented by the collapse in the Eastern bloc. He could not reconcile himself to the fact that Gorbachev had launched reforms for which the Soviet Union was unprepared.

His meetings with Gorbachev during the last years were an even more painful and oppressive experience and the 1 July 1989 meeting was a mere formality. Todor Zhivkov had no illusions about Gorbachev's feelings towards him. He realized that the two of them belonged to different ages and nothing could be done to draw them closer. Moreover, all Soviet channels – diplomatic, intelligence, or through the direct contacts between the two countries' intellectuals – carried negative information about the situation in Bulgaria and about Todor Zhivkov himself. There was a disrupted market which rallied everybody, irrespective of their political platform and ideas, against the system with Todor Zhivkov at the top. He felt cornered and desperately sought a way out. But the time for active and decisive moves had ran out. There was little room to manoeuvre in terms of time and geopolitical space.

Over the last few years trade with the Soviet Union was causing serious difficulties. The 1986–90 period saw a steep decline in the amounts of raw materials which we received from there. The supply of oil was reduced by 6,855 thousand tons, that of coal by 3,000 thousand tons, coke by 1,500 thousand tons and fuel oil by 100 thousand tons. The deliveries of manganese ore, pyrite and apatite concentrate, steel ingot and plate, rolled iron, soot, cement, coniferous timber and cellulose also decreased. This shortage of raw and prime materials had to be set off by imports from the West valued at 500 million leva annually. This closed even more tightly the vicious circle of our economy.

Todor Zhivkov found himself in a trap he had never expected. 'If it continues like this, we'll have to blow our brains out,' he said in one of our conversations. At the same time, he was unable to adapt our economy to the 'special' terms of the Western market and to obtain preferential treatment, nor did he want to declare openly a stagnation of personal consumption.

I insisted that we raise the prices to protect the market from overconsumption, but he would not hear of it. Neither did he want to close certain branches of business and to declare their bankruptcy, even though we discussed the matter on several occasions. He became touchy when he heard predictions that the 'modern' branches of electronics and mechanical engineering were losing money in Bulgaria and faced even more bleak prospects against future trends.

Together with several experts from the economic department we proposed to him a package of measures to turn some projects in tourism, the food industry, agriculture, light industries, electronics and mechanical engineering into concessions. We motivated those proposals, citing the example of the petroleum concession in the Soviet Union at the time of Lenin, but this option seemed complicated to him and besides, we didn't have the legal framework. I still believe that that was and is one of the ways to save the Bulgarian economy.

At the beginning of September 1989 Todor Zhivkov returned from vacation, but had not been able to have a good rest. As usual, in Varna, he had had numerous meetings and talks.

His first words were, 'Boys, what's happening to socialism? It's a goner. Socialism is lost as a system.' After that he made a brief commentary on the situation in Hungary, Poland, Czechoslovakia and the Soviet Union.

He ordered the preparation of a plenum of the Central Committee of the Bulgarian Communist Party which was to consider a report on the work done and to raise some 'theoretical problems'. In those days Todor Zhivkov was very busy working on a development of the ethnic issue. It was assigned to Professor Todor Ivanov, another aide of his, who I think made a wonderful job of the assignment. He consulted a large number of experts in different fields and, for the first time, the ethnic issue was presented free of illusions and ideological bombast. Sensible compromises and fair solutions were suggested. But the whirlpool of events did not allow these ideas to be made public and put into practice.

The secretaries of the communist parties in charge of international affairs met in Varna from 24 to 27 September 1989. There Todor Zhivkov conferred with Alexander Yakovlev who created the impression of being a person of exceptionally high moral standing and a real representative of that Russian intelligentsia which had achieved many intellectual and moral triumphs in human history. In his talk with Yakovlev, Todor Zhivkov resolutely upheld the thesis that we cannot let Romania, the People's Republic of Korea and the German Democratic Republic mould the communist movements' opinion of the world because their views dated from the 1950s.

He once again advanced the thesis that on a global scale, the all-out pressure in socialism can be reduced on the basis of two points. First, if we go ahead with a large-scale, wide-ranging improvement of relations with China, for which all conditions were available. And, secondly, if we demolish the Berlin Wall, allow the unification of Germany and wait for centrifugal forces to develop in the Western alliance within several years.

He believed that a united Germany would never accept putting its colossal human and economic capability 'behind bars'. Now that German reunification has taken place Europe will surely face many questions.

The meeting ended in an interesting way. Leaving the table, Todor Zhivkov declared, 'Tell Comrade Gorbachev that if Marx and Engels were alive, they would have told us, "Boys, it is still too early to rename our parties social democratic and to struggle for capitalism. Our society and our economy are not yet ready for that."' He burst out in his usual loud and hearty laughter.

I took that joke as an afterthought of an idea. He elaborated before Gorbachev: that we should yield and reform the system but that we should do it concertedly, playing by 'the rules of the game'. Otherwise, the balance of interests in Europe and the world would be upset.

The morning coffee meeting on 5 October 1989 had a stormy beginning.

Turkey had taken an intransigent stand at the United Nations. Our delegation was to leave for the celebrations in Berlin. In this connection Todor Zhivkov said, 'We are going to a memorial service. The leadership here will hold out for just a couple of weeks.'

After that he discussed the situation in the country and the mounting tension over the depleted consumer goods market. 'We must prepare for dramatic manoeuvres,' he pointed out. 'The restructuring has ground to a halt. The cadres are demoralized. The government is not implementing the policy of the Central Committee. The minister of economy and planning is incompetent and cannot put anything into practice. He is a "mummy's boy". I was mistaken to have him appointed and the disgrace falls on me. I was wrong and I take the blame.'

It was then mentioned that the foreign debt was growing disastrously.

Future researchers will have a lot to think about. The government which took office when Bulgaria had a net foreign debt of 5,000 million dollars, contrived to have it rise to 10,500 million in four years. And yet its annual reports and statistics of the period never sounded the alarm. Why? Was the government afraid? Or was it hiding behind Zhivkov's back? I think the reason was incompetence combined with manoeuvring and time wasting in the hope of surviving in the coming days. After the change on 10 November 1989, Prime Minister Georgi Atanassov laid the entire blame for the grave situation on Todor Zhivkov, unperturbed and without the slightest remorse.

Meanwhile, the debt continued to rise even after 10 November 1989. By February 1990 it grew monthly by 200 million dollars but the government continued to excel in refusing truly to acknowledge the problem. The situation was already dictated by the street and could not be controlled despite the desperate attempts which sounded all too hollow.

But then on 3 October 1989 Todor Zhivkov told about the situation in the German Democratic Republic and the mood of the German leaders who were crestfallen. He described Karoly Gross as a weakling 'in these times for Hungary'. Of Jaruzelski he said he was pleased with his politics and that he had calmed down and his conduct showed it. He was particularly worried by the emergence of new parties in Hungary and Poland. He assessed the situation in the Soviet Union as critical and said that we here in Bulgaria could not hold out alone.

The preparations for the CSCE meeting on environmental protection began. The informal organizations and societies stepped up their activities. Some of them had tried to stage a public demonstration involving around 30 people. Some of those assembled tried to jeer at them but Todor Zhivkov said, 'Don't be misled. Now they are 30, they will be 300 and 3000 and 300,000 in a year's time. That is the logic of the struggle.'

I was always surprised by the fact that while sometimes he displayed realism and foresight, on other occasions it was the awkwardness of a feeble attempt to prevent or defer the end.

And when having predicted the growth of the opposition, instead of using his vision and imagination for sweeping political action, together with Politburo member and secretary of the Central Committee Dimitar Stoyanov and Velko Palin, head of the Social and National Security Department, he started to form 'political units'. They were supposed to fight against the informal organizations. Some called them 'our stormtroopers'. While the protesters still numbered several dozen, these units could achieve something, but when the number of protesters grew, they became useless and even pitiful.

At a suitable moment I told Todor Zhivkov that the people were somewhat confused and if Simeon came the people would vote for him. He did not reply. It seemed he agreed.

Here is yet another curious episode, which characterizes both the situation and Zhivkov's assessment of those around him.

Several months earlier, I insisted on the establishment of diplomatic relations with South Korea and Israel. I told him that I had acquaintances who had been trading with them for a long time, who knew their top business people and could hold informal talks on the establishment of at least wider business contacts. He agreed and left for Vienna and Bonn in August 1989. Our trade officials initiated informal talks with South Korean representatives. Things got off the ground and in mid-October South Korea agreed to send to Bulgaria a large delegation for talks and agreements.

Delighted, I went to tell him. He cheered up too. I asked him who would take over. He replied, 'The competent authorities.' 'Then I should phone Andrei Loukanov?' I suggested. 'No!' he snapped. 'Not him. Call Petko Danchev.'

Both of them, Andrei Loukanov and Petko Danchev, were deputy chairmen of the Council of Ministers. But Zhivkov almost openly endorsed Petko Danchev as a future prime minister of Bulgaria, and that was one of the personal changes he was planning for the forthcoming plenum.

I phoned Petko Danchev but it turned out he was in Japan at the head of a delegation and would not be back until the end of the month. I returned and reported to Todor Zhivkov that we would waste time and, I again insisted, that Andrei Loukanov was the most competent person to take charge of the preparations for the visit. 'No, under no circumstances,' Zhivkov replied stubbornly. 'This phenomenon [that was what he called Andrei Loukanov] must be wiped out.' I realized why Zhivkov had been collecting material and facts related to the sensitive field of Bulgaria's foreign economic relations. He was undoubtedly clearing the way for Petko Danchev. At the forthcoming plenum, Andrei Loukanov was to be relieved of his party and government posts. An indication of this was the isolation in which Zhivkov had been keeping him over the last few years.

On 25 October 1989 I crossed the garden opposite Kristal where members of Ecoglasnost collected signatures on an appeal against the Rila and the Mesta hydroengineering projects. I stopped and listened to the speakers. Young people were heatedly canvassing the passers-by. Everything seemed normal or, at least, peaceful. There was alarm only in the secret service bulletins and in the special reports which lent an entirely different political colour to these actions against the background of the European meeting in Sofia and the activation of the diplomatic circles.

I shared my impressions with Zhivkov. I told him what was going on and that a crackdown was out of the question. After all, they were talking of air, water and soil. We could do nothing except join that movement. It had to be granted political recognition and legalized. If the government thought in a modern way, it should give them money and organize a competition between the two national projects. He listened attentively but said nothing. I think he agreed with me and I felt contented.

About noon, however, when I was leaving the Central Committee headquarters, I saw a colleague of mine who indignantly told me of the clash between the security forces and the Ecoglasnost activists. I went back to my room. It was clear that the repressive system was functioning and that nothing could change it. It had gone into action according to its own laws and mechanisms. I don't know who gave the orders and in what way (afterwards there was a prolonged controversy over what had happened and what had gone wrong in the communication between the security forces and the party). It was a shame that in those days we could not find the courage, the human and the political will, the imagination and the flexibility to shape an honest policy which would halt the escalation of mutual mistrust. Because during this first wave of the opposition, many of the participants were people with whom we could do business and who did not seek confrontation for its own sake.

It became worse and much more difficult when the second wave surged, consisting of people who sought vengeance and chanted 'Down! Down and death!' and were not concerned about pollution. That too, should have been foreseen. Another category of people should be added to the several hundred thousands who resented the repressions in the 1940s and the 1950s.

Some 20,000 people are convicted in this country of economic crimes and criminal offences. In just one decade their number grew to a size which, if somebody managed to rally, would create a strike force driven not by ideals and justice, but hatred, vengeance and destruction.

Besides, judging by the history of the communist states, once it stops producing fear, the repressive machine proves surprisingly weak. They have no points of support of their own. In a capitalist state, ownership plays the role of a stabilizing factor. Owners there are interested in having order and justice within the law. They form a permanent cushion which absorbs the abrupt motions in the political and social sphere. Depersonalized state property has no such cushion. Precisely for this reason, at the time of restructuring which we are now experiencing, the conduct and actions of the communist states with a totalitarian system is unpredictable. They are dangerous not only for their own people because they can subject it to violence, but also for the necessary balance of interests in international relations.

By the end of October it became clear that Todor Zhivkov and Peter Mladenov, Politburo member and minister of foreign affairs, were at odds.

The Politburo met to discuss some issues of the 'regenerative process'. Peter Mladenov was absent. He was not ill.

What had happened?

On 24 October 1989 Mladenov had sent a strongly worded letter to Todor Zhivkov, expressing disagreement with his style and methods of work. The letter was addressed to Todor Zhivkov himself, to the Politburo and the Central Control and Auditing Commission. By that letter Mladenov handed in his resignation. The letter was received only by Todor Zhivkov.

How did Zhivkov react?

He called the Politburo members alone to several long meetings to seek a way to hush up Mladenov's resignation. The only possible and plausible motive was 'on health grounds'. This was very convenient, because Mladenov had undergone major surgery. Zhivkov did not want scandals. He sent truce envoys: Dimiter Stoyanov and Pencho Koubadisnki who nearly persuaded him to withdraw the letter. On 27 October he called Peter Mladenov himself to a 30-minute talk but, obviously, failed to reach agreement. I saw Peter Mladenov coming out of his office with a frown on his face.

As the meeting in Kuwait with the Turkish foreign minister Mesut Yilmaz was forthcoming, the conflict could not be hushed up. The deputy chairman of the Council of Ministers Georgi Yordanov had to go to the meeting instead of Mladenov.

Todor Zhivkov called the leadership of the delegation together with Peter Mladenov, but he refused to come, pleading illness. When he learned that, Todor Zhivkov said, 'Oh, really?' in a tone suggesting that was the first time he had heard of it. He was very skilfully hiding the conflict, even from us.

Several days later Todor Zhivkov had to receive a number of ambassadors at the State Council on a protocol call. Peter Mladenov turned up for the meetings.

It appeared that the storm had blown over.

But still, no one but Peter Mladenov took the risk of making a stand against Todor Zhivkov in those days. In the time until 8–9 November 1989 he was alone, nobody backed him in the Politburo.

Thus there was no 'coup conspiracy'.

There were many disgruntled people who bided their time.

Still the letter was the catalyst that set the process in motion, at the end of which, around 8–9 November, everybody found out that it was not so terrible to switch sides, especially when they saw that Zhivkov was immobilized and could not decide to counteract the situation without Soviet support.

Because rumours of coup and gory plots still circulate in Bulgaria, I can't help telling about the events which took place in the days immediately before 10 November 1989.

On 31 October Todor Zhivkov called me to dictate his remarks on the health service decree. Next on his schedule was a meeting with the editor-in-chief of the mass media. When we had finished he asked me, 'Is that all?'

He wasn't sitting at the far end of the table but in the middle, creating an atmosphere for candour and encouragement to tell the truth. I was unhappy with the fact that the materials of the plenum released for publication were entirely overlooked by the mass media and the public. That state of affairs was unbearable. That is why I spoke tensely, 'Comrade Zhivkov, what I am going to tell you might be taken as the fruit of intrigue or go-getting. If you take it that way, I will resign here and now and I will never set foot in your office again. The materials about the forthcoming plenum were published five days ago. They hate us so much, that there is not the slightest reaction, not even by the professional panegyrists. The report is once again academic and theoretical, with divine allusions to "processes and stages". It offers no concrete solutions. The report contains inscrutable political generalities and quasi-scientific phrases.'

He kept silent, all ears and tense, but he listened readily. At other times he would become bored and you had to shut up, but now he was restrained. I eagerly went on, 'You personally and the entire party are going disarmed to that plenum. We are on the brink of an acute currency and food crisis. The people are very anxious. The cadres are demoralized. I expect a rebellion at the plenum itself because even some Central Committee members cannot stand this any longer. What is more, there are clear indications that you are internationally isolated among our allies.'

Unexpectedly Zhivkov replied, 'Yes, yes, I agree.' He said it straightforwardly, without faltering or quibbling. 'I should prepare myself and deliver a forceful speech,' he said. He stood up and energetically paced his office.

I left happy that he had not become angry and had accepted everything in a businesslike manner. He knew that intrigues were made against him but continued to talk about the introductory speech and not about plots or their frustration by police methods.

Until 10 November 1989 (the start of the plenum) he had enough time to take countermeasures, including the use of the arm of repression.

It was 31 October, 1989.

The Soviet ambassador was out of Bulgaria until 2 November. On 3 November he had a meeting with Todor Zhivkov. The meeting began at eleven in the morning and ended at half past midday. Obviously, Zhivkov had tried to see how things stood with the Soviets, to win time and allies. It is not known what they discussed.

On 4 November in the morning we discussed the Ecoglasnost march on the National Assembly. Todor Zhivkov asked us how to handle their registration with the court. He was already contemplating having the movement legalized, especially after the mass action.

Around noon I asked to see him to brief him on the forthcoming plenum. Zhivkov had estimated the shortage of raw and prime materials which we were not going to receive, the condition of the food reserves and had outlined the situation with its growing danger of unrest. He was in a militant mood. The fatigue had disappeared and he vigorously questioned me.

In the meantime Peter Mladenov had left on an official visit to China.

On the day of the reception at the Soviet embassy on the occasion of 7 November, Zhivkov had another meeting with the Soviet ambassador. The discussion had obviously been hard because Zhivkov arrived at the reception one hour late.

Zhivkov showed no signs of worry for his position. At the reception he shook hands with everyone, he talked cheerfully, and only those who knew that he was engaged in a struggle could sense some tension in his glance and conduct.

On 8 November 1989 in the morning, we discussed the snowballing elections at the higher educational establishments which were won by people who were not trusted by the party leadership. The losers were those who had been connected with the party and the state apparatus. The wave of discontent with the official cadres came as a complete surprise. The leading posts were taken by political opponents or malcontents.

At eleven in the morning Todor Zhivkov met a group of former members of the Chavdar detachment, all of them senior party functionaries: Dobri Djourov, Yordan Yotov and Dimitar Stanishev. They had come to urge him to resign.

They openly voiced their concern over the situation in the country. In the course of the conversation Todor Zhivkov asked, 'Wouldn't it be better if I hand in my resignation?' Asked pointblank, the three of them agreed with 'his' decision and tried to persuade him that his resignation would be painless.

Todor Zhivkov, however, talked of resigning at the next plenum of the Central Committee and not at the forthcoming one. (He obviously planned to confirm Petko Danchev's nomination for the prime ministry. Danchev, along with several other nominees for regional party secretaries, was to fill the vacancies in the Secretariat and the alternate member circle of the Politburo. But he needed some more time for that.)

In such cases, however, there is always too little time for the decisive move. The three of them supported this idea unanimously. Yordan Yotov even pointed out that in this way the change would be carried out much more easily without the use of force, pressure or confrontation.

That brought their conversation to an end.

Todor Zhivkov left for his residence in Bankya.

In the afternoon at three-thirty the protocol department of the Soviet embassy phoned, requesting an appointment between the Soviet ambassador Sharapov and Todor Zhivkov. (He often had meetings with him.) I answered the phone in his office. The message was received. In a little while, around four o'clock, Todor Zhivkov phoned and, as usual, asked 'What's up?' I relayed the message that the Soviet ambassador wanted to see him. He said briefly, 'Tell him to come at five o'clock to Bankya.' The subject of their talk remains a mystery.

On 9 November the morning coffee session began on time. Todor Zhivkov came in, wearing a formal dark suit. The atmosphere was oppressive. He stared vacantly, he could not concentrate, something weighed heavily on his mind.

The briefing on the current public developments was gloomy: the events in the German Democratic Republic, the fate of socialism at home and abroad. Alarming news arrived from everywhere. No one mentioned the events unfolding around us. As I said, he exercised marvellous self-control. He was a strong willed and secretive man. His daughter Lyudmila Zhivkova used to say in this connection 'Success takes several things: you have to want, to know, to be capable and to keep silent. The last is the most difficult.'

The conversation switched to the subject of socialism which we continued to identify with the crumbling political system in those countries. I threw in the following off the cuff remark: 'Socialism is going away and it is so because the people never wanted that sort of socialism. It was foisted on them on the tips of the bayonets.' Surprised, as if he didn't quite catch what I said, he asked 'What, what?' I repeated what I had said.

He pondered and said weakly, 'It was the same in Bulgaria, too.' That was the end of the coffee session.

Todor Zhivkov knew that they were working on his resignation. People had spoken with his guards to prevent possible attempts at counteraction on his part, and the security people had told him.

I am convinced that Todor Zhivkov did not plan any actions for organized repressive resistance although he did have opportunities for such actions. I am stressing all this because I think that the rumour about lists containing thousands of names earmarked for arrest and execution, of a confrontation between the army and the police and of the menace of a blood bath are quite unfounded. These fabrications place a stigma on State Security. Some of the top-ranking members of State Security knew about the processes unfolding at the Central Committee. They had enough time to act if they had wanted to do anything. Conversely, some excitedly and expectantly phoned and indirectly questioned me. But not one of them was prepared to counteract. On the contrary, to all of them this was just a long awaited change because nobody knew better than them how things stood at the top echelon of power in Bulgaria. In Bulgaria, in the party and in the security forces, there has never been such a situation or people who would have thought of something rash like that. These rumours only incited hatred and stirred up tension among the people. The entire party lost. The rumours presented it as a moral and political force capable of going to war with its own people and intelligentsia. But this could not happen in this country. Not in Bulgaria.

Todor Zhivkov's working day on 9 November, 1989 began with the coffee session with his aides, after which he had several successive appointments. At ten o'clock he conferred with Alexander Fol, minister of science, culture and education, he then called for a talk Grigor Stoichkov, deputy chairman of the Council of Ministers; at about eleven-thirty he called his friends from the hunting party – Georgi Djagarov, Anguel Balevski and Pantelei Zarev. His meetings ended at one o'clock in the afternoon.

At these meetings he tried to obtain information and possibly to learn whether he could rely on their political support at the plenum. He realized that the battle at the Politburo would be lost since he knew that the key Politburo members themselves were making arrangements for his resignation. On this account, he probably wanted the support to come at the plenum. There he could rely on many of the Central Committee members whom he had handpicked and who were loyal to him.

At one o'clock Zhivkov retired for a rest. After four he asked to see Yordan Yotov. No sooner had he come in when he asked,

'What is Djourov bustling about?' It is interesting to know how he had learned about this, since the 'contact' between the members and alternate members of the Politburo and the secretaries of the Central Committee was assigned to Nacho Papazov, chairman of the Central Control and Auditing Commission. Some people after 10 November shouted 'Down with Nacho Papazov', but they did not know what it was like to fight when you were merely a cog in the totalitarian machine. How much more difficult it is to stay courageous when you have to choose daily between your official duties, on the one hand, and your honour and civic conscience, on the other.

Yordan Yotov told him that Djourov was an honest revolutionary and that if he was bustling about something, it was only for the best. At that same moment Djourov himself entered the room: he had an appointment for four-thirty. They decided to call Dimiter Stanishev, too.

In his conversation with them, Zhivkov once again announced his resignation; this time however, he said he would resign not at the next plenum but at the forthcoming one. He told them that they had misunderstood him the day before and that he had in mind the forthcoming plenum. (Obviously something in the meantime had made him change his mind.) 'I have made mistakes, but I have not committed any crimes.' That was how he summed up his readiness to retire.

The meeting passed peacefully. Djourov was almost in tears at this historical moment.

At five o'clock the Politburo began its meeting.

As soon as he walked in, Todor Zhivkov declared, 'One year ago I raised the question of my resignation, and it was declined. Now I insist that you accept it.' (It was true that he had enacted his resignation once, but the Politburo did not accept it at that time unanimously, because it was actually not being handed in.)

One after another, all those who had been informed beforehand took the floor. They all approved his decision to resign and assessed it as a new manifestation of his foresight.

Only two of them were surprised: Milko Balev and Dimitar Stoyanov (Grisha Filipov was at that time in Czechoslovkia and came back for the plenum itself).

Milko Balev said, 'Some of us think otherwise, Comrade Zhivkov,' while Dimitar Stoyanov added, 'I am surprised. No one has talked to me about this. Why don't we wait for the congress to make this change?'

But their remarks went unnoticed. In the end they also agreed to support his resignation.

They went on to the second item on the agenda: the election of a new general secretary. Todor Zhivkov put forward Georgi Atanassov who immediately declined and nominated Peter Mladenov. The rest of the Politburo members and its secretaries supported the nomination of Peter Mladenov, and the meeting was closed at about a quarter to eight in the evening.

After the meeting, Todor Zhivkov retired to his office and was followed there by Peter Mladenov, Dobri Djourov, Georgi Atanassov, Andrei Loukanov and others. Todor Zhivkov ordered brandy and wine. (Peter Mladenov asked for whisky. The rest took wine and loukanka.)

Todor Zhivkov told them that they would go on seeing each other in the future and that they would still have coffee together.

In such a civilized manner, peacefully, without excesses, 9 November 1989 passed before my eyes.

Zhivkov remained to make the last move – the plenum of the Central Committee, scheduled for the following day.

The session began at nine in the morning. Some members were called beforehand and were assigned to make statements on item two of the agenda: the resignation. I saw some of their statements. In some of them I deleted the 'historical' evaluations and raptures over Todor Zhivkov (that was how they were ordered to write them – as eulogies).

Some of the participants in the plenum knew nothing until the last minute, and had prepared their statements on item one of the agenda in the traditional style. Others learned about it at the last moment and hastened to cross out 'the name of God'. That was probably my last chance to watch the grimaces of people. Expressions and moods changed. Some Central Committee members feverishly but awkwardly tried to switch allegiances. Others tried to find favour with the new leadership. All this as if in a street theatre, took place in a hall and was played out in a matter of hours.

Todor Zhivkov made an introductory speech on item one. He spoke vehemently, with a specific analysis, with a lot of energy and fervour. He wanted to appeal to the audience, to cope with the situation and to postpone the end, at least for a while.

During the break he came to us, his aides and summoned us as usual. He asked us about his speech, whether it had been well received. All of us already knew about the resignation approved by the Politburo and instead of replying, one of my colleagues asked why he was not keeping at least one post for himself? He even reminded him that everything now would be laid on him and he would not be able to defend himself. Zhivkov replied, 'No, I am determined to go. I cannot do anything more with this government. Our friend whom we made prime minister has let us down. It turned out that he could not cope with things. Let such people take over who can make decisions and carry them out. Besides, you see what the international situation is. As to the criticism, if it is fair, then we too have something to say. Moreover a politician should be able to stand criticism.'

I watched his hands which at that moment were mechanically crumpling a paper serviette, tearing it into long strips which he kept holding and tearing up.

The statements on item one continued. Towards the end of the discussion, he suddenly left the honorary Presidium and came over to his aides. He asked anxiously, 'What shall I say in my closing speech?' None of us had thought about that. He went on insistently, 'What do you think is the main point?'

We tried to improvise but nothing came out of it. He left us and started resolutely, and took his place in the Presidium.

When the discussion on item one was over, Dimitar Stoyanov, who was presiding over the session suddenly announced a break until three o'clock.

Todor Zhivkov stood bewildered as he had expected to say some closing remarks to item one.

During the break, at lunch, the news had already spread.

The discussions at three began with the reading out of Todor Zhivkov's resignation.

The usual statements followed; evaluations, praise, tributes, compliments, acknowledgements and gratitudes for the outgoing Zhivkov and praises of Peter Mladenov. Everything was going smoothly when, suddenly, one Central Committee member upset the scenario – Ivan Maslarov, the party veteran, stood up and put forward Alexander Lilov as general secretary. Another Central Committee member, academician Nikolai Iribadjakov, pointed out that the plenum was not ready to elect a new general secretary. He moved that the post be opened to competing candidates with their platforms and at the plenum they should then choose the best candidate. Nikolai Iribadjakov was not in Todor Zhivkov's inner circle. What happened in practice, however, was that Todor Zhivkov had wanted a deferral of the decision on the resignation.

The session was interrupted. A break was announced. During the break Todor Zhivkov made a timid attempt to offer resistance, appealing to some of his friends to help him. They assured him that they would help – and immediately informed 'the new ones' that Todor Zhivkov was preparing to resist.

The session was resumed. Some of the Central Committee members were assigned to take a more categorical stand so as to foil any attempts to put off the decision.

Todor Zhivkov, who still had some hopes and harboured some illusions, suddenly realized that he had lost, and that it was final. He completely changed. He collapsed as an old war horse who after a lash of the whip had managed to rise at the end of his tether but could not take one more step. Life had drained all his strength. What was left was a ball of nerves, ambitions and desire always to be number one. But that was no longer possible.

The session closed at five o'clock.

Todor Zhivkov headed for the lift alone. He was seen off by Peter Mladenov.

Epilogue

The reader of this book can hardly fathom the gravity of the crisis into which Bulgaria has now been plunged if he is unfamiliar with certain economic and political factors which for decades on end have left their imprint on all public life in Bulgaria. For some of them there was no alternative. They were simply inevitable in view of the geopolitical facts and the real historical processes.

The most important of them was the complete dependence of the Bulgarian economy on the economy of the Soviet Union. Recent events have been an objective lesson on the effect of a drop in the energy supply from the Soviet Union. As far as Bulgaria is concerned, this dependence is fateful indeed. We are totally dependent on our sole and therefore crucial source of raw materials, the Soviet Union. A slight disruption in the steady inflow of energy is enough to upset our manufacturing processes and the life of the Bulgarian population.

The road that links us with the Soviet Union, however, is of two lanes. Most of the industrial feedstock and energy products we needed came on one lane. The other turned the Soviet Union into our major trading partner because its boundless market absorbed the bulk of the output of the Bulgarian economy. Now, however, both lanes seem problematic and will become even more so in the face of the deep-rooted changes in the Soviet Union, in Bulgaria and all over Europe.

While political restructuring and the detachment from a political bloc could take a short period of time, in the economy this can only happen in the course of years and even decades.

I appreciate the appeals to find a 'road to Europe'. But for the time being they remain more or less in the realm of political sentimentalism, being unmatched by feasible constructive ideas on the fastest practical way out of the isolation and on avoiding a possible entrapment in a hopeless economic autarchy or some new triumph of an authoritarian or totalitarian management model. Integration into Europe is a difficult process especially in its economic dimensions. In Bulgaria the economic change amounts to starting from scratch. It is illusory to assume that this could happen by switching over from one source to another. It is even more illusory to hope that not only politicians, but also owners and bankers in the West will welcome us with open arms. Or that there will be another Brezhnev who with one stroke of a pen would 'sign us up' for supply from some state source. All this is an illusion which could throw Bulgaria – and not only Bulgaria – into a fever. This unclear and uncertain future of our country should be projected against the background of the world's historical processes. The time has gone when political, ideological and military confrontation modelled a bipolar, distinct world of two radically different systems: capitalism and socialism. Each one of them saw the other as the ideal target and, paradoxically, world stability was guaranteed by the arms race.

The world, however, has changed dramatically. Communism has ceased to be one of the two geopolitical centres of the planet. History has embarked on its own unexpected road and the breath-taking events have already drawn a new line of demarcation which is gradually shaping two new poles of confrontation: the rich and the poor. The tendencies of this confrontation were evident much earlier in the retarded development of the so-called Third World countries. Now, however, these two poles begin to escalate tensions in the European geopolitical space, too. For the present there is no theoretical scheme or political doctrine which could outline in most general terms the future profile of the new confrontation. Now what matters most is the practical question.

Is the West prepared to pay for the shift of priorities in the countries of Eastern Europe? This would imply higher taxes for the population in the West, restricted consumption by their own peoples and a lower standard of living. If this does not happen, nothing will be left of the market of ideas, of the human rights appeals, of the spirit of Helsinki. The poor and economically paralysed Eastern Europe will come to hate the rich and economically vibrant Western Europe. This hatred could even lead to a conflict motivated by the maxim, 'We want to live, too.'

This picture is not illusory. If the Soviet Union continues its headlong disintegration, then its leadership driven by noble and moral motives (which I, for one, do not call into question) may reduce Russia to its size under Ivan the Terrible. But this will hardly happen. As in China, one day political changes will come to an abrupt end in the face of the threat of national disintegration.

The greatest tragedy will occur if a military–political group in the Soviet Union sums up Gorbachev's time in terms similar to the following: we compromised with our ideas; we renounced entire periods of our history; we withdrew our forward-based nuclear arms from Europe; we stirred up ethnic passions and strife; living conditions are worse than ever. What did we get out of all that? A pat on the back and sentimental acclaim for Gorbachev. Then the pendulum will swing, the inherent instinct of self-preservation will be activated for years, and the Russians will try to make up for the decades of failure. By the end of the century the situation will become unpredictable, insidious and sinister. Add to this the new page which is already being written in the history of the age-old struggle between Christianity and Islam. We should not dismiss with a sneer the claims that world tensions now run high not only because of the conflict between poor and rich nations but also due to the regional clash between the cross and the crescent.

The poor nations in Eastern Europe have been given a taste of democracy and Western luxury. This has made them impatient and embittered. Unless things improve they can say with the desperation of a loser, 'Either you give or we'll pull the trigger!' Brezhnev deployed the SS-20 missiles in Europe in the most cooperative years following Helsinki. He told Todor Zhivkov complacently, 'Now we've got them in the bag.' What will happen in the atmosphere of hunger, misery and social desperation which is now arising in Eastern Europe?

The present transition from totalitarianism spells a serious threat to the Western world because it takes place in societies which, on the whole, have no stable democratic traditions. This implies explosive changes and inherent strife and excess in the rejection of the former values. It is precisely this that should put the businesslike and rational West on its guard. A slower pace of change is required in Eastern Europe. Only then could the democratizing political structures control the reforms and channel them into a mainstream that would be convenient and, most of all, safe for the Western world.

This world will either have to drop an iron curtain or be prepared to pay for the active policy which attracted people to its model of social organization and development. If this does not happen, the Slav nations' exasperation will compound Asian and African poverty and Islamic fundamentalism. The Soviet Union is already nearing the brink of civil war. If it breaks out it will cast a menacing shadow on the countries of Eastern Europe as well, due to their vital economic dependence on the Soviet Union.

The world is facing an unclear future. The only certain thing is the ever more urgent opportunity for multivariant development.

This situation makes it possible to resort to blackmail in all its versions, from the military threat, to the eco-terror of the nuclear power stations and chemical factories, and the severing of transport links. In addition, while the West has the power of capital and modern technologies, the Soviet Union controls many of the raw material sources. The European basket is becoming increasingly small for the number of eggs it carries. Each shake and shift may break them; and this is precisely what is going on at the moment.

Moreover, in our countries, totalitarianism as a system is far from eliminated. There is still no stable economic or political structure similar to that of the West. The old structure can reproduce in a matter of days because the fast and often chaotic dismantling does not always signify an irreversible integration into the general drive of democratic changes.

On the other hand, Bulgarian society is not prepared psychologically nor does it have the necessary historical prerequisites for a return to primary accumulation. The sale of businesses would hardly help, with little prospect for the buyers themselves.

And yet, the logic of economic necessity will make us repeat stages and phases in the development of a market economy which were characteristic of Western society back in the nineteenth century. It is an elementary truth, however, that the repetition of past laws of history in modern times have always been a painful process in social, political and ethno-psychological terms. To say nothing of the difficulties and the traumatic dimensions of this process in the economy.

In Bulgaria, we have no waged workers. Due to the character of the system, they have been dependent, among other things, because they contributed a limited amount of socially productive labour to social production. The labour intensity which they confronted in the private sector started to scare them. At this point this fear was partially compensated by good pay compared to the previous state wages. But then the worst defect of the former command and administer system came into play: it had accustomed a large part of the population to rely on others and to hate work.

The market economy dynamism will logically lead to a socio-economic stratification and internal confrontation in Bulgarian society. It will no longer be stratified on a nomenclature basis. Its driving forces will be ownership, market demand and supply, enterprise and high productivity of labour.

The clash with these categories in real life will definitely bring about social discontent, which does not rule out the possibility of further political cataclysms with a dramatic end result clad in the familiar attire of a new totalitarian regime.

An economy is not managed by technocratic economists alone. It is managed by the respective class as a historical formation. In Bulgaria the change from a centrally planned to a market economy still does not have a class base; at least, the term 'social class' has yet to be redefined. The fast emergence of such a class may prove more disastrous and harmful than the rushed industrialization of the Bulgarian economy in fulfilment of Georgi Dimitrov's idealistic slogan to achieve in twenty years what others have done in a hundred. It may also resemble Lenin's abortive attempt to skip an entire age in the objective development of society in Russia.

In general, I am afraid that the emphasis on an instant change will plunge the country into another crisis if a steady, though tense, transition to new structures is not secured, and it cannot be secured without the help of outside forces. A first step in this direction could be a remission of our foreign debts – to give us some 'economic breathing space' and to allow us to spare the money for primary accumulation.

In this connection I should stress yet another concern of the citizens of little Bulgaria. Since its liberation from the Turkish yoke it has always been externally dependant on the great European powers; it has always been tacked on to one great power or another, either Slav (latterly Soviet) or European. The hopes of Bulgaria have always been reckoned along with the interests of foreign political powers.

The foreign economic dependence has always been a fact of our international life. The few active champions of Bulgaria's full diplomatic emancipation such as Stefan Stambolov never achieved any lasting practical result.

Today the Bulgarian citizen is ever more clearly aware that the great powers still have Bulgaria at their beck and call according to their own European, international or even world interests.

It is once again the major world capitals that seek our partnership and not *vice versa*. Nominally, Bulgaria now enjoys a measure of foreign political independence which it has not had since 1876. But we do not know what to do with our independence because the comprehensive crisis is forcing us to hold out our hand for charity to both sides of the ocean.

Besides, Bulgarians have an ever keener sense of historical forsakenness. There is a spreading conviction that they have been sold to the West. The West, for its part, is all too eager to support and praise the changes in this country but does not omit to warn us that 'business is business'. Besides this, the Munich Accords before World War II, the Yalta Division of Europe, the Soviet government's diffident protests over the US military intervention in Panama and the US neutrality on the question of Lithuania's independence clearly show that Eastern Europe is turning into a bargaining chip in something more than European policy.

The great powers have obviously laid their cards on the table of world politics. I still have the feeling, however, that they underestimate the future global role of the giant China. It remains communist and its huge potential bodes uncertainty. Uncertainty has always been frightening or, at least, has created insecurity.

On the other hand, our people, just as the other peoples of Eastern Europe, would hardly put up with the position of a Cinderella in the new home, to which the historical circumstances are pushing them. Playing at independence in conditions of total social and economic dependence cannot justify the game of empty hopes which we are now being offered. The one-sided foreign interest in Bulgaria is clearly evident, among other things in the one-sided foreign propaganda on Bulgaria in all Western-supported mass media. When a country turns into a sphere of foreign and conflicting interests, the most common result is a civil war with only the people on its receiving end. Now, more than ever before, Bulgarians realize that they continue to be the pawn of alien interests, that outside forces determine their destiny. We now painfully feel the lack of a real national foreign policy in which the three major components – a real national interest, national concept and national doctrine – could really guarantee Bulgaria's state sovereignty.

In this connection I would like to point out two important circumstances.

EPILOGUE

The conduct of the political top crust in our country throughout the postwar period has actually been a political tragedy which cannot be judged in black and white terms as entirely positive or entirely negative. At a meeting with United States business executives, Todor Zhivkov had told in jest the bitter truth that, even if he wanted to, he could not break away from the Soviet Union. The moment he tried to do this, the people in Bulgaria would depose him. On the other hand, he told Soviet officials on numerous occasions that he could not disregard Bulgaria's historical links with the rest of Europe. This was the political conduct not just of a leader, but of an entire nation. The fast, almost indecent, swing to the West on the part of the intelligentsia is indicative of the all-nation drama and the feeling of the Bulgarian people that their country is just a puppet.

Here once again we confront the feeling of historical inferiority, so typical of the majority of small nations. For Bulgaria, however, it can only have dramatic effects in view of the dire straits in which the country has found itself. The abrupt shift of foreign political orientations is not just a doubtful way of gaining international prestige. It also has nasty historical reminders of the time when the wavering and vacillation between different foreign political patrons have brought only misery to the nation; they have put it at a disadvantage in the Balkan peninsula even in periods when the region was dominated by the desire for a peaceful alternative in interstate relations.

Drawing on past experience, we must admit that Georgi Dimitrov's old idea of a Balkan federation of people's democracies – an idea for which he paid dearly – is becoming increasingly relevant. It was probably not only an expression of dissatisfaction, but also of a clear awareness that small countries can best survive if they become large countries. Dimitrov simply gave expression to the traditional reaction of the small states which, under the threat of the great powers, seek the umbrella of various kinds of interstate alliances in order to survive.

In early 1949 Stalin abruptly cut short the Balkan federation idea because he was fully aware of its threat to Soviet influence in the Balkans. What are the chances of survival that have now been left to the small states? How can they hold out effectively against the pressure of the large ones? In this connection, some other Bulgarian historical parallels may also serve as a lesson. Bulgaria's contemporary history makes us take a closer look at the fate of the people who have been running the country. Several years after its liberation from the Turkish yoke, bowing to pressure from contending great powers, our country went as far as to break off its diplomatic relations with its liberator, Russia.

One of the remarkable figures of the young state at that time, Stefan Stambolov, sought new dimensions for Bulgarian foreign policy towards its European allies. He was assassinated in the street under the loud roar of the mob who had branded him a 'murderer', 'gambler', 'traitor', 'profiteer' and 'black marketeer'.

His life was sacrificed in the struggle between Russia and the Western powers for dominance in Bulgaria.

World War I proved politically lethal for a number of Bulgarian leaders. Some of the leading political figures ended up in prison as a result of the events which had brought about a national catastrophe. Their political and non-political fate was once again sealed in the contention between the great powers, in the rivalry between the warring entente (Britain, Russia and France) and central powers (Germany and Austria–Hungary).

World War II turned Bulgaria into a mini-battlefield for the Soviet Union and Germany. This divided the political world and plunged the Bulgarian political forces into a bitter strife. Then Tsar Boris III – a scion of the Bourbons and the Orleans, the royal houses which had ruled Europe for centuries – could not evade the ill-fated role of a leader of a small nation trying to preserve its independence. His reign was a series of tortuous manoeuvres between the pro-Soviet political movement and the pro-German opposition. He failed because on the geopolitical chessboard of the great powers, small Bulgaria and its monarch were merely pawns which had to be moved but which could not make strategic moves on their own.

After 9 September 1944 the establishment of new rule was accompanied by a series of show trials against a number of leaders of political parties, including top people from the ruling Communist party.

Foreign political preferences sealed the fate of many political leaders when they motivated decisions backstage of the courtrooms and very often on the political forestage.

Todor Zhivkov managed to accommodate the correlation of the forces in Europe and ruled for over 35 years. But when this correlation changed, he was forced to go, and subsequently found himself under judicial investigation.

Thus the fate of the Bulgarian leaders appears more or less to be a delicate function of the East–West correlation of forces. This is not a tragic predestination but a fatal law of history, not only in Bulgarian history but also in the past of other small countries.

There has hitherto been a balance and order in international relations based on the axis between the two politico-military blocs. But the fast disintegration of the Warsaw Treaty and of the Soviet Union itself will undoubtedly liberate the negative energy that has been building up for decades. All peoples must seek a new balance as a basis for their security. But in order to achieve this they will have to go through a cataclysm, on the basis of which new organization and order in the world will be built. The question is from where and how will this cataclysm appear?

Above all, it should be expected from the large nations of the planet which are poor and hungry. The new conditions in the world, where there is only one world superpower – the United States – will give rise to the natural need to seek another pole. This need is almost as forceful as the physical laws of the planet because the harmony of the macrocosm as a matter of principle underlies all human activity and every human structure. Whoever does not realize or would not realize this law of nature, is doomed to experience bitter disappointments. For the moment we are still experiencing the foretaste of these disappointments which will leave us stranded for some time in the labyrinths of historical truth and political justice. It is difficult for everyone to find on his own the thread in these labyrinths and an answer to the question, 'Where is this world going?'

The restructuring underway in the Soviet Union will have its exorbitantly high price not only in an internal but also in an international aspect. To build his new foreign political image, Gorbachev needed a new generation of East European leaders suiting his vibrancy and sharing his modern vision of the fate of world socialism. The old ones were replaced in a strikingly short time, but the new ones did not stay at the top for very long either. Gorbachev had hardly expected that these changes would trigger off that mechanism which led to dramatic social changes with a marked pro-Western orientation in the East European countries. There is no doubt that the void in the former space of the socialist community will be filled with West European civilization, technology, capital, and culture.

Gorbachev and his team simply failed to foresee the depth of the built-up socio-political discontent which left behind the wave of cardinal changes, ignoring the relatively slow pace of reform. The Soviet leader suddenly found himself in the unenviable position of that familiar magician who had let the genie out of the lamp and could not put it back again.

How will the Soviet Union meet this challenge? Will it let itself be overwhelmed by its troubles or will it find a chance to regroup its forces for a new offensive in Europe? It needs a new policy and a new ideology to protect its national interest. This could be expected to happen quite soon in that country and it will probably pass through several phases. Above all, the leadership may be changed and a new leader may establish himself to replace the vain Gorbachev. In the long run, after five years at the helm, one can claim that he is running the country more like a provincial boss than a leader who has the Russian geopolitical school of philosophy and action in his genes.

I find it difficult to agree with those who see Gorbachev as a politician capable of a strategic step back in order to run and take a leap. This theory seems debatable on a number of grounds in the actual political life of the old continent and of the entire planet.

The dividends which Gorbachev won by selling out Eastern Europe are quickly melting away. The West was flattered and, at the same time, spellbound by the easy prey. The Western politicians will pay a high price in the foreseeable future for the fact that they built for themselves a fascinating image and became carried away with it. Still, nobody knows what will be the result of an effective and even attractive foreign policy, combined with a disastrously ineffective reform policy in his own country. This imbalance will have serious, even catastrophic consequences. The first to disintegrate and break away will be the Baltic states and the Transcaucasian republics. The future of the Asian peoples within the boundaries of the Soviet Union, as well as of the Ukraine, is under a big question mark; conflicting political processes are also tearing apart the social texture of the Russian federation.

Still the Soviet Union holds 90 per cent of all raw materials and this umbilical cord can hardly quickly be broken off by the nations and states which have extricated themselves from this Russian embrace. Western Europe neither can nor intends to turn into their alternative source of raw materials: Lithuania is a case in point.

The disintegration of the Soviet Union will lead to the emergence of new, uncontrollable structures and reactions. Entire sectors of the economy will operate clandestinely in the hands of obscure groups and people. Organized crime is already taking over distributive trade, in much the same way as highwaymen struck terror in travellers all over Russia in the distant past. Barter will supersede the market and equivalent exchange in trade. Individual groups may be making adventurist plans to seize missile launch sites or nuclear power stations with the purpose of espionage and terror.

The annals of history will show how dangerous it is to live on class hatred engendered by revolution. Under the new conditions, when classes will be anachronisms, only hatred will remain. The Soviet Union has experienced its first ethnic-based unrest. But if this hatred acquires a social basis it can lead to self-annihilation.

It is then that a new Peter the Great, Stepan Razin, Pugachev, Lenin or Stalin can be born. The genetically programmed code of the great Russian state and the great Russian people to be at the head of the world historical movement will be activated. The new thinking will be a new thinking, but this time for the defence of Russia's interests. The ideological basis of the new policy will not be socialism with its postulates but probably a latter-day Pan-Russian nationalism. Russia will seek rapprochement with the large and poor peoples of China and India. They will be joined by the Arab nations, among whom anti-Americanism is already bearing bitter fruit. They will also be joined by those countries of Eastern Europe which will inevitably be disappointed by the transition to a market economy and the inevitable drama of this transition. The natural basis of this rapprochement will not follow the logic of political laws and international relations but the biological laws of the hungry and impatient peoples who would not forgive the wealthy peoples their egotism and affluence.

Totalitarian Bulgaria, for example, had visa-free entry regulations with half of the Western states but now, with the indisputable democratic changes, its citizens face drastic restrictions on travel. The roles are gradually reversed. The poor nations of the East will be campaigning for human rights, while the rich will hide behind barbed wire, police dogs and soldiers. Eastern Europe lifted the iron curtain, Western Europe is hastening to drop it back again in its own defence. The political paradox is on the way to becoming a historical one. As a result, the geopolitical landscape of the world will become even more menacing and no one knows how far one can give way to evil. Violence, which is already a component of the perverted mind of the peoples of Eastern Europe, will awaken the dormant instinct of extermination.

The arc of instability will probably begin in the Balkans, passing through Turkey and the Middle East, through the Soviet Union and reaching China, India and Pakistan. It is there that the new geopolitical centre will arise. The world will acquire the dimensions of the existing bloc system but in a far more unstable and dangerous situation. There will be no contending ideologies of different colours but primitive psychological necessities. The new banners under which the nations will march will, in place of 'Socialism' or 'Communism', read 'Good Poorman versus Bad Richman'. Instead of supreme philosophical values, the relations between the new structures and centres in the world will be based on the age-old hatred of the poor for the rich. The decline of ideology in existing relations will usher in a brutal psychology in these relations. Its malignant outgrowths will spread to all of the poor societies without running into any moral barriers.

Ironically, while the countries with a totalitarian regime kept an iron grip on the revolt of the disgruntled peoples, this deterrent role will now have to be played by the rich democracies.

The latter will have to buy indulgences for past as well as for future sins. The forthcoming historical period will be so complicated that some will see in it an agony and others a birth. The West, too, will arrive at the sad conclusion that it had too hastily and cruelly condemned the political past of the Eastern societies.

As to Bulgaria, its survival strategy probably consists of looking for allies in all directions. I say 'probably', because it is difficult to prescribe a remedy for an organism which suffers from many diseases.

The twentieth century showed that reliance on a single ally faces us with unpredictable situations. In these situations only the large nations survive; for the small ones, it is a different story. A third national catastrophe for Bulgaria will not be limited to economic and political crises, which are gaining momentum in our country. The crises after World War I and World War II were rather tragic episodes in our country's contemporary history caused by the state of war. We must regard the third national catastrophe in a different historical aspect. Now it is a question of the survival of the Bulgarian people and state. Bulgarian statehood perished twice: once under the blows of Byzantium, and the second time under the wave of the Turkish invasion in Europe.

History often becomes tired of creating variety and repeats its lessons. Six centuries ago, the surge of the Turkish conquest found the Bulgarians divided into three small, hostile states. The present-day challenges of history again found us divided, stuck in two warring political tendencies. Italy opted for the Piedmont way of unification, the small German states chose the Prussian way. Even trilingual Switzerland united in a single state. Bulgaria's ship is on the way to wrecking in a sea of ascending Balkan nationalism. This may be the catastrophe, which will consign the Bulgarian state to the ashheap of history.

It will be a mistake if Bulgaria ignores its former ally, the Soviet Union, with which it has historical, ethnic, religious, cultural and geopolitical connections. Apart from everything else, moral considerations should also be taken into account. We cannot flirt with every great power and abandon our allies. In this way, we will lose our own self-reliance. For its part, the Soviet Union should prove, materially and morally, that despite its serious internal problems it is not inclined to desert one of its closest allies of the recent past. Otherwise, the Kremlin's morality and ambitions to keep up the reputation of the USSR as a great country and a great power may once again be called into question.

Dependence on America is, for some, perfectly satisfactory; but for Bulgaria, America is too far and too indifferent. Moreover, Turkey is and will remain a priority ally for the United States. The large European states and above all Germany deserve more attention.

In the final analysis everything depends on whether we will be clever enough to achieve the status which is available: as a bridge between Europe and Asia. Such a status combines strategy with politics and economics. Let us recall Austria which, pursuing its own specific policy between two bristling blocs of states, profited from the transfer of technologies, tourism, transport and banking. For the time being we have a geopolitical advantage over that small Central European country; we are the closer and the more convenient door between Europe and the Orient. Does the future have further advantages or at least further hopes in store for us?